Springer Series on Asian Criminology and Criminal Justice Research

Series editor

Jianhong Liu
University of Macau
Macao, China

More information about this series at http://www.springer.com/series/15738

Xiaoyu Yuan

Restorative Justice in China

Comparing Theory and Practice

Springer

Xiaoyu Yuan
School of Criminal Justice
Shanghai University of Political Science and Law
Shanghai, China

Springer Series on Asian Criminology and Criminal Justice Research
ISBN 978-3-319-63921-5　　ISBN 978-3-319-63922-2 (eBook)
DOI 10.1007/978-3-319-63922-2

Library of Congress Control Number: 2017952374

Printed on acid-free paper

This Springer imprint is published by Springer Nature
The registered company is Springer International Publishing AG
The registered company address is: Gewerbestrasse 11, 6330 Cham, Switzerland

To my grandfather

Acknowledgments

This book is based on my PhD thesis conducted at the Leuven Institute of Criminology, KU Leuven, under the supervision of Prof. Dr. Ivo Aertsen. I owe a huge debt of gratitude to my supervisor. Without his great patience and tolerance, without those years of support and guidance, this project would not be possible.

I would also like to thank cordially Professor Carine Defoort and Professor Ching Lin Pang for the encouragement and attention throughout the project and all the constructive suggestions and comments. I also thank sincerely Professor Lode Walgrave and Professor Michele Panzavolta for the helpful comments and suggestions. I am deeply grateful to Professor Jianhong Liu from University of Macau, whose profound insight has been a continual source of inspiration. I am indebted to Professor Xiaohua Di from Nanjing University for offering opportunities, discussion, and support. My special thanks to Springer Series on Asian Criminology and Criminal Justice Research for making this work accessible to a wider audience.

I am also indebted to those who have contributed to the successful completion of the empirical phase of this project. My sincere thanks to Ms. Guan, Ms. Wang, and Mr. Guo who are working at the China's local justice department, as well as many other research participants, whose names cannot be listed here, for their time, assistance, and invaluable inputs.

I had a lovely and inspiring stay in Leuven because of the presence of a group of lovely and kind colleagues and friends. In particular, I would like to thank Monica, Monique, Loes, Edit, Inge, Katrien, Bruna, Daniela, Elli, Helene, and Huma for offering encouragement and support and for sharing ideas and conversations. My Chinese companions, Yingying, Qiao, and a few others have also filled my spare time with lots of laughter and fun.

I also thank the China Scholarship Council for financing my doctoral project.

Last but not least, I would like to appreciate the understanding and support from my family. I thank my parents, Daolin Yuan and Yunxiang Wang, and my brother Hengxin Yuan for letting me go for what I want. I also thank Dr. Shiqiang Du, a geographer, for, while teasing my lack of sense of direction, mapping out accurately our path from Leuven to Shanghai.

Contents

Part III Empirical Findings

Part IV Doing "Restorative" Justice: China and the West

List of Abbreviations

CCP	Chinese Communist Party
CPL	Criminal Procedure Law
CL	Criminal Law
FGC	Family Group Conferencing
JPO	Juvenile Prosecution Office
JC	Juvenile Court
MR	Mediation Room
PMC	Peacemaking Circles
PRC	People's Republic of China
RJ	Restorative Justice
UNODC	United Nations Office on Drugs and Crime
VOM	Victim-Offender Mediation

About the Author

Xiaoyu Yuan has a PhD in Criminology from KU Leuven (Belgium). She was born in Jiangsu Province at the People's Republic of China. From June 2012 to March 2016 she worked as a doctoral researcher at the research line Restorative Justice and Victimology at LINC (Leuven Institute of Criminology, KU Leuven). Before that, she obtained her master's degree in Criminal Law from China University of Political Science and Law (Beijing) in 2011 and bachelor's degree in Law from Southwest University of Political Science and Law (Chongqing) in 2008. She also passed China Bar Exam in 2008. She is now an Assistant Professor at Shanghai University of Political Science and Law. Her current research interests include restorative justice, juvenile justice, Chinese criminal sentencing, and community corrections.

Introduction

The field of restorative justice (RJ) is bustling today, full of legal philosophers, spiritual leaders, project managers, empirical researchers, mediators and facilitators, and others. Eglash (1977) has often been credited with coining the term, but RJ did not achieve wide acceptance until the 1990s. Zehr (1990), a key figure in this movement, called for a lens change, setting its tone as a different paradigm from retributive justice. There are unsettled debates over the relationship between restoration and retribution and between process-oriented conceptions and outcome-focused conceptions. In this context, another study of RJ is likely to make this chaotic world more turbulent rather than to restore order and soberness. Yet restorative justice is a buzzword that is not easy to avoid.

As a Chinese native, I was very puzzled by its meaning and its discourse. It appeared to be an ideological puzzle, having Western discourse on the one hand and Chinese realities on the other. Hence, the ambition of the exploration initiated in this study was not to resolve all the debates mentioned above. At best, it provides answers to an individual quest that may be shared by academics in China. That is, when we discuss restorative justice, what are we talking about? Is it feasible for this "foreign import" (*bolaipin*, 舶来品) to be replicated in China? Does China necessarily have to follow the same path as that pursued by the Western world?

The starting point of this book is what is currently practiced in China – mediation/reconciliation in the Chinese criminal justice context. A new phenomenon, or perhaps "old wine in new wineskins," stimulated the public and scholastic nerve approximately a decade ago. It probably cannot be dissociated from the Chinese soil, as it has been nurtured by Chinese uniqueness in terms of its prevailing culture, as well as the contemporary societal context. Indeed, China has a rich tradition of mediation. However, its relationship with Western restorative justice is not yet self-evident. For instance, why should the development of RJ consider what is happening in today's Chinese society and what is being practiced in non-Western legal systems? While we have witnessed an eagerness among Chinese scholars to look beyond their borders, we have not found many Western scholars who are truly concerned about RJ's destiny in a non-Western society, except when they are seeking evidence to support their arguments or to satisfy their curiosity about a new world.

That said, we do not ascribe "ethnocentrism" to this perceived ideology, because in doing so, we might fall into another type of ethnocentrism.

To break through the obstructions created by scattered information in the literature, as well as the exposure and interpretations by the media, this study calls for an elaborate field investigation. Drawing on the data obtained, this study aims to answer the following questions: How should we understand reconciliation within Chinese criminal justice settings and within its contemporary societal, cultural, and political context? Is there any space for the restoration model developed in Western societies to take root in China?

Synopsis

This book consists of four parts. Part I, entitled *Introducing the Topic*, comprises Chaps. 1, 2, and 3. In Chap. 1, we discuss the research background, define the phenomenon we intend to approach, and present the scholarly contemplation. In addition, the research questions and methodology are introduced.

In Chap. 2, we shed light on the evolution of conflict resolution in China. As Confucius was "arguably the most influential thinker about restorative justice the world has known" (Braithwaite 1999, p. 12), we look back on the traditional dispute resolution that was sustained by the traditional Chinese culture and social structure. The convergences and divergences between traditional Chinese mediation and modern Western restorative justice are discussed. We also examine mediation in the more recent periods, namely, the republican period and the socialist period. We conclude this chapter by expressing some concerns, as well as by pointing out the implications that Western restorative justice may have for reforms of Chinese mediation.

In Chap. 3, we discuss the place of mediation in the contemporary Chinese criminal justice context, both "in the books" and "in action." Based on a literature review, we identify problems and concerns revealed by domestic scholars.

Part II of this book is entitled *Discovering Realities: A Naturalistic Inquiry*. This part mainly elaborates on the methodological approaches and methods that were utilized in our field investigation in China. Condensed into one chapter, this part consists of the choice of methodology, the issues of access and sampling, data collection, research ethics, and data analysis. The implementation of the empirical work, while respecting the rules and standards developed in Western social science, also had to adapt to local cultural rules and practical settings. The access to a local district's prosecutor's office, a court, and a mediation room situated at a police station was largely facilitated by a Chinese criminologist. Readers will find the steps taken and other pertinent information in the relevant section.

Thus, an understanding of mediation in criminal cases in China has been developed, and we present the findings in Part III, *Empirical Findings*. We provide a short case summary and case descriptions (Chap. 5), undertake a thematic analysis (Chap. 6), and finally, discuss the findings (Chap. 7). We conclude that the harmony approach does not fully address individual needs and rights but instead prioritizes societal order and abstract social relationships.

This brings us to the last part of the book, Part IV, *Doing "Restorative" Justice: China and the West.* In Chap. 8, we return to and delineate the rise and development of RJ in the West. The stakeholders, such as the victim, the offender, and the community, deserve analysis, especially the place of society and the state in the RJ literature. Additionally, we discuss the values that have so far been established within theory and practice. The modalities of RJ practices are also briefly described.

In Chap. 9, we examine RJ practices and review the evaluation studies of a large number of restorative justice programs that have been developed in Western societies. This attempt enables us to see how restoration has been understood in these programs and the terms according to which the stakeholders are claimed to have been restored. We construct a restoration model, which is built upon voluntariness, neutrality, empowerment, and storytelling. Each of these concepts is analyzed, and the question of their applicability to another cultural society is discussed. We also revisit the unsettled issues revolving around the minimalist and maximalist conceptions of RJ.

In Chap. 10, we discuss whether China should follow the path of developing a restoration model to restore harmony in social relationships. Next, we focus on the feasibility of such a model through an analysis of neutrality, voluntariness, storytelling, and empowerment. Finally, attention is drawn to whether we can move beyond the restoration model and embrace a Chinese model of restorative justice.

In the concluding chapter, Chap. 11, we particularly discuss what lessons the "lived" Chinese experiences captured in this study can have for Western restorative justice and how the current study helps to enrich the understanding of restorative justice. Likewise, consideration is given to how to reform and improve current Chinese practices to better serve China's citizens. Looking back, the methodological problems involved in this study deserve serious attention, and we hope they will contribute to and inspire any future studies.

References

Braithwaite, J. (1999). Restorative justice: Assessing optimistic and pessimistic accounts. *Crime and Justice, 25*, 1–127.

Eglash, A. (1977). Beyond restitution: Creative restitution. In J. Hudson, & B. Galaway (Eds.), *Restitution in criminal justice* (pp. 91–129). Toronto: Lexington Books.

Zehr, H. (1990). *Changing lenses: A new focus for crime and justice*. Scottsdale, PA: Herald Press.

Part I
Introducing the Topic

Chapter 1
Introducing the Topic

1 Who Is Qiuju? Old Wine in New Wineskins

Twenty years ago, the story of Qiuju appeared on screen, attracting attention and interpretation from critical scholars and an entertainment-seeking audience.[1] The basic storyline goes like this: A village chief kicks a man so severely that he is left unable to work. The man's wife, Qiuju, is upset by the act, as well as the attitude of the village chief. She first seeks mediation from the local police officer, who asks the village chief to pay 200 yuan in compensation. However, when Qiuju goes to the village chief, he throws the notes on the ground and refuses to apologize. Qiuju then goes to the county, and the verdict from the district police is that the village chief must pay 250 yuan. Nevertheless, the latter still refuses to apologize. Finally, Qiuju goes to the city and finds a lawyer who helps her to initiate a lawsuit. The court determines that the decision made by the district is correct, and the fine remains at 250 yuan. Qiuju is still unhappy and makes another appeal to a higher level. As part of the lawsuit, Qiuju's husband is X-rayed.

The story does not end there. One night, Qiuju goes into labor with difficulty and nearly dies. The village chief calls on several men to help carry Qiuju to the hospital. Qiuju safely gives birth to a healthy boy.

Qiuju and her husband invite the village chief to the "1-month-old party" for the baby out of gratitude for his help. However, on that day, the village chief is taken away by the police and sent to jail for 15 days. At the end of the movie, Qiuju watches the police car leave with a puzzled look.

Different opinions and interpretations about this movie and about the character Qiuju have been brought forward. For some, Qiuju is a fighter for individual rights against bullying officials; for others, what Qiuju seeks can perhaps never be provided

[1]The movie was titled The Story of Qiuju (or Qiuju Goes to Court), released in 1992 and directed by Zhang Yimou.

X. Yuan, *Restorative Justice in China*, Springer Series on Asian Criminology and Criminal Justice Research, DOI 10.1007/978-3-319-63922-2_1

by the law or the courts.[2] We are not going to unfold or expand on all these discussions. Instead, an interesting question for this study might be: What does justice mean for Qiuju? Obviously, what Qiuju seeks is not the punishment imposed on the village chief and not even the 200 yuan; she seeks an apology. Nevertheless, an apology does not come out of the mouth of the village chief. However, the village chief also does not refuse to offer help when Qiuju's family comes to his door. The interpersonal relationship continues to be maintained when the village chief is cordially invited to attend the baby's 1-month-old ceremony. What is disturbing, perhaps, is what a Western audience would applaud, namely, that the village chief is taken away by the police. We wonder if Qiuju and the village chief can remain in harmony after the latter is released from jail. Will the village chief still offer help without hesitation if Qiuju's family again seeks any type of favor?

2 Research Background: Restorative Justice

In parallel to this movie, an academic term is gaining popularity and achieving acceptance in the Western world: restorative justice (*huifuxing sifa*, 恢复性司法). Albeit different opinions exist, a common idea is that Eglash (1977) coined this term (Maruna 2014). Yet it was unknown to Chinese academics until 2002, when it began to circulate through encounters and exchanges between scholars at home and abroad at international conferences (Huang 2010).

Anyone can opine about the meaning of the term, which has unavoidably led it to be a controversial and heated topic (Strang 2013; Walgrave 2013). Walgrave (2011) warned that the lack of clarity in the concept of restorative justice is detrimental to both practice and research.

The ambiguities around the concept itself, however, have not prevented restorative justice practices from taking off in many jurisdictions throughout the world. Ever since the 1970s, when the first instance of mediation was attempted in North America by a probation officer to deal with vandalism by two young offenders, many European countries have introduced mediation into their criminal justice systems. For example, in France, the law of 23 June 1999, in Article 41-1 of the Code of Penal Procedure, introduced the possibility, among other alternatives to prosecution, of informing the offender of "proceeding, with the agreement of the parties, to a session of mediation between the offender and the victim" (Faget 2012, p. 148). In Germany, Article 46 of the Penal Code prescribes that when

[2] More comments on this movie can be found online, such as http://www.nytimes.com/movie/review?res=9E0C, E2D6143CF931A35753C1A964958260&partner=Rotten%2520Tomatoes, http://www.washingtonpost.com/wp-srv/style/longterm/movies/videos/thestoryofqiujupgkempley_a0a382.htmhttp://www.washingtonpost.com/wp-srv/style/longterm/movies/videos/thestoryofqiujupgkempley_a0a382.htm, and http://www.washingtonpost.com/wp-srv/style/longterm/movies/videos/thestoryofqiujupghowe_a0afb9.htmhttp://www.washingtonpost.com/wp-srv/style/longterm/movies/videos/thestoryofqiujupghowe_a0afb9.htm.

certain conditions are met, such as making an effort to reconcile with the victim and make reparations, the offender may get a reduced punishment or even be exempted from punishment (Lenz et al. 2012). In Belgium, penal mediation was regulated by the law of 10 February 1994, which introduced the new Article 216ter in the Code of Criminal Procedure (Aertsen et al. 2006). "Mediation for redress" ("herstelbemiddeling," sometimes translated as "restorative mediation") concerns another provision and program, as legally established by the law of 22 June 2005, which introduced Article 553 and ff. in the same Code of Criminal Procedure. "Mediation for redress" requires more than "penal mediation" – based on a clear restorative justice philosophy, defining mediation as a communicative process and guaranteeing the principles of confidentiality and voluntariness (Miers and Aertsen 2012). The main difference lies in their scope of application: Whereas penal mediation works as a type of diversionary measure for less serious crimes that can be adopted by the prosecutor, mediation for redress can be applied to crimes of every degree of seriousness across all phases of the criminal justice process (Aertsen 2015).

The introduction and development of mediation in criminal procedures in European countries must be examined in light of the existing legal instruments at the European level. As early as 1985, the Committee of Ministers of the Council of Europe recommended that the member states examine the possible advantages of mediation and conciliation schemes in its document *Recommendation No. R (85) 11 on the position of the victim in the framework of criminal law and procedure*. In 1999, the Committee of Ministers recommended that member states adopt mediation in penal matters, taking the proposed principles into account. The general principles are voluntary participation, confidentiality, general availability and availability at all stages of the criminal justice process, and sufficient autonomy for the mediation services (Willemsens 2008).

Above all, the United Nations ECOSOC Resolution 2002/2012 on *Basic Principles on the Use of Restorative Justice Programmes in Criminal Matters* (hereafter UN Principles) encourages the member states of the United Nations to implement restorative justice programs in the criminal justice system. What are the so-called restorative justice programs according to this resolution? They are indicated under the use of terms: Both restorative processes, such as mediation, conciliation, conferencing, and sentencing circles, and restorative outcomes, such as reparation, restitution, and community service, are regarded as components of restorative justice programs.

Still, this legislation can hardly describe the variety that exists in restorative justice practice. Although all this legislation concerns mediation in the criminal justice context – which is the predominant restorative justice model in the European landscape – studies have revealed different focuses in these mediation programs as they are performed by NGOs across different countries: e.g., they may be either offender oriented or victim oriented (Dünkel et al. 2015). Within the criminal justice context, these programs aim to repair the harm and to engage all parties in resolving the conflict.

At the risk of being simplistic, restorative justice can be considered as an umbrella term for a set of "new" or "old" practices. Being "new" suggests that these practices differ significantly from the dominant punitive practices, while being "old" indicates that these practices were widespread in Western societies before the modern criminal institutions were established and are still prevalent today in many traditional non-Western societies (Weitekamp 2000; Braithwaite 2002). Nevertheless, RJ is a term now used to include a set of practices that are primarily oriented toward repairing the harm in a consensual way after a crime happens. Citing Marshall (1999, p.5), "[r]estorative justice is a process whereby all the parties with a stake in a particular offence come together to resolve collectively how to deal with the aftermath of the offence and its implications for the future." This definition is said to be the most widely accepted so far; nevertheless, we will return to the discussion on the definitions of RJ in the last part of this book.

3 Understanding of Restorative Justice in China

The concept of restorative justice was received by Chinese academia as a foreign import (舶来品) (Dong 2007; Li 2009a, b). The translation of the term differs slightly between mainland China, Taiwan, and Hong Kong due to the two-tier meaning of justice in Chinese. In both mainland China and Taiwan, restorative justice is translated as *huifuxing sifa* 恢复性司法, and in Hong Kong, it is called *fuhe gongyi* 复和公义 or *xiufuxing zhengyi* 修复性正义 (Wang 2007). The connotation of this term can vary depending on whether *sifa* 司法 or *zhengyi* 正义 is used.

The term *sifa* semantically refers to the justice system. Consequently, it is likely that restorative justice is initially associated with the formal way of settling disputes, situated within the criminal justice system. Other scholars have pointed out that an interpretation of justice as *sifa* is inappropriate, because, derived from a Western language context, restorative justice is meant to counteract the current criminal justice system (Li and Zhang 2006). A distinction should also be made between *huifu* (restore) and *xiufu* (mend), because not all harm can be remediated to restore victims to their original status (*huifu*), although a harmonious status is worth striving for (*xiufu*) (Li and Zhang 2006). Hence, *xiufuxing zhengyi* instead of *huifuxing sifa* is preferred by some scholars. Generally speaking, restorative justice in the Chinese language consists of the following Chinese terms: *huifuxing zhengyi*, *huifuxing sifa*, *fuhe gongyi*, and *xiufuxing zhengyi*.

Restorative justice is generally regarded among Chinese scholars as a reform movement addressing the crisis in Western criminal justice systems (Chen and Ge 2006; Liu 2010). It encourages participation and negotiation and pursues reconciliation between victims and offenders; it attends to victims' needs in material, emotional, and social terms; and it also reintegrates both offenders and victims into the community (Liu 2010; Di 2006).

3.1 "Chinese Practice" and "Chinese Context"

Some scholars do believe that restorative justice finds a local model in China, which is the practice called *xingshi hejie* (刑事和解). *He (和)*, in Chinese, means harmony, while *jie* (解) means understanding and reconciliation. *Xingshi* (刑事) means criminal matters. Translated into English, it is sometimes called criminal mediation, mediation in criminal matters, criminal reconciliation, penal mediation, victim-offender mediation, or simply mediation.

The practice of *xingshi hejie* has been regarded as restorative justice with Chinese characteristics (Shi 2008). Shen and Antonopoulos (2013) considered that the Chinese criminal justice system has now incorporated restorative justice values into handling juvenile matters. Wong and Mok (2010) also reported restorative practices within Chinese criminal justice systems. Admittedly, *xingshi hejie* has been widely applied to juvenile offenses, especially those involving minor physical harm (Yao 2007), diverting young offenders away from the criminal justice system based on their acknowledgment of guilt and making direct reparations to victims (Yao 2007; Shen and Antonopoulos 2013).

Other than dealing with juvenile offenses, *xingshi hejie* has also been widely used to deal with adult offending, across different stages of criminal proceedings, depending on the type of conflicts and the relationships between victims and offenders (Song and Yuan 2009; Song 2009).

The "Chinese context" of RJ appearing in the literature includes but is not limited to the following aspects: the political agenda of building a harmonious society has offered the prospect of lessening punitiveness (Trevaskes 2010, 2011; Liu 2010), a characteristic that had long captured the criminal justice system; the ineffectiveness of executing civil judgments pursuant to criminal sentences; and the increasing overpopulation of prisons (Trevaskes 2009). The merits that *xingshi hejie* can achieve are specifically perceived in relation to the "Chinese context." As claimed, confrontation within society among citizens has been resolved in terms of reduced "petition letters" or "appeals" to authorities; victims' interests have been satisfied through timely compensation from offenders; and judicial costs have been significantly decreased (Song 2008).

3.2 Does Restorative Justice Fit Chinese Realities?

Restorative justice seems to receive praise on its perceived merits in addressing the problems associated with the current Chinese criminal justice system. These merits can be summarized as resolving interpersonal disputes and building a harmonious community, restoring victims' losses, helping relieve the courts' case burden and pressure (Du 2010; Fu 2006; Liu 2007; Shao 2005), and contributing to the rehabilitation of the offender (Shao 2005). Restorative justice fits the contemporary context of building a harmonious society (Liu 2007), as well as traditional Chinese culture, which values harmony and forgiveness (Wong 2013). Scholars have deliberated upon how to construct and perfect *xingshi hejie* with reference to Western RJ theory and practice, while recognizing the boundaries to integrating restorative justice into the Chinese sentencing system (Liu and Xiao 2007).

It is assumed that *xingshi hejie* shares commonalities with the Western notion of RJ in giving the victim a role in resolving the conflict. In other words, the focus of both is not on punishing offenders but on addressing the harm in order to resolve the disputed issue (Li 2007). In opposition to the conventional state monopoly, *xingshi hejie* emphasizes participation and negotiation in resolving the conflict for both sides (Shi 2007).

Because the underlying assumptions of *xingshi hejie* and Western restorative justice seem to concur – repairing the harm to victims and achieving harmony in interpersonal relationships and social harmony – the question remains of how this operates in practice. How is harm understood, and how is it repaired in Chinese society through *xingshi hejie* practices? What is the place of interpersonal harmony, and how is it experienced? Based on the answers to these questions, to what extent does Western restorative justice fit Chinese realities?

4 Clarifying Mediation Under Examination

There is a need to further clarify the mediation practices that will be examined in this project. To be exact, this study is about *xingshi hejie* practices in China. I use the term criminal mediation as an alternative to refer to this practice.

However, in the RJ literature, *mediation* and *victim-offender mediation* seem to be used interchangeably. Native English speakers use the term *mediation* when they address the practice of *victim-offender mediation*, while non-English speakers are more accustomed to the latter term.[3] The truth is that when the concept of *huifuxing sifa* and its *victim-offender mediation* model were introduced to China, the Chinese translation of *victim-offender mediation* was, on many occasions, mingled with *xingshi hejie*. It is hence no surprise to see that attempts have been made to distinguish these two terms or the two sets of practices they represent.

We will proceed by clarifying the terminology regarding what this project entails and excludes – setting the boundaries for this study. "Chinese mediation" is more well-known in the English-language literature; hence, again, this project must be differentiated from the study of "Chinese mediation."

Chinese mediation is not foreign to many Western scholars. As a matter of fact, it has received wide attention domestically and internationally, particularly since the Chinese government launched its open-door and reform policy in the late 1970s. Due to the fact that the Chinese government became open to foreign researchers who were intrigued by Chinese mediation, literature based on field

[3] Email exchange with Martin Wright on June 12, 2013.

examinations or empirical findings exploded. A few examples among these studies explored community mediation, court mediation, and conflict resolution. As Chinese society has progressed, this body of literature from the 1980s and 1990s now appears outdated. Further, more often than not, their results were contradictory, possibly triggering confusion for non-Chinese specialists. For instance, while Wall and Blum (1991) concluded that China is the "most heavily mediated nation on earth" (p. 4), Diamant (2000), one decade later, raised a challenge to this conclusion by demonstrating that mediation is "but one of several methods of conflict resolution in China" (p. 543) and that the preference for mediation largely correlates with region, class, and gender and, therefore, does not constitute a national pattern.

Since the beginning of the 1990s, continuous academic output engaging different methodologies[4] has been produced, falling under the following areas: (1) mediation provided by residents' committees (RC) in the cities and villagers' committees (VC) in the countryside; (2) mediation by higher-level committees in the urban street offices and the rural townships; (3) mediation within associations, organizations, or enterprises, such as the National Women's Federation; (4) mediation by unofficial intermediaries, mostly related to interpersonal conflicts; and (5) judicial mediation by the courts. Among these instances, the RCs and the VCs together constitute a vast apparatus of social control mechanisms maintained by the state. Under the RCs and VCs, people's mediation committees are set up to which local residents can resort when disputes arise. The themes under study involve but are not limited to the following: (1) the techniques and strategies employed by Chinese mediators; (2) the communication process; (3) the preference for mediation in relation to region, gender, class, etc.; (4) the evolution of mediation throughout history; (5) underlying cultural values; and so on.[5]

All these studies have focused on mediation as a form of civil dispute resolution. Official sources in China, such as the China's Law Yearbook, release information each year on how many cases have been mediated by people's mediation committees during the last year. Cases handled by these grassroots mediation committees are categorized into family disputes, neighborhood squabbles, and other relational conflicts.[6] This does not exclude the possibility that some of these conflicts, as some legal scholars would argue, may emerge from minor criminal offenses.

Nonetheless, this project looks at mediation in the criminal justice context – how conflicts are resolved through reconciliation under the contemporary Chinese crimi-

---

[4] Apart from Wall and Blum (1991) and Diamant (2000), other studies, to name a few, include Utter (1987), Ma (1992), Chen and Ma (2002), Halegua (2005), Huang (2006), Read and Michelson (2008), Cao (2008), Di and Wu (2009), Peerenboom and He (2009), Hu (2011), Ali (2013), Hawes and Kong (2013), He and Ng (2013), Wang (2013), Zhang (2013), Ng and He (2014), and Li (2009a, b).

[5] Based on the aforementioned scholarship, the themes and topics can thus be broadly categorized.

[6] In this book, we use conflicts and disputes interchangeably, without making distinctions between conflicts and disputes as Burton (1990, as cited in Tidwell, 2001) and Tidwell (2001) preferred.

nal justice settings. The Chinese term for this, as mentioned before, is *xingshi hejie*. It is best, at the outset, not to make any erroneous assumptions or to impose any preconceived notions but rather to describe and conceive it as a practice.

5 Research Purpose

This exploratory study intends to bridge the dialogue about doing justice in a restorative way between China and the West. First, it sheds light on how we can better understand the reconciliation/mediation practices in the current Chinese criminal justice context. This beckons historical, cultural, and societal insights, as well as a knowledge of the place of mediation in the Chinese legal framework. Second, because restorative justice in the West started initially with practice, rather than following a clear theory, it is necessary to highlight the typical way, as said in China, to achieve restoration. Finally, this study hopes to enrich the discussion and understanding of RJ in the West by drawing on the empirical and theoretical inputs gained from China. Equally, concerning current Chinese mediation/reconciliation, it would be interesting to discover what lessons can be learned from the Western restoration model to better advance China's domestic practices. This study does not consider East/West as a binary; reference to this term within this book is for the convenience of discussion and exchange.

6 Research Questions

Today, both China and the West have embraced nonpunitive and reparative efforts in addressing crimes in their respective jurisdictions. In comparison with the abundant RJ literature in the West and its continuing export to China, Chinese domestic practices remain under-theorized and "behind the door." To fill this gap, this book attempts to gain insights into the mediation practices in China within its contemporary social, political, and cultural contexts.

The questions addressed in the book are centered around the following:

1. *How is the restoration of harm and interpersonal relationships embodied in current criminal mediation as a means of conflict resolution*? This question consists of several sub-questions, in particular: (1) How have conflicts (including crimes) historically been resolved in Chinese society? (2) What is the role of mediation? (3) In what legal framework is the current criminal mediation situated, and what findings and discussions have occurred?
2. *In what ways do Chinese mediation practices converge with and diverge from RJ in the West*?
3. *To what extent can the restoration model in the West be replicated in China? What adaptations should be made?*

7 Research Methodology

To answer the first question, we will start by examining the historical path of resolving conflicts in China, as well as the cultural underpinnings that have sustained its popularity. A historical analysis is presented. Moreover, a literature review is undertaken to differentiate the themes and topics regarding the status quo of criminal mediation in China. The missing themes and topics, which await further examination enabled by fieldwork, are highlighted.

The first and the second questions require a field visit. The exploratory nature of the field inquiry implies that any predesigned instrument may risk being refined or altered when the researcher is confronted with the realities. The essential concerns for the researcher are how to leave the research questions as open as possible and how to effectively cope with new issues or topics that may emerge. This may be particularly true for China, because its door has only been open for less than four decades, and the associated uncertainties can only be addressed during the course of the fieldwork itself. Moreover, the direct application of the theory and concepts that arise from a Western understanding of its own social realities to a different place, such as China, can be problematic. In this circumstance, the researcher cannot be led by what a theory has told her to seek nor can she cram the data into an inappropriate framework. A grounded approach is needed and is well suited for this study.

Thus, attempts are made to understand the realities from the perspectives of all those involved in criminal mediation in their natural settings. This requires a detailed documentation of what people say and how people behave in certain settings, as well as their opinions about what is happening to them. Unfolding the social realities from the perspectives of the participants gives this research enterprise an ethnographic edge. The naturalistic paradigm (Lincoln and Guba 1985) provides a framework for the empirical inquiry, as it views realities as "multiple, constructed and holistic" (p. 37), vastly different from the positivist paradigm, which sees realities as "single, tangible and fragmentable" (p. 37). A naturalistic study requires the investigator to enter the natural setting and be part of the context. Instead of requiring a preprepared instrument, it treats humans as the instrument and enables the investigators to maximize the information.

This study also positions itself as a case study: placing the phenomenon of criminal mediation in the contemporary Chinese social context and linking its practices and occurrences to the actual societal developments. According to Yin (2009), the use of a case study can better answer "how" and "why" questions, as it "investigates a contemporary phenomenon in depth and within its real-life context, especially when the boundaries between phenomenon and context are not clearly evident" (p. 18).

To answer the third question, due to the language barrier, only the English language and Chinese literature will be consulted. We will discuss what we have learned from Western RJ theory and practice and construct the prevailing restoration model. We will not, for instance, compare the findings from Chinese practices with the findings from the international literature on RJ, because that would be an endless endeavor. Instead, a comparative analysis of the different cultural, societal, and institutional realities, as well as the micro-dynamics with regard to resolving conflicts between China and the West, will be offered. This analysis will be built upon the findings from the fieldwork and will be informed by approaches from neighboring fields, such as psychology, sociology, and sinology.

References

Aertsen, I. (2015). Country reports: Belgium. In F. Dünkel, J. Grzywa-Holten, & P. Horsfield (Eds.), *Restorative justice and mediation in penal matters: A stock-taking of legal issues, implementation strategies and outcomes in 36 European countries* (pp. 45–87). Monchengladbach: Form Verlag Godesberg GmbH.

Aertsen, I., Daems, T., & Robert, L. (Eds.). (2006). *Institutionalizing restorative justice*. Cullompton: Willan Publishing.

Ali, S. (2013). The jurisprudence of responsive mediation: An empirical examination of Chinese people's mediation in action. *The Journal of Legal Pluralism and Unofficial Law, 45*(2), 227–248. doi:10.1080/07329113.2013.796759.

Braithwaite, J. (2002). *Restorative justice and responsive regulation*. Oxford: Oxford University Press.

Burton, J. W. (1990). *Conflict: Resolution and prevention*. New York: St Martin's Press.

Cao, Y. (2008). Social conflicts and modes of action in China. *The China Journal, 59*, 89–109.

Chen, G., & Ge, L. (2006). Initial exploration on penal mediation [*xingshi hejie chutan*]. *China Legal Science, 5*, 3–14.

Chen, G. M., & Ma, R. (2002). *Chinese conflict management and resolution*. Westport: Greenwood Publishing Group.

Di, X. (2006). Restorative justice from the perspective of psychology [*xinlixue shiye xia de huifuxing sifa*]. In D. Luo, X. Di, & A. Ma (Eds.), *Criminal Justice Psychology Study* [xingshi sifa xinli yanjiu] (pp. 12–21). Beijing: Qunzhong Press.

Di, X., & Wu, Y. (2009). The developing trend of the People's mediation in China. *Sociological Focus, 42*(3), 228–245.

Diamant, N. J. (2000). Conflict and conflict resolution in China beyond mediation-centered approaches. *Journal of Conflict Resolution, 44*(4), 523–546.

Dong, S. (2007, May). An overview of studies on Chinese restorative justice (zhongguo huifuxing sifa yanjiu zongshu). *Journal of Shandong Police College, 93*, 32–40.

Du, Y. (2010). The conceptual framework of victim-offender mediation: Centering on comparison of five dimensions [*xingshi hejie de gainian kuangjia—yi wuzu fanchou de bijiao wei zhongxin*]. *Zhongshan Law Review, 8*(1), 306–329.

Dünkel, F., Grzywa-Holten, J., & Horsfield, P. (2015). *Restorative Justice and Mediation in Penal Matters in Europe: A stock-taking of legal issues, implementation strategies and outcomes in 36 European countries*. Monchengladbach: Form Verlag Godesberg GmbH.

Eglash, A. (1977). Beyond restitution: Creative restitution. In J. Hudson & B. Galaway (Eds.), *Restitution in criminal justice* (pp. 91–129). Toronto: Lexington Books.

Faget, J. (2012). Restorative justice in France: A hard fight against penal logic. In D. Miers & I. Aertsen (Eds.), *Regulating Restorative Justice: A comparative study of legislative provision in European countries, studies in criminology and forensic sciences* (Vol. 2). Monchengladbach: Verlag für Polizeiwissenschaft.

Fu, J. (2006). Re-examining restorative justice [*zaiyi huifuxing sifa*]. *Gansu Agriculture, 2006*(3), 13.

Halegua, A. (2005). Reforming the People's mediation system in urban China. *Hong Kong Law Journal, 35*, 715.

Hawes, C. S., & Kong, S. (2013). Primetime dispute resolution: Reality TV mediation shows in China's "harmonious society". *Law & Society Review, 47*(4), 739–770. doi:10.1111/lasr.12046.
He, X., & Ng, K. H. (2013). In the name of harmony: The erasure of domestic violence in China's judicial mediation. *International Journal of Law, Policy and the Family, 27*(1), 97–115.
Hu, J. (2011). Grand mediation in China. *Asian Survey, 51*(6), 1065–1089. doi:http://dx.doi.org/10.1525/as.2011.51.6.1065.
Huang, P. C. C. (2006). Court mediation in China, past and present. *Modern China, 32*(3), 275–314. doi:10.2307/20062641.
Huang, Z. (2010). How to integrate Chinese and western Laws? Morals, rights and utility [*zhongxi falv ruhe ronghe? daode, quanli yu shiyong*]. *Peking University Law Journal, 22*(5), 721–736.
Lenz, S., Weitekamp, E. G. M., & Kerner, H.-J. (2012). Depicting the development of victim-offender mediation: Empirical research on restorative justice in Germany. In I. Vanfraechem, I. Aersten, & J. Willemsens (Eds.), *Restorative justice realities: Empirical research in a European context* (pp. 121–147). The Hague: Eleven International Publishing.
Li, H. (2007). Criminal reconciliation: A challenge to traditional conceptions of criminal law [*xingshi hejie: yizhong dui chuantong xingfa linian de tiaozhang*]. In J. Huang & Z. Zhen (Eds.), *Criminal reconciliation under the context of harmonious society [hexie shehui yujing xia de xingshi hejie]* (pp. 362–377). Beijing: Qinghua University Press.
Li, J. (2009a). A response to "the developing trend of the People's mediation in China": An institutional transformation of grassroots mediation in conflict resolution: Where is China headed? *Sociological Focus, 42*(3), 246–253.
Li, W. (2009b). Discussion on the relationship between victim-offender mediation and restorative justice [*shilun xingshi hejie yu huifuxing sifa de guanxi*]. *Journal of China Youth University of Political Science, 5*, 79–84.
Li, J., & Zhang, S. (2006). Restorative justice: Ethics based on criminal justice [*xiufuxing zhengyi: jiyu xingshi sifa zhankai de lunli*]. *Morals and Civilization, 6*, 54–57.
Lincoln, Y. S., & Guba, E. G. (1985). *Naturalistic inquiry*. Newbury Park, London and New Delhi: Sage Publications, Inc.
Liu, R. (2007). Restorative justice and harmonious society. *Journal of Fujian Public Safety College, 2007(1)*(95), 4–10.
Liu, R. (2010). Pursuing 'No Harm' and win-win justice [*zhuiqiu wuhai shenzhi duoying de zhengyi*]. *Observation and Reflection, 2010*(6), 56.
Liu, Z., & Xiao, H. (2007). Criminal reconciliation: Local construction of restorative justice [*xingshi hejie: huifuxing sifa de bentuhua goujian*]. *Journal of Liaoning Administrators' College of Police and Justice, 2007*, 20–23.
Ma, R. (1992). The role of unofficial intermediaries in interpersonal conflicts in the Chinese culture. *Communication Quarterly, 40*(3), 269–278.
Maruna, S. (2014). The role of wounded healing in restorative justice: An appreciation of Albert Eglash. *Restorative Justice: An International Journal, 2*(1), 9–23.
Miers, D., & Aertsen, I. (Eds.). (2012). *Regulating restorative justice: A comparative analysis of legislative provision in European countries, studies in criminology and forensic sciences* (Vol. 2). Monchengladbach: Verlag für Polizeiwissenschaft.
Ng, K. H., & He, X. (2014). Internal contradictions of judicial mediation in China. *Law & Social Inquiry, 39*(2), 285–312. doi:10.1111/lsi.12034.
Peerenboom, R., & He, X. (2009). Dispute resolution in China: Patterns, causes and prognosis. *East Asia Law Review, 4*, 1.
Read, B. L., & Michelson, E. (2008). Mediating the mediation debate conflict resolution and the local state in China. *Journal of Conflict Resolution, 52*(5), 737–764.
Shao, J. (2005). Debating on pros and cons of restorative justice [*huifuxing sifa de libi zhizheng*]. *Law Science, 2005*(5), 113–115.
Shen, A., & Antonopoulos, G. A. (2013). Restorative justice or what?: Restorative justice in the Chinese youth justice system. *European Journal of Crime, Criminal Justice, 21*, 291–315.
Shi, L. (2007). Criminal reconciliation: The "third realm" of criminal dispute settlement [*xingshi hejie: xingshi jiufen jiejue de disan lingyu*]. *Tribune of Political Science and Law, 25*(6).

Shi, Y. A. (2008). On restorative justice practiced in China. *Frontiers of Law in China, 3*(2), 294–323.
Song, Y. (2008). Empirical research on China's victim-offender mediation [*xingshi hejie shizheng yanjiu*]. *China Legal Science, 5*, 123–135.
Song, Y. (2009). Empirical analysis of the status quo of criminal mediation in China [woguo xingshi hejie xianzhuang shizheng fenxi]. Paper presented at the *Criminal Mediation and Improvement of the Criminal Procedural Law*, Beijing.
Song, Y., & Yuan, J. (Eds.). (2009). *Theory and practice of criminal reconciliation in China*. Peking: Peking University Press.
Strang, H. (2013). Conferencing and victims. In E. Zinsstag & I. Vanfraechem (Eds.), *Conferencing and restorative justice: International practices and perspectives* (pp. 83–100). Oxford: Oxford University Press.
Tidwell, A. (2001). *Conflict resolved?: a critical assessment of conflict resolution*. London and New York: Continuum.
Trevaskes, S. (2009). Restorative justice or mcjustice with Chinese characteristics? In M. Farquhar (Ed.), *21st century China: Views from Australia* (pp. 77–96). Newcastle upon Tyne: Cambridge Scholars Publishing.
Trevaskes, S. (2010). The Shifting Sands of punishment in China in the era of 'Harmonious Society'. [article]. *Law & Policy, 32*, 332–361.
Trevaskes, S. (2011). Political ideology, the party, and politicking: Justice system reform in China. *Modern China, 37*(3), 315–344. doi:10.1177/0097700410394776.
Utter, R. F. (1987). Dispute resolution in China. *Washington Law Review, 62*, 383.
Walgrave, L. (2011). Investigating the potentials of restorative justice practice. *Journal of Law & Policy, 36*(9), 91–139.
Walgrave, L. (2013). The need for clarity about restorative justice conferences. In E. Zinsstag & I. Vanfraechem (Eds.), *Conferencing and restorative justice: International practices and perspectives* (pp. 33–46). Oxford: Oxford University Press.
Wall, J. A., & Blum, M. (1991). Community mediation in the People's Republic of China. *Journal of Conflict Resolution, 35*(1), 3–20.
Wang, P. (2007). *Restorative Justice Forum: Vol. 3 [huifuxing sifa luntan: zong di san juan]*. Beijing: Chinese Procuratorial Press.
Wang, J. (2013). To divorce or not to divorce: A critical discourse analysis of court-ordered divorce mediation in China. *International Journal of Law, Policy and the Family, 27*(1), 74–96.
Weitekamp, E. G. M. (2000). Research on victim-offender mediation. Findings and needs for the future. In European Forum for Victim-Offender Mediation and Restorative Justice (Ed.), *Victim-offender mediation in Europe* (pp. 99–121). Leuven: Leuven University Press.
Willemsens, J. (2008). The role of the European Union in the further development of restorative justice. In *Restorative justice: an agenda for Europe*. Leuven: European Forum for Restorative Justice.
Wong, D. S. W. (2013). Restorative justice for juvenile Dlinquents in Hong Kong and China. In K. S. V. Wormer & L. Walker (Eds.), *Restorative justice today: Practical applications*. Los Angeles, London, New Delhi, Singapore, Washington DC: Sage Publications, Inc.
Wong, D. S. W., & Mok, L. W. Y. (2010). Restorative justice and practices in China. *British Journal of Community Justice, 8*(3), 13–23.
Yao, J. (2007). Practces and prospects of restorative youth justice in China [*huifuxing shaonian sifa zai zhongguo de shijian yu qianjing*]. In X. Di & Z. Liu (Eds.), *Theory and practice of restorative youth justice [huifuxing shaonian sifa lilun yu shijian]* (pp. 381–394). Beijing: Qunzhong Press.
Yin, R. K. (2009). *Case study research: Design and methods*. California, New Delhi, London, Singapore: Sage Publications, Inc.
Zhang, H. (2013). Revisiting people's mediation in China: Practice, performance and challenges. *Restorative Justice: An International Journal, 1*(2), 244–267.

Chapter 2
Conflict Resolution in China: Cultural Then Political?

Braithwaite (1999, p. 12) once opined that "Confucius [was] arguably the most influential thinker about restorative justice the world has known." Deeply influenced by Confucian values and philosophies, Chinese society, as compared with its Western counterparts, is supposed to exhibit a higher degree of interdependency and communitarianism, two characteristics believed to be conducive to the reintegrative shaming of the wrongdoer. Restorative justice, as an umbrella concept – covering various programs that endeavor to bring the wrongdoer and the victim together – did not establish itself until the early 1990s (Strang 2002). It claims to have roots in community conflict resolution mechanisms in the early histories of various societies. The concept of restorative justice may be unknown to the Chinese (Johnstone and Van Ness 2007), but its ideals and values are not new to Chinese society and its people. Mediation, as a peaceful way of resolving conflicts, is a historical reality and continues today. In fact, there are remarkable convergences between restorative justice principles and the Chinese traditional legal culture (Liu and Palermo 2009), although one cannot neglect their distinct differences in terms of their respective value-driven practices (Wong and Mok 2013).

Knowing the past helps us to better understand the present. This chapter comprises three parts. The first part (Sects. 1, 2, and 3) delineates the traditional Chinese culture and social structure and its sustaining traditional dispute resolution model. The convergences and divergences between traditional Chinese mediation and modern Western restorative justice are discussed. In the second part (Sects. 4 and 5), we examine mediation in more recent periods, namely, the Republican period and the Socialist period. For this part of the analysis, we relied on the literature and historical materials retrieved from the Century Journals Project in CNKI (China National Knowledge Infrastructure) as well as English and Chinese scholarly publications. In the third part (Sect. 6), we conclude by expressing some concerns as well as by pointing out the implications that Western restorative justice may have for reforming Chinese mediation.

X. Yuan, *Restorative Justice in China*, Springer Series on Asian Criminology and Criminal Justice Research, DOI 10.1007/978-3-319-63922-2_2

1 A Glimpse of Traditional Chinese Culture

1.1 Harmony Culture

Perhaps the term that best represents Chinese culture is "harmony" (*he*, 和). There are many proverbs in Chinese (Mandarin) associated with *he*, such as *he wei gui* 和为贵 (harmony is the most precious thing), *he qi sheng cai* 和气生财 (harmony brings wealth), *jia he wan shixing* 家和万事兴 (a peaceful family will prosper), etc. The emphasis on harmony is rooted in Confucianism. The Analects of Confucius[1] articulate *he* many times, and the one that is probably cited the most is: "In hearing litigations, I am like any other body. What is necessary, however, is to cause the people to have no litigations."[2] The ideal society, for Confucians, is a land without litigation. People maintain harmonious interpersonal relationships and exert mutual love and respect, which is for the greater good and ultimately benefits the whole society. The Confucian ideal of harmony is said to have been borrowed from another Chinese philosophy, Taoism, which believes in the existence of a corresponding relationship between the human world and the cosmic order. A disturbance in society is a disruption of harmony in the cosmos. Therefore, harmony in society should be well preserved.[3] Another school, the Legalists (*fa*), which is opposed to Confucianism, emphasizes heavy penalties to keep people's behavior in line. However, the Legalists share the Confucian pursuit: People should live in peace and harmony without being bound to external constraints such as the law. In other words, the purpose of punishment was to restore social order and harmony, thus restoring relationships to their original state.

To attain the status of harmony, Confucianism also developed a comprehensive set of norms for the social interactions between people in various relationships. Among these norms, two core concepts are *ren* 仁 (benevolence) and *li* 礼 (rites). Ren refers to showing love and affection to one's counterparts in social interactions (Chen 2002). The truly cultivated gentleman would not allow himself to be drawn into a dispute or a lawsuit against his fellows; such involvement was itself a sign of moral failure (Huang 2006). If a dispute arose, he would nevertheless rise above it by practicing yielding (*rang*) and forbearance (*ren*).

The other core element of Confucianism, *li*, refers to propriety and respect for social norms (Yum 1988, as cited in Chen and Ma 2002). Each human being should behave in accordance with his status in the hierarchical structure categorized by five relationships: parents and children, inferiors and superiors, teachers and students, elders and youngsters, and friends. Hence, harmonious relationships are characterized by "benevolence from the father, filial piety from the son, gentleness from the elder

[1]A collection of ideas and notions attributed to Confucius and his disciples, also known as the Confucian Analects or the Analects.

[2]Translated by James Legge, retrieved from http://ctext.org, 10 February 2016. The original in Chinese: 子曰: "听讼, 吾犹人也, 必也视无讼乎!".

[3]For a discussion on *he* in Confucianism and Taoism, see Jun (1994).

brother, obedience from the younger, uprightness from the husband, submission from the wife, benevolence from elders, deference from juniors" (Zhang 2013b, p. 144). In short, the maintenance of harmony and the containment of interpersonal conflict are highly valued principles of social regulation in Chinese society (Hwang 2012). The belief in harmony leads the Chinese people to pursue a conflict-free society in which they can attain "a feeling of security, a feeling of togetherness, a joyful feeling of interacting, and a feeling of being benefited from the interaction" (Chen 2002, p. 14).

1.2 *Shame Culture*

Chinese people believe that a human being should have a sense of shame. A man without a sense of shame is a shame in itself. Since the seminal book by Benedict (1946), *The Chrysanthemum and the Sword*, Eastern culture, influenced by Confucianism, has generally been regarded as a *shame culture*, while Western culture has been perceived as a *guilt culture*. While a popular distinction between shame and guilt suggests that shame is a more public emotion, whereas guilt is a more private affair, this idea has been challenged by another influential distinction proposed by Lewis (1971, as cited in Tangney et al. 1996, p. 1257) that "a fundamental difference between shame and guilt centres on the role of the self in these experiences." Lewis argued that the experience of shame is directly about the *self*, while in guilt, the focus is on the *thing* done or undone (as cited in Tangney et al. 1996, p. 1257). Despite these psychological endeavors regarding the differences between shame and guilt, the role of shame in people's lives and in Chinese society cannot be neglected.

1.2.1 Shaming as Punishing

As in any other society, punishment was pervasively used in ancient China, although it may have meant different things. Punishment could consist of a variety of cruel penalties imposed by the sentencer, such as casting out, exile, imprisonment, etc. It may also refer to the rationalities behind the way the sentencer treats the perpetrator. What has distinguished the punishments in China from those in its Western counterparts historically may lie in the fact that shaming was used both in formal settings and informal settings to punish offenders. While the formal setting refers to a formal court procedure, the informal setting refers to close-knit niches: the family, the neighborhood, the clan, the village, etc.

Formal shaming seemed to have been used much less than informal shaming. Historically, the state justice was only sought for the most serious crimes, which defied the royal rule or broke the fundamental ethics of the Confucian society (MacCormack 1990). The penalties imposed by courts, recorded as *wu xing* (five penalties), were largely for the purpose of shaming the offender, such as beating with a light stick, beating with a heavy stick, penal servitude, and life exile. Arguably, there was no such thing as "imprisonment" because the ancient Chinese did not believe that throwing the offender into prison could turn a bad man into a good one (Mühlhahn 2009). State punishments, with exceptions such as execution, were resorted to with the purpose of arousing the offender's sense of shame so that he could repent and renew himself.

1.2.2 Reintegrative Shaming Practices

Social sanctioning, an informal shaming used by the family and the neighborhood, was widely used to bring offenders in line (Leng 1967). Historically, the family and the neighborhood have been important institutions of informal social control in China (Lu et al. 2002). One illustration is *baojia* (*jia*, 10 households; *bao*, 100 households), a system in existence since the *Qin* state[4] to ensure interdependency, the reinforcement of mutual obligations, and the supervision of neighbors.

The fact that the state had difficulty extending its power into the vast rural lands contributed to the growing number of local societies comprised of families, clans, villages, or counties. Governance was performed by these local institutions, which were not formally integrated into the governmental system. They had the duty to resolve disputes related to family, marriage, property, and minor criminal cases. When a dispute arose, the family and clan organization were the first to settle it, and if this failed, the village headmen were then consulted. A wrongdoer violating the values or morality maintained by the larger group for community life was encouraged to reform himself – which was the process by which he could be reintegrated back into the community (Mascolo et al. 2003, cited in Li et al. 2004). If he did not show a sense of shame, people may have felt an urge to condemn him not only for his shameful act but mainly for the person's unwillingness to amend himself (Li et al. 2004). Surrounded by the community and caring people, the perpetrator was placed under great pressure to demonstrate shame and remorse for his behavior. In societies with a high level of communitarianism, offenders are viewed as "whole complex personalities" whose behavior is seen as shameful, but the self is not stigmatized as deviant (Braithwaite 1989). Shaming is more likely to end in reintegration: He who shows repentance is accepted back into his original community.

1.3 Interdependent and Communitarian Society

1.3.1 Families and Neighborhoods

In Confucian political philosophy, the family and the state are not very distinct from each other. The relationship between the emperor and his subjects was akin to the relationship in a family between the father and his subordinates, including the son,

[4]The *Qin* state conquered all the other warring states and established the first dynasty in China in 221 BC, although the dynasty was short-lived (14 years).

the wife, the daughter, the grandchildren, etc. A stable state and family require everyone to behave according to their roles and status in society and the family.

One of the fundamental ethics in Confucian philosophy is the "filial piety" (*xiao*, 孝) that children should practice toward their parents. Children should obey the teachings of their parents and behave as is expected of them, i.e., they should be good members of their family and law-abiding members of society. While a person's achievement is a source of pride to the whole family, his bad deeds are also shameful for all members of the family. A shameful circumstance even goes beyond the present members, reaching to their ancestors. One might say a good achievement "grants face" to the ancestry, while a bad one "loses face" for the ancestry.

Children are usually socialized through shaming: They learn that what they have done is not acceptable when their parents exert disapproval. This disapproval may include care and hope, but it can also be very harsh, disrespectful, hateful, etc. Nevertheless, as long as bonds with the family remain central in one's social life, the family's role in deterring and preventing negative social behavior is significant.

Neighbors may play both good and bad roles. As the Chinese saying goes, "a close neighbor is better than a distant cousin" (*yuanqin buru jinlin*, 远亲不如近邻), because the good neighbor provides social support when it is needed. However, he can also spread bad/shameful news to others. Gossip remains a very powerful weapon in a highly interdependent community. When one member of the family commits a reprehensible act that shames all the family members, this event cannot be kept only within the family. The neighbors always hear about it and work as important messengers; as another saying goes, "good things stay indoors while bad things will go far away" (*haoshi bu chumen, waishi chuan qianli*; 好事不出门, 坏事传千里). Consequently, family members may suffer from anxiety, worries, embarrassment, etc. because their shame has been exposed to the community. This may act as an important but very pervasive informal social control and crime prevention strategy in Chinese society. Nevertheless, the power of shaming cannot be divorced from the basic societal structure, which is dominated by interconnectedness.

1.3.2 Interconnectedness and Mutual Obligation

The modern reintegrative shaming theory proposed by Braithwaite (1989) hypothesized that interdependence and communitarianism are two social conditions that are conducive to reintegrative shaming. While Western culture emphasizes independence, in which "the self is conceived of primarily as an autonomous entity," Asian cultures like China emphasize interdependence, which is defined as "the inherent connectedness among different individuals" (Kitayama et al. 1995, p. 442, as cited in Stipek 1998, p. 616).

Chinese society is widely regarded as an "acquaintance society" (*shuren shehui*, 熟人社会). Connections play an extremely important role in people's lives. For the Chinese, each person's identity is intimately and essentially defined by their many relationships within the intricate network of Chinese society (Utter 1987). One anthropologist (Fei 1985) pointed out that the Chinese categorize their relationships by steps, from the self outward, much like the ripples created when a stone is thrown into a lake. He defined this cultural feature as a "differential mode of association (*chaxu geju*, 差序格局)." The Chinese view the self as "the totality of relationships touching one's life" (Utter 1987, p. 396), thus preserving a relationship is paramount. Moreover, because people are closely connected with each other, interpersonal conflict never affects only the primary parties; rather, that "which touches one person must inevitably reverberate through the lives of a host of others" (Utter 1987, p. 394).

In contrast to the individualism and liberalism in Western societies, Chinese society reinforces one's obligations to others, i.e., those in the network of family, friends, neighbors, colleagues, etc. There is no such a thing as an individual "right" in Chinese legal culture (Liang 2011). The bearer of the "right" is the one whose properties, interests, or feelings have been harmed – the "victim" according to the Western concept. However, if the "victim" raised his claims, he would be laughed at or treated as an outcast by the community, because by doing so, he would violate the mutual obligation that everyone within the same community owes to each other. An encouraged virtue would be *ren* 忍 (forbearance). Due to their obligations to others, those faced with injuries and suffering are supposed to exert endurance and even forgiveness. This orientation toward obligation was well captured by Montesquieu et al. (1748):

> The principal object of the Chinese legislators was to have their people living [in] tranquility. They wanted men to have much respect for each other; they wanted each one to feel at every instance that he owed much to the others; they wanted every citizen to depend, in some respect, on another citizen. Therefore, they extended the rules of civility to a great many people. (p. 317)

2 Traditional Dispute Settlement in China

Recourse to litigation was definitely a breakdown in an interpersonal relationship and hence was greatly discouraged by rulers throughout Chinese history. A good man must not have issues with others, while those who brought lawsuits were usually considered morally reprehensible. Such a repressive attitude toward conflict stemmed, on the one hand, from the need for governance; on the other hand, it embodied a pursuit of harmony in society. Under the harmony mores, the law was to teach people to avoid conflict with each other, rather than to specify a person's rights in the conflict as in the Western legal system. Overall, the responsibility of the state and the mission of the law were not to coordinate people's conflicts but to eliminate conflicts (Liang 2011). However, just as in any other society, conflicts could not be eliminated entirely; therefore, mechanisms for resolving conflicts had to be functional and accessible.

Throughout Chinese history and over the extensive rural areas in China, mediation has been dominant in dispute resolution (Cohen 1966; Lubman 1967; Huang

2006; Utter 1987). Dispute settlement was mainly performed by the county organizations (Jun 1994), comprised of a system of families, villages, clans, guilds, etc. The mediation was based on the Confucian social norms of *li* and, hence, was recognized or given tacit consent by all the dynasties. Only the most serious cases in a village were referred to the officials; most matters of conflict or crime were specified for settlement at the village level, and the officials were ordered not to interfere.

Although the village was given the maximum autonomy in managing and administering its own affairs, the central authority still monitored it via the rule exercised indirectly through the local elites to make sure that the community order conformed to the state sovereignty. The founder of the *Ming* dynasty (1368 AD–1644 AD), for example, attached importance to penetrating the villages and ensuring that the local populace's behavior and beliefs conformed to the ideals advocated by the government (Farmer 1987). The elders and the village leaders had the duty to settle local disputes and establish a positive moral influence over the community. In the *Qing* dynasty (1644 AD–1911 AD), the reach of the official state apparatus was quite limited, and much of the work of government was undertaken in "a third realm" in which the state and society collaborated (Huang 1993). The local magistrates incorporated community and kin mediation in dealing with civil matters: There was mediation or conciliation both in court and in the community. According to Huang's study of Qing's civil justice, in these cases, an out-of-court resolution of the dispute through the efforts of community or kin mediators was very common. As he described based upon an examination of the historical archives:

> *Upon satisfactory resolution of the matter, the plaintiff was expected to petition to close the case, explaining how it had been settled. Alternatively, the group of mediators—community or kin leaders, the local xiangbao, or one or more local notables—might submit the petition to close the case and recount how the dispute had been settled. Such petitions usually mentioned that the two parties had observed the appropriate ritual of apologizing to one another* (bici jianmian fuli [or peili]), *or that the offender had apologized or otherwise made amends, and that both parties wished to end the suit* (juyuan xisong). *In the event injury was involved, some reference also would be made to the fact that the wounds had healed* (shang yi quanyu). (Huang 1993, p. 266)

The magistrates usually granted the petitions from the plaintiff and the offender, or from the mediators, to close the case, showing leniency to the parties in dispute and respecting local customs and culture. They would attach a note of warning, e.g., "if this person should cause trouble again, the matter will be dealt with severely," or "if this person should engage in such unseemly behavior again, he will definitely be arrested and punished" (Huang 1993, p. 266).

In addition to the cooperation between the official and unofficial processes, village mediation was a typical "third realm" dispute resolution mechanism at the grassroots level.

> First, the invited or self-appointed village leaders come to the involved parties to find out the real issues at stake, and also to collect opinions from other villagers concerning the background of the matter. Then they evaluate the case according to their past experience and propose a solution. In bringing the two parties to accept the proposal, the peacemakers

> have to go back and forth until the opponents are willing to meet half way. Then a formal party is held either in the village or in the market town, to which are invited the mediators, the village leaders, clan heads, and the heads of the two disputing families. The main feature of such a party is a feast. While it is in progress, the talk may concern anything except the conflict. The expenses of the feast will either be equally shared by the disputing parties or borne entirely by one of them. If the controversy is settled in a form of 'negotiated peace', that is, if both parties admit their mistakes, the expenses will be equally shared. If the settlement reached shows that only one party was at fault, the expenses are paid by the guilty family. If one party chooses voluntarily, or is forced, to concede to the other… it will assume the entire cost. When the heads or representatives of the disputing families are ushered to the feast, they greet each other and exchange a few words. After a little while they will ask to be excused and depart. Thus, the conflict is settled. (M.C. Yang 1945, p. 165–166; as cited in Jun 1994, p. 27)

According to Jun (1994), this type of village mediation was sought only when informal mediation proved unsuccessful, the family and clan organization proved too weak to settle the dispute, or the disputing parties were from different clans, causing difficulty in solving the problem.

> In settling disputes, the heads of the family and clan concerned, the gentry or other respected persons were often invited to mediate the conflict jointly. Disputes were frequently settled at the village or town tea-house, which was often found to provide a congenial as well as a neutral and public setting for restoring harmony (Jun 1994, p. 26).

Settling disputes in a peaceful way and restoring harmony within communities mostly applied to ancient Chinese society (Jun 1994). A number of criminal matters were also settled this way, even if they were supposed to be reported to the authorities. The exact proportion of these cases remains unknown due to the limited amount of historical data. McKnight (1981) assumed that in the late imperial times (from the end of the first millennium to the last imperial dynasty), there was an increase in the proportion of criminal matters dealt with by agencies other than the state. As he explained, the foreign dynasties (or alien states) ruling the Chinese had less of a capacity to dispense official justice. Because the body of officials remained *Han* Chinese, influenced by Confucian philosophy, they may have been more concerned with preserving traditional culture, e.g., by respecting local customs and harmony.

The preference for local community settlement, such as mediation or peacemaking, although primarily driven by Confucian philosophy and values, also had something to do with the traditional legal structure. Chinese law, with very few clauses regulating civil affairs in the imperial formal codes, criminalized almost every type of civil dispute, allocating guilt and punishment to the parties in dispute, instead of differentiating rights from obligations. For fear of official sanction, the ordinary people entrusted their disputes to local organizations by seeking help from a respected or elder authority from the same community. Most civil cases and minor offenses were resolved within the community and attended by all the affected members. According to Lubman (1999), in the local community settlement, the "peace-talkers" or guild/clan leaders usually tried to bring the parties to a compromise without imposing a decision on them.

For traditional Chinese people, offenses were understood not in an official sense but as a violation of human feelings and community bonds. The aim of the settlement was not to exclude the guilty from the community or to impose suffering on him. Rather, the ideology was to achieve the greatest harmony possible among the parties and, more importantly, the community. Thus, a breakdown in social harmony far outweighs an individual concern.

3 Traditional Chinese Mediation and Western Restorative Justice: Convergences and Divergences

The Confucian philosophy, which stresses the virtue of harmony, has produced very strong social pressure against conflict and in favor of mediation and compromise. The community is not composed of equal individuals; rather, everyone's status and prestige is predetermined and known to the community members. To resolve conflicts within the community, the moral authorities from families, clans, and villages are all invited to decide upon the matters. This mechanism protects against state coercion and relies on a community's own resources. The agreement reached signifies harmony between the disputing sides and within the community and, thus, restoration.

Although it has been said that restorative justice (RJ) was commonly found in non-Western communities' early methods of resolving conflicts, the process comprising Chinese mediation can be totally different from what modern restorative justice would appreciate. However, both seek to resolve conflicts within the community. Restorative justice practices give decision-making power to the participants. In Chinese mediation, the mediator represents the moral authority in the community and has great influence on both sides, while the mediator/facilitator in many Western RJ settings is usually a trained volunteer or professional and has no moral weight in the disputants' lives. Braithwaite (2002), despite promoting the democratic decision-making model, recognized that "it might be wrong to persuade Asia to democratize their restorative justice practices. There may be merit in special efforts to recruit exemplars of virtue, grace, *mana* (italic in original), to participate" (p. 53).

Chinese mediation does not specifically attach importance to personal needs or rights but places greater emphasis on the solidarity and harmony within the community or society. In collectivist societies, individuality is devalued, and the individual's rights and needs are repressed. Rather, one's obligations and duties to others are stressed. In Western RJ, however, the victim is acknowledged as the direct bearer of the harm. Following that perspective, victims should be given the opportunity to tell their story of suffering, to be vindicated, and to be empowered when they walk out of the room. In Chinese mediation, individuals are considered selfish if they only care about their own needs or interests, therefore neglecting the harmony of the whole community. Perhaps there is not an obvious distinction between the perpetrator and the victim, because when a relational dispute occurs, both suffer the harm resulting from the broken relationship.

The judgment of what is right and wrong during Chinese mediation is based on *qing* 情 (human feelings) and *li* 理 (customary rules), rather than a clear legal responsibility set by the law, as may be embraced by many of today's restorative justice practices. Braithwaite and Pettit (1990) used the concept "dominion" to counter criticism from just desert theorists on the grounds of a lack of protection of legal rights. "Dominion," meaning freedom as non-domination, represents the minimum standard for safeguarding both offenders' and victims' rights in restorative justice. The criminal justice system supervises and takes care of any failure in the restorative justice process. In Chinese mediation, substantive justice has priority over the "due process" paradigm; there can be no such "Sword of Damocles" hanging over the parties in dispute, because the courtroom is generally believed to be impersonal, distant, and less relevant.

In order to achieve a resolution between the two sides, Chinese mediation may involve many techniques, such as persuasion, lecturing, education, etc. In some RJ practices, a "script" or "peace stone" is used in order to facilitate an equal dialogue. Facilitators/mediators cannot push the perpetrator or the victim into any settlement. If there is unwillingness, the process can stop at any time if one side so chooses. In Chinese mediation, the mediator, the community representatives, and other participants all make efforts to persuade each side to compromise and take a step back. The pressure from those involved is certainly tolerable. A final agreement that restores harmony is greatly appreciated.

Although Christie (1977) sounded the alarm that in Western societies, "conflict" has been stolen from the community by the state, we have probably seen how conflict was resolved in non-Western societies, despite the great divide between the approaches and the values of the East and the West. Triandis (1995), in *Individualism and Collectivism*, wisely pointed out: "[M]any problems of modernity in the West can be linked to too much individualism, whereas a lack of human rights can be attributed to too much collectivism" (p. 2). Not only are there differences in the approaches to crime, there are also nuances between the fundamental assumptions of restorative justice and the perceptions of conflict resolution in China.

3.1 Defining Harm

Chinese "mediation" is a term for bringing people together to resolve conflict. It is not, however, as limited as the modern concept of "victim-offender mediation," in which only the victim and the offender or, at most, their respective parents (in the case of juveniles) are invited. For the Chinese, the conflict is perceived as a community affair, and all those involved on both sides, as well as the community leaders and respectful persons, join the "circle" or "conference" to see the issue resolved.

In RJ, harm has been defined very broadly, including "material losses, physical injuries, psychological consequences, relational troubles and social dysfunctions" (Walgrave 2000, p. 260). Although the RJ literature to date has comprehensively focused on harm toward the victim, theoretically, it has defined harm at the individual, relational, and societal levels (Walgrave 2008). Thus, RJ theorists have supported the claim of a balanced attention to the needs of the victim, the community, and the offender (Bazemore and Maloney 1994).

However, the traditional practice in China seems to initially treat harm as relational and as having an orientation toward the community or the society. If one has a conflict with another, their relationship has been broken; therefore, as community members, the conflict between them interrupts the harmony (peace) within the community or, in a larger sense, in the society. Community leaders thus feel a need to restore peace within the geographical place over which they have authority.

3.2 *Defining the "Victim"*

Restorative justice places the victim at the center of attention and tries to meet the victim's needs. In Chinese society, because the harm is relational, all sides – the offended, the perpetrator, and their families – suffer from the occurrence of the conflict. In particular, the offender's family is affected to a greater extent, because it now bears great pressure and blame. As stated above, having a delinquent family member is considered as "losing face" (*diulian*, 丢脸), and all the family members can only bow their heads in front of their neighbors. The family then must stand up and make an apology for the wrong caused. This, presumably, shifts the attention from the person who is directly affected to the offender and his family. Mawby and Walklate (1994) critically commented that victims do not necessarily enjoy better treatment in non-Western systems of dispute settlement than they do in Western industrial societies. We would argue that in a collectivist culture, in which individuality is downplayed, the definition of a victim is different from that in Western societies.

Chinese mediation emphasizes the pursuit of harmony within the community and within interpersonal relationships, a goal shared by modern Western restorative justice. However, as discussed above, there may be differences with Western restorative justice, but the fundamental divergence may lie in the following: While Western restorative justice has defined a crime as "a violation of people and interpersonal relationships" (Zehr 1990, p. 19), implying one individual against another, Chinese mediation places interpersonal relationships and harmony above the individual. Thus, the understanding of a "victim" in the Western sense does not necessarily apply in a non-Western society such as China.

4 Mediation in the Republic of China (1912–1949)

The traditional dispute settlement was recontextualized to include new functions and roles in the "new China," which was founded in 1949 after the Communist Party finally took control over mainland China through violence and revolution. It might be worthwhile to briefly describe the period prior to the Communist takeover. Throughout the first half of the twentieth century, even though Chinese society frequently suffered civil wars and engaged in the War of Resistance against the Japanese (1937–1945), mediation survived this societal turbulence. As demonstrated below in this section, mediation continued to function as the primary way of resolving conflicts throughout the vast rural land, where peasants accounted for the largest portion of the population. In the cities, the courts, the police, the prosecutors, and the prisons were increasingly influenced by Western legal systems in terms of the way they functioned. It was a widely shared belief among intellectuals and reformists that Confucian culture and the two thousand years of feudalism it sustained were the reasons that China was backward and bullied (Lin 1979). The way out, according to these intellectuals and reformists, was to modernize Chinese society. Apart from developing industry, another crucial solution was to overhaul the traditional criminal justice system and to replace it with a whole set of advanced Western legal systems (Michael 1962). The German legal system was heavily emulated. However, these endeavors experienced very little success (Tay 1968). Still, traditional mediation had great vitality during the Republican period in counteracting the legal system as an instrument of modernization, and it largely operated on the basis of community autonomy with limited state intervention (Li 2009).

Early in the Republic of China, a nationwide mediation organization was yet to be established, but traditional civil organizations (*minjian zuzhi*, 民间组织) continued to play a significant role in resolving conflicts. In the period of the Nanjing Nationalist Government (1928–1949), *xi song hui* 息讼会 and *xi zheng hui*[5] 息争会 were built across the country. Although most of the constitutions for these committees did not specify the scope for mediation, a variety of disputes could be addressed (Luo 2013). For instance, the Constitution for Village *Xi Song Hui* 乡息讼会 in Hebei Province prescribed that "except death and theft cases, as long as the sides involved in the dispute request mediation and reconciliation, (the cases) should be decided fairly" (Luo 2013, p. 136). Usually, when hearing the case, *renqing* 人情 (human emotions) and *gong li* 公理 (common sense) were observed, while persuasion and peace were held as the key principles.

Based on some constitutions of *xi song hui*, a set of procedural requirements can also be identified. The mediators (*gong duan yuan*, 公断员) should remain fair and neutral, for instance, the "*gong duan yuan* should claim based on conscientiousness, conduct mediation in a proper way; (he/she) should not be influenced by private feelings such as closeness of relationship (*qinshu*, 亲疏), reciprocity and resentment, likeness and anger" (Luo 2013, p. 136). Moreover, *gong duan yuan* must not accept gifts beforehand or rewards afterward, and any violators would be punished. The mediation process was generally made public with a few exceptions, and at least half of all the committee members participated.

Later on, these *xi song hui* and *xi zheng hui* were replaced by mediation committees. In 1929, the Nationalist Government promulgated the Town Self-Governance

[5] Literally translated, they are the quenching litigation committee and the quenching conflict committee, respectively.

Implementation Law and the District Self-Governance Implementation Law, both prescribing that mediation committees be set up to resolve civil and criminal matters withdrawn from the court. More legal efforts can be found in the national 1931 Rules of Competence for *Qu* 区, *Xiang* 乡, *Zhen* 镇, *Fang* 坊 mediation committees and the national 1943 Organizational Rules on *Xiang Zhen* 乡镇 mediation committees. In addition, each province, county, and town laid down their own rules or regulations based on the local circumstances.

Note that the matters listed in the Organizational Rules on *Xiang Zhen* mediation committees comprised rape by means of guile (Article 229, Criminal Law of Republic of China), incest (Article 230), infringing marriage and family (Articles 238, 239), assault and battery (Articles 270-1, 281, 284), infringing freedom (Articles 298-1, 360), endangering reputation and credit (Articles 309-1, 310, 312, 313), infringing confidentiality (Articles 315, 316, 317, 318), theft (Article 324-2), encroachment (Articles 338, 324-2), fraud (Articles 343, 324-2), and damage (Articles 352, 354, 355, 356). Additionally, criminal matters that had been brought to court could still be mediated by the mediation committees.[6]

The following is an account of the work of a mediation committee in an administrative village of Sichuan Province in 1948 under the Nationalist regime (Barnett 1963, as cited in Cohen 1968):

> The Mediation Committee in the Hsiang Government is a five-man board (according to the regulations, there should be seven) responsible for administering justice. There is no court of law in the Hsiang. All disputes that can be handled locally are settled by this committee on the basis of equity. For example, if a man is accused of robbery, his neighbours escort him to the Mediation Committee, which hears both sides of the case, decides whether or not the man is guilty, and then proposes some sort of settlement that is accepted by all concerned. Crime is not a serious local problem, however. In the rare cases where a serious crime is committed, the man is sent to the Chungking Local Court for trial. Normally, he would be sent to the Hsien Local Court, but Pahsien has no court of its own and uses the one nearby in Chungking.
>
> The Mediation Committee holds its sessions on market days, and at each session a minimum of three committee members must meet to handle the cases brought before them (they average two to six cases each market day). Decisions must have the concurrence of at least two committee members and the committee's chairman. If the disputes are trivial and informal, the meeting is held in a teahouse. If they are more serious and a formal written report is presented, then the session is held in the Hsiang Office. All the current committee members are old men who have the respect, and command the deference, of the entire community. Four of the five belong to the group of twenty-one gentlemen [leaders] already mentioned. None of them receives any salary for serving on the committee.
>
> The cases brought before the Mediation Committee in Hsieh-mahsiang include petty criminal cases such as stealing, commercial disputes, personal arguments, debt trouble, and landlord-tenant disputes. (p. 129–130)

Only serious crimes were brought to court, while larger numbers of crimes were dealt with by the nongovernmental committees. With no intent to generalize, the

[6] See Luo (2013). The original is in Chinese; as such, the English translation is by myself.

above material may provide an indication about the notion of crime as it was understood by most of the population. That is, in most cases, crime was not understood as an offense against the state, and the offenders were not ostracized. This was a great contrast with the Western notion of crime. In the modernization of the criminal justice system in the Late Middle Ages in Europe (Langbein 2003), the state had taken over conflicts, distancing the offenders and victims and taking revenge in a "legitimized" form by sentencing the offender to prison. Because the crime occurred in the community, its solution should be provided by the local people within the same community. Even when some of the disputes were brought to the officials, the idea was not to alienate but to bring peace.

Cases brought to court could also be mediated by the judges in the Republican Era. Interestingly, an order issued by a judicial administrative minister on 3 June 1943 addressed how the judges should conduct mediation:

> *First, he should depart from the judge's ground, behaving himself as a mediator. When observing and listening, he should express the intent to resolve the disputes and let people have peace (*xishi ningren, 息事宁人*), making sure that both sides are convinced and contented, willing to mediate; then (he) should deliberately investigate the causes and development of the disputes, the character of the disputing parties, their experience, and their daily contacts and relationships. The aim is to identify the root causes, offer an equitable solution based on the time and the context, and inform both sides of the advantages, disadvantages and the policy. When a quarrel of greater intensity emerges, it is preferable to have a temporary interval, hold private discussions with each side and try to persuade them separately. If they are accompanied by relatives and friends, they should be allowed to be present should they so wish, or stay outside and assist in the persuasion. When an antecedent mediation is suitable, a recess is ordered, and mediation should come first. All in all, (if the mediators) are not afraid of fatigue and expenses, and harbour good will, then nothing is impossible for a willing heart, and mediation is more likely to achieve an effect.*[7]

According to Huang's (2006) investigation into the documentation, as well as the civil cases preserved in the country's archives (Huang 2006; Chen 2008), the business of the courts was mainly to adjudicate, while mediation was done extrajudicially by community and kin. In no case would a court make a serious effort to push the two sides toward a mutually acceptable settlement. Mediation operated to greater effect in the Republican period in society itself, and community mediation continued to play a significant role in the justice system as a whole (Huang 2006).

The Nationalist Government, which made substantial efforts in advancing China toward the Western model of the rule of law, acted progressively – albeit with difficulty – in respecting and preserving Chinese traditions (Chen 2008). As a result, crime remained a local problem and was dealt with by the local community with the help of mediation committees and their mediators. Community autonomy was respected and shielded from state intervention. However, the Nationalist Government retained only nominal control over China, and the Communist Party ruled over most of the country (Leng 1967).

---

[7]The 3098 order by the judicial administrative minister on 3 June, the thirty-second year of the Republic of China, in the Wartime Judicial Summary, 1948, p.165; as cited in Luo (2013, p. 142), my translation.

5 Mediation in the People's Republic of China

5.1 Early Period of the Socialist Regime (1949–1978)

5.1.1 Politicalizing Crime and Conflict

Following the triumph of the Chinese Communist Party (CCP) and the founding of the "new China," the socialist regime led by Mao immediately endeavored to consolidate its leadership. The notion of conflict suddenly fell within the ambit of "class struggle." Throughout the continuous revolutionary campaigns and reforms, Chinese society was split into "the people," i.e., those who were in favor of the socialist regime, and "the enemies," i.e., those who were against the CCP. Likewise, "conflict" was also classified as "between the people" and "between the people and the enemies." For conflict "between the people," a milder approach was used, such as self-criticism and socialist education. For conflict "between the people and the enemies," repression was the rule, although leniency could be granted when these reactionaries agreed to reform through labor and turned themselves in to the new socialist regime. According to Huang (2001), in the wider form of criminal process, harsh treatment, stigmatization, and exclusion were imposed on these enemies.

After all the previous legal codes enacted by the Nationalist Government were abolished, for a period, there was neither criminal law nor criminal procedure law in China. However, the trials of these enemies continued based on the regulations and policies made by the party itself. Criminality was defined as acts that did harm to the socialist state, and those who were against or presumably opposed to the socialist regime were offenders. "The state apparatus, including the army, the police and the courts, is the instrument by which one class oppresses another. It is an instrument of the oppression of antagonistic classes; it is violence, not 'benevolence'..." (Mao 1967, vol. 4:445–446, cited in Mühlhahn 2009, p. 200). The criminal justice system, established in the absence of a criminal code and a criminal procedure code, was based solely on the socialist ideology. As Michael (1962) commented, "[l]aw in the sense of norm no longer exists… the social order is to be reduced to that of a monist Communist power system, the totalitarian state" (p. 147). Crime was defined by the interests of the socialist regime. The 1979 Criminal Law and Criminal Procedure Law continued to be characterized by this notion.

5.1.2 "Institutionalizing" Mediation

While a formal criminal process was almost nonexistent during the first 30 years of Communist China, large numbers of conflicts were handled in an informal way. In fact, not long after the founding of the socialist regime, the State Council promulgated the Provisional General Rules for the Organization of People's Mediation Committees (25 February 1954), the first legislation specifically regulating mediation throughout the country. A People's Mediation Committee, according to this regulation, was defined as the masses' organization, working under the guidance of the local people's governments and the people's courts (Article 2). The task of the mediation committees was to mediate ordinary civil disputes among the people and minor criminal cases, and through mediation, they also had to conduct policies concerning propaganda-education, laws, and decrees (Article 3). The mediators should be selected from among those "whose political appearance is clear and who are impartial, linked with the masses, and enthusiastic about mediation work" (Article 5). By the end of 1954, in less than 10 months, 155,100 people's mediation committees had been set up in both the countryside and the cities (Jun 1994). Perhaps the most astonishing figure in the Chinese criminal justice system is the number of cases (this will be touched on in the next section) that have been handled by this mass organization since the founding of the People's Republic of China (PRC).

The dramatic departure of the semiofficial mediation organization from traditional Chinese mediation perhaps lies in its politicization. This process was compounded by the frequently launched political campaigns aimed at protecting the socialist regime, the high point being the 10-year Great Proletarian Cultural Revolution. The practices of the people's mediation committees during that period may provide some insights about how they worked. The following description is based on an article by a headman of the court at the county level on the role of mediation. People's mediators voiced their support for the party's policy and ideology, "under the Party's as well as Mao's leadership…we promise to work hard, diligently and with creativity, and will never be afraid of trouble." It was also asserted that "mediators should under the uniform leadership of the party, be equipped with more intensive political and ideological education."[8] To benefit the socialist production and reinforce solidarity among the people, the mediators spared no expense to provide mediation services. Cited in the same article, a divorce case involving assault was discussed in which the wife was persuaded as follows:

> Only the people's government would come to persuade you. If it were the reactionary government in the past, even if you died ten times, who would care about you? Yin mediator did not eat one meal at your home, and he also criticized your husband and he admitted mistakes. Others persuaded you with such patience only for your own sake, that if you continued with the quarrel, you may feel ashamed about this.

It was said that the wife was greatly touched and did not claim divorce or suicide, and they both lived peacefully.[9] It was not uncommon to find that the policies and interests of the party were cited during the mediation process in order to convince the disputants to surrender. While minor criminal offenses among "the people" were also dealt with by mediation, it arguably also helped the wrongdoers to correct their mistakes and induced conforming behavior.

Besides mediation, other forms of informal sanctions were widely used by local units (work units, residential committees, etc.). These sanctions were summed up by

[8] The script was taken from Zhao (1958).

[9] Ibid.

Mühlhahn (2009, p. 214) as follows: "Private criticism education through a member of the local unit, usually a party cadre; private warning by a functionary or an official; criticism in front of a small group; criticism in front of a larger group; censure as a harsher degree of criticism, involving oral or written statements of self-denunciation, self-examination, and repentance; discussion session to make the offender see reason; struggle session involves shaming and public humiliation and physical intimidation."

Given that most disputes arose among the people, not between the people and the non-people (the enemies), a series of measures were used according to the context and the circumstances. The policy for handling these disputes and misdemeanors was formulated in an explicit way in the following quotes (Cohen 1968):

> Our firm and unchanging policy for handling disputes among the people is to use persuasion-education and mediation. The basic method is energetically conducting socialist and communist education of the vast masses of people and propagandizing socialist law and discipline, thereby heightening the political awareness of the masses of people and their concept of law and discipline and preventing or reducing the occurrence of disputes. When we say that in resolving disputes one should persist in persuasion-education and in mediation, we certainly do not mean to reject the use of appropriate coercive sanctions when they are necessary. Persuasion-education and mediation have principles and a standpoint. Their principles are the benefiting of unity among the people and the benefiting of production and construction; their standpoint is the use of proletarian concepts to analyse affairs and to resolve problems. They are not vulgar mediation methods that rely on some abstract, supra-class "fairness" and "humanitarianism" or that in an unprincipled way make big matters into small matters and small matters into nothing. If we do not censure those who ought to be censured and if we do not give sanctions to those who must be sanctioned, then we cannot effectively educate the parties and the vast masses of people.

> Family meetings resolve family disputes. Since family disputes are problems within the same family, a meeting of the family members living within the same household may be held so that they can take the initiative in discussing the problem and resolving them. When necessary, they may invite relatives, friends, or neighbours to participate in the discussion in order to clarify right and wrong so as to arrive at a resolution of the dispute. It is their own affair, and this is a method whereby they themselves analyse and resolve it.[10] (pp. 141–142)

During the initial 30 years of the socialist regime, the party-state had gradually extended its influence deep into the lives of ordinary people, which manifested itself by politicizing informal organizations into semiofficial apparatuses. The wider part of society, which had not been touched by the past regimes, had now been incorporated into the socialist program, which has exerted its role as an instrument of propaganda-education and social control ever since. It was through its organizational web that the party's authority over the mediation process was distributed and wielded (Lubman 1967). This observation is also supported by the sociolegal analysis of Li (2009). His study suggested that "from 1949 to the mid-1970s, we notice a clear pattern of the ruling political party's gradual organizational penetration into the grassroots level of society, a situation that had never been seen before in Chinese history" (p. 249). Meanwhile, the Maoist ideology of mediation, which bore stark

[10] Chiang Shih-min et al., "Correctly Handling Disputes Among the People," CFYC, 4:29, 30 (1959). Cited in Cohen (1968, p. 141-142).

differences from the earlier Confucian ideology, expanded the meaning of mediation, giving it a far more aggressive and interventionist nature, irrespective of the will of the disputing parties (Huang 2006).

5.2 *Conflict Resolution After the 1978 Opening Up and Reform*

5.2.1 Defining Criminality Through Legislation

In the late 1970s, the party, under the leadership of Deng Xiaoping, was determined to steer the country back onto the right track, ending the chaotic political upheavals. The bold program of Opening Up and Reform was established as the state policy. A well-rounded legal system had to be put in place to facilitate economic development. Early in 1979, the Chinese criminal law (hereafter CL) and the criminal procedure law (hereafter CPL) were passed, respectively, by the National People's Congress. From the onset, both of these laws were strongly saturated with the ideology of the Communist state, with the Marxist-Leninist-Mao ideal as their guiding principle (Article 1, CL and CPL). The goal of the implementation of the criminal justice system became to punish criminals and protect the people (Article 1, CPL). A standard criminal process, similar to those in the Western world, was laid down, consisting of proceedings ranging from investigation, prosecution, pretrial, trial, and court sentencing to execution.

The 1979 Criminal Law consisted of eight categories of crimes: (1) counterrevolutionary, (2) endangering public security, (3) undermining the order of the socialist market economy, (4) infringing upon the rights of the person and the democratic rights of citizens, (5) encroaching on property, (6) disturbing the public administrative order, (7) disturbing marriage and family, and (8) dereliction of duty. The power to regulate crime was seemingly centralized to the state, in contrast to the relatively scattered approaches to crime before 1979. For instance, violently intervening in marriage freedom now constituted a crime based on CL and needed to be handled through the formal court procedure. In conducting a criminal lawsuit, the people's courts, the people's prosecutors, and the public security organs had to divide their responsibilities, coordinate their efforts, and check each other to ensure the correct and effective enforcement of law (Article 5, CPL).

The 1979 Criminal Law was later replaced with the 1997 Criminal Law, and the 1979 Criminal Procedural Law was replaced with the 1996 Criminal Procedural Law. To conform with the spirit of the legal systems of many other countries, the new CL established "nulla poena sine lege (no crime without law)" (Article 3), equality before the law (Article 4), and proportionality (Article 5) as its fundamental principles (Qu and Chen 2008). The categories of crime were provided with the following slight adjustments: (1) endangering national security (i.e., espionage), (2) endangering public security (i.e., arson, sabotaging public transportation), (3) undermining the order of the socialist market economy (i.e., smuggling, financial fraud), (4) infringing upon the rights of the person and the democratic rights of citizens (i.e., murder, rape), (5) encroaching on property (i.e., theft), (6) disrupting the order of the social administration (i.e., drug trafficking, organizing and forcing prostitution, manufacturing and selling obscene publications), (7) endangering the interests of national defense (i.e., sabotaging military weapons), (8) graft and bribery, (9) dereliction of duty (i.e., governmental official abuse of power), and (10) crimes of the violation of duty by military personnel (Lu and Kelly 2008). The order of this arrangement revolved around the severity of the harm each crime caused to society or the public interest, where applicable. The principles underlying the Chinese criminal justice system had changed. Crime was now seen as a rebellion against the state. Tackling crime became the monopoly of the state, including the public security organs, the prosecutor's office, and the courts.

If crime had been previously perceived as being not among "the people," but committed by the "enemies," there was now a perception of rising disorder, whereby crime challenged the entire modernization program and the power of the party. In dealing with this, the new leadership, led by Deng Xiaoping, believed firmly in the use of harsh punishment. The criminal justice system, since its establishment in 1979, has been marked by the frequent use of strike hard (*yan da*) campaigns, namely, in 1983, 1996, 2001, and 2004.[11] Being swift and brutal, strike hard campaigns were launched at the expense of offenders' rights and judicial fairness (Chen 2004a, b). Harshness in itself became the core of the argument in criminal justice policy (Bakken 2011). All these campaigns were launched in an attempt to halt the rising crime, to free society from hard-core criminals through harsh penalties and executions, and to frighten the population away from criminal involvement (deterrence). Capital punishment was used extensively, covering crimes ranging from the most severe to very minor and, sometimes, the slightest violations. Although data on crime prior to 1983 was unavailable, data on the crime rates from 1984 to 1988 showed that this draconian campaign did not manage to achieve any long-term effects (Bakken 2000). What ensued, however, was the fostering of a punitive culture in society. As Bakken (2011) asserted, changes in public attitudes toward harsh punishments are highly dependent on the state's own practices of punishment. Offenders were perceived as the "other" and, therefore, as deserving punishment with no mercy. Arguably, it was presumed that the state's interests lie in social stability; when the crimes jeopardize the social order, they deserve to be dealt with by criminal law.

5.2.2 People's Mediation in Handling Conflicts

People's mediation has appealed to international scholars (Goh 2002; Cohen 1967; Wall and Blum 1991; Lubman 1967; Cloke 1987). Here, we briefly examine the legislative efforts to bring the people's mediation committees under the framework of the rule of law, as well as the challenges and weaknesses associated with its functioning in the new broader societal context.

[11] The one launched in 2004 particularly focused on organized and gang crimes, violent crimes, and thefts.

People's mediation committees expanded quickly, as can be illustrated by the following figures. By 1979, there were 410,000 committees and 3,000,000 mediation workers (Yu and Liu 2007). Three decades later, by 2010, there were 818,000 committees and 4,669,000 mediation workers. In 2010, 8,418,000 cases were handled by these local mediation organizations, which was more than those handled by the courts, namely, 7,022,000 (Law Yearbook of China Editor Committee 2011).

The 1982 Constitution recognized the People's Mediation Committee as an important form of self-governing mass organization. In resolving conflicts in neighborhoods between groups, organizations, and individuals, it aims at promoting public morality and a sense of neighborhood (Wong 1999). Consistent with the practices formulated during the early years of the PRC, the committees handled a large number of disputes that may be qualified as "criminal" cases in Western legal systems. The mediated civil disputes include family disputes, housing disputes, conflicts between neighbors, damages and compensation, and a variety of other situations. Criminal cases could appear within some of these categories, such as conflicts between neighbors, damages and compensation, and so on.

In 1989, the new Organization Rules of the People's Mediation Committee were approved by the State Council. Note that in this regulation, the authority over minor criminal offenses was withdrawn from the people's mediation organization. Instead, the cases it addressed were of a civil nature, occurring in neighborhoods, among acquaintances, colleagues, etc.[12] They included those concerned with divorce, inheritance, parental and child support, alimony, debts, real property, production, torts, etc. Mediation committees are branches of the villagers' committees in the towns and villages and residents' committees in the cities. They are also under the guidance of the local government and the local people's court to conduct mediation. The mediation must clearly observe the stipulations of law, the regulations, and the party policies, and when they are not in place, the norms of public morality shall be observed.

People's mediation has undergone reforms along with the national goals of the CCP (Halegua 2005). Legal scholars in China have questioned the legitimacy of people's mediation on the grounds of problems with their approaches, in an era when there is an increasing demand for personal rights and legal protection. Yet the government perceives a need and an interest in increasing the use of people's mediation to resolve conflicts in society. In 2010, the National Congress passed the People's Mediation Law of PRC, granting the agreements reached through people's mediation legal weight in court. The People's Mediation Law requires that people's mediation committees shall abide by the laws, regulations, and policies of the state (Article 3) and that the mediator shall report in a timely way to the local public security organ or another competent department when he finds that a dispute may become a public security case or a criminal case (Article 5). It stipulates that in mediating a dispute, one or several people's mediators from the people's mediation committee can either be designated or chosen by the parties. After obtaining consent from the parties, the mediators can invite relatives, neighbors, colleagues, or people with certain expertise to participate in the mediation (Articles 19, 20).

[12] The original term was *Minjian jiufen* 民间纠纷, my translation.

An examination is required to understand exactly how mediation based on the law is being conducted (Halegua 2005). The members of the committees are selected or appointed based on their political integrity and ideology. Many of them are retired party cadres paid by local justice bureaus. Interference from the government is likely to occur in these circumstances in the form of pressure on the mediator to favor the party's interests and ideology when deciding upon the matter (Zhang 2013a, b). The parties may not be able to choose the mediator they want, and voluntariness during the mediation process, as well as in the final outcome, cannot be secured.

As one of the most informal social control mechanisms in Chinese society (Chen 2004a, b; Wong 1999), the main function of people's mediation is to maintain social order and social harmony, as written in the People's Mediation Law of the PRC 2010. Progressive efforts made by the government to promote people's mediation in recent years, including the passage of the People's Mediation Law 2010, need to be interpreted as responding to the intensified social conflicts that have manifested themselves in various types of negative incidents such as mass events (Halegua 2005; Wang 2013). The official utilization of comprehensive societal management in the name of social harmony has given rise to a quest by governmental offices and the judiciary to mobilize conflict solving – the "grand mediation" (*da tiaojie*, 大调解) (Zhang 2013a, b; Hu 2011). As in the past decades, the state has remained an active player in resolving disputes, although a proportion of these conflicts are between the people and the state (Hu 2011).

The extent to which mediation is used led Wall and Blum (1991) to name China the "most heavily mediated nation on earth." Whether or not this argument was made with care, mediation declined in the 1990s (Di and Wu 2009), and since 2002, there has been a tendency to rely more on the courts to resolve a broad range of disputes and conflicts (Zhang 2013a, b). Di and Wu (2009) explained this evolution in relation to the broader social structure and social changes. They cited economic development, social transformation, and cultural changes, which are more evident in urban China. They maintained that, as a result of increasing economic activities, conflicts have increased in number, type, and complexity, posing new challenges to people's mediation. The societal transition from an "acquaintance society" to a "stranger society" has weakened people's traditional bonds with their work units or neighborhoods. Therefore, when a dispute arises today, traditional reasoning such as collective interests and social harmony no longer has the same persuasive power. On the road to modernity, with people's enhanced awareness of rights and democracy, people's mediation will inevitably face old problems, as well as new challenges.

6 "The End" After the End

Braithwaite (2003) considered that, with regard to restorative justice, "Asian legal traditions are a more useful resource than Western ones" (p. 17). When we examined conflict resolution in Chinese legal history and the important philosophies and values from which it was formed, we share a similar opinion, although there are great divergences between China and its Western counterparts. As China modernizes under the socialist regime through the politicalizing and statizing of Chinese society, traditional mediation has been mobilized and transformed into people's mediation. According to some scholars (e.g., Hu 2011), people's mediation offers a place for the party-state to implement its ideologies and policies and to oversee every activity that may endanger the socialist order. Perhaps traditional mediation still exists in very rural villages or minor ethnic groups, where informal mediation by families, friends, neighbors, and colleagues is still favored (Cao 2008). One study by Song (2003) estimated that in the villages of Shandong Province, the number of criminal cases that are privately settled could be as much as 25%, although this is now prohibited by the law. Given the level of transformation to which the society has been subjected, this figure is dubious. A seed has been planted that the act of failing to hand a criminal over to the state is a crime in itself. A well-known recent example was that, in order to capture an escaped death-row prisoner, every corner of a village in a rural county installed CCTV and deployed well-equipped military personnel. A relative of the prisoner bound the prisoner when he came in for food and waited for the police to come. Suffering great guilt ever since, the relative murmured to the journalist: "No matter who he is, he would do the same."[13]

According to Wong (1999) and Braithwaite (1999), mediation-based informal control in China is the aspect that is the most similar to Western restorative justice. Indeed, in many respects, they bear a striking resemblance. For instance, they both aim to restore broken relationships and bring peace to disputing parties and the community (Mok and Wong 2013). Both emphasize negotiation and communication, rather than confrontation (Nie 2006). Both stress the role of community in crime prevention. Further, mediation programs in modern China and restorative justice practices in the West seem to have grown along parallel paths so far.

China's modernization process, which has been salient in recent decades, has transformed the nature of mediation and the voluntary settling of differences through third-party facilitation or intervention by a state-sponsored or state-controlled program, the "grand mediation" launched in recent years (Zhang 2013a; Hu 2011). This seems to have contrasting implications. Di and Wu (2009) believed that China's modernization and democratization process promises a bright future for people's mediation in terms of involving and empowering the community. By contrast, Li (2009) suggested that empowering the community has become an unattainable dream in the face of a strong party-state. Conflicts in the form of demonstrations, protests, and collective complaints have habitually been perceived as a threat to its regime, rather than as a legitimate way of articulating citizen interests (Hu 2011). While the trends of community participation in Chinese civil society remain marginal due to the monopolized power exercised by the CCP (Taylor 2004), organizations have also emerged to strengthen civil society and enhance people's participation in the decision-making processes affecting their daily lives (Taylor 2004).

Which of these developments provides a more accurate representation of the mediation being conducted today? What lessons can the Western restorative justice

[13] Retrieved from http://news.qq.com/a/20140912/071607.htm. 25 October 2014.

movement, which calls for the empowerment of the community, learn from China's resolution of conflicts and achievement of harmony? Conversely, what are the implications of the theory and practice of Western restorative justice for reforms in Chinese mediation?

References

Bakken, B. (2000). *The exemplary society: Human improvement, social control, and the dangers of modernity in China*. Oxford: Oxford University Press.
Bakken, B. (2011). China, a punitive society? *Asian Journal of Criminology, 6*(1), 33–50.
Bazemore, G., & Maloney, D. (1994). Rehabilitating community service toward restorative service sanctions in a balanced justice system. *Federal Probation, 58*, 24–35.
Benedict, R. (1946). *The chrysanthemum and the sword: Patterns of Japanese culture*. Boston: Houghton Mifflin.
Braithwaite, J. (1989). *Crime, shame and reintegration*. Cambridge: Cambridge University Press.
Braithwaite, J. (1999). Restorative justice: Assessing optimistic and pessimistic accounts. *Crime and Justice, 25*, 1–127. doi:10.2307/1147608.
Braithwaite, J. (2002). *Restorative justice and responsive regulation*. Cambridge: Cambridge University Press.
Braithwaite, J. (2003). Principles of restorative justice. In A. V. Hirsch, J. V. Roberts, & A. Bottoms (Eds.), *Restorative justice and criminal justice: Competing or reconcilable paradigms?* (pp. 1–20). Oxford: Hart Publishing.
Braithwaite, J., & Pettit, P. (1990). *Not just deserts*. Oxford: Oxford University Press.
Cao, Y. (2008). Social conflicts and modes of action in China. *The China Journal, 59*, 89–109.
Chen, G. M. (2002). The impact of harmony on Chinese conflict management. In G. Chen & R. Ma (Eds.), *Chinese conflict management and resolution* (pp. 3–17). Westport: Greenwood Publishing Group.
Chen, X. (2004a). Discussion on advantages and disadvantages of severe cracking down on criminal activities [*yanda libi zhiyi*]. *Journal of Henan Administrative Institute of Politics and Law, 5*, 120–123.
Chen, X. (2004b). Social and legal control in China: A comparative perspective. *International Journal of Offender Therapy and Comparative Criminology, 48*(5), 523–536. doi:10.1177/0306624x04265225.
Chen, J. (2008). *Chinese law: Context and transformation*. Leiden/Boston: Martinus Nijhoff Publishers.
Chen, G. M., & Ma, R. (2002). *Chinese conflict management and resolution*. Greenwood Publishing Group.
Christie, N. (1977). Conflicts as property. *British Journal of Criminology, 17*, 1–15.
Cloke, K. (1987). Politics and values in mediation: The chinese experience. *Conflict Resolution Quarterly, 17*, 69–82. doi:10.1002/crq.38919871709.
Cohen, J. A. (1966, August). Chinese mediation on the eve of modernization. *California Law Review, 54*, 1201–1226.
Cohen, J. A. (1967). Chinese mediation on the eve of modernization. *Journal of Asian and African Studies, 2*(1–2), 54–76.
Cohen, J. A. (1968). *The criminal process in the People's Republic of China 1949–1963: An introduction*. Cambridge, Ma: Harvard University Press.
Di, X., & Wu, Y. (2009). The developing trend of the People's mediation in China. *Sociological Focus, 42*(3), 228–245.
Farmer, E. L. (1987). Social order in early Ming China: Some norms codified in the hung-wu period. In B. E. McKnight (Ed.), *Law and the state in traditional East Asia: Six studies on the sources of east Asian law*. Hawaii: University of Hawaii Press.

Fei, X. (1985). *Native China*. Beijing: Life, Study and New Knowledge SanLian Bookstore.
Goh, B. C. (2002). *Law without lawyers, justice without courts: on traditional Chinese mediation*. Farnham: Ashgate.
Halegua, A. (2005). Reforming the People's mediation system in urban China. *Hong Kong Law Journal, 35*, 715.
Hu, J. (2011). Grand mediation in China. *Asian Survey, 51*(6), 1065–1089.
Huang, P. C. C. (1993). Between informal mediation and formal adjudication: The third realm of Qing civil justice. *Modern China, 19*(3), 251–298. doi:10.2307/189346.
Huang, P. C. C. (2001). *Code, custom, and legal practice in China: the Qing and the Republic compared*. Stanford: Stanford University Press.
Huang, P. C. C. (2006). Court mediation in China, past and present. *Modern China, 32*(3), 275–314. doi:10.2307/20062641.
Hwang, K.-K. (2012). *Foundations of Chinese psychology: Confucian social relations*. New York: Springer Science + Business Media.
Johnstone, G., & Van Ness, D. (Eds.). (2007). *Handbook of restorative justice*. Cullompton: Willan Publishing.
Jun, T. (1994). *A Historical, Philosophical and Legal Analysis of Chinese Mediation, University of Lapland Pulications in law, Serie B 22*. Rovaniemi: University of Lapland Faculty of Law.
Langbein, J. H. (2003). *The origins of adversary criminal trial*. Oxford: Oxford University Press.
Law Yearbook of China Editor Committee. (2011). *Law yearbook of China*. Beijing: China Law Yearbook Press.
Leng, S.-C. (1967). *Justice in communist China: A survey of the judicial system of the Chinese People's republic*. New York: Oceana Publications.
Li, J. (2009). A response to "the developing trend of the People's mediation in China": An institutional transformation of grassroots mediation in conflict resolution: Where is China headed? *Sociological Focus, 42*(3), 246–253.
Li, J., Wang, L., & Fischer, K. (2004). The organisation of Chinese shame concepts? *Cognition and Emotion, 18*(6), 767–797. doi:10.1080/02699930341000202.
Liang, Z. (2011). *Seeking harmony in natural order: Study on traditional Chinese legal culture [xunqiu ziran zhixu zhong de hexie — Zhongguo chuantong falv wenhua yanjiu]*. Taipei: National Taiwan University Press.
Lin, Y. (1979). *The crisis of Chinese consciousness: radical antitraditionalism in the May fourth era*. Madison: University of Wisconsin Press.
Liu, J., & Palermo, G. B. (2009). Restorative justice and Chinese traditional legal culture in the context of contemporary Chinese criminal justice reform. *Asia Pacific Journal of Police and Criminal Justice, 7*(1), 49–68.
Lu, H., & Kelly, B. (2008). Courts and sentencing research on contemporary China. *Crime Law and Social Change, 50*(3), 229–243. doi:10.1007/s10611-008-9132-6.
Lu, H., Zhang, L., & Miethe, T. D. (2002). Interdependency, communitarianism and Reintegrative shaming in China. *The Social Science Journal, 2002*(39), 189–201.
Lubman, S. (1967). Mao and mediation: Politics and dispute resolution in communist China. *California Law Review, 55*, 1284–1359.
Lubman, S. B. (1999). *Bird in a cage: Legal reform in China after Mao*. Stanford: Stanford University Press.
Luo, J. (2013). The mediation system in the period of Republica of China [*minguo shiqi de tiaojie zhidu*]. In X. Xu (Ed.), *Mediation: China and the world [tiaojie: Zhongguo yu shijie]* (pp. 134–147). Beijing: Press of China University of Political Science and Law.
MacCormack, G. (1990). *Traditional Chinese penal law*. Edinburgh: Edinburgh University Press.
Mascolo, M., Fischer, K., & Li, J. (2003). The dynamic construction of emotions in development: A component systems approach. In R. Davidson, K. Scherer, & H. Goldsmith (eds.), *Handbook of Affective Science* (pp.375–408). New York: Oxford University Press.
Mawby, R. I., & Walklate, S. (1994). *Critical victimology: International perspectives*. London: Sage Publications.

McKnight, B. E. (1981). *The quality of mercy: Amnesties and traditional Chinese justice.* Honolulu: The University Press of Hawaii.
Michael, F. (1962). The role of law in traditional, nationalist and communist China. *The China Quarterly, 9*, 124–148. doi:10.2307/651697.
Mok, L. W., & Wong, D. S. (2013). Restorative justice and mediation: Diverged or converged? *Asian Journal of Criminology, 8*(4), 335–347.
Montesquieu, C., Cohler, A. M., Miller, B. C., & Stone, H. S. (1748). *The spirit of laws (K. T. Nugent, trans., Cambridge texts in the history of political thought).* Cambridge: Cambridge University Press.
Mühlhahn, K. (2009). Criminal justice in China: A history. Cambridge, Massachusetts, and London. England: Harvard University Press.
Nie, Z. (2006). Deliberative justice: A new choice for criminal justice system [*xieshangxing sifa: xingshi sifa de xin xuanze*]. *Journal of Law Application, 9*, 92–94.
Qu, X., & Chen, X. (Eds.). (2008). *Criminal law*. Beijing: Press of Chinese University of Political Science and Law.
Song, Z. (2003, September 5). Why phenomenon of "siliao" in criminal cases became more rampant? [weishenme xingshi siliao xianxiang lvjin buzhi?]. *Semimonthly*.
Stipek, D. (1998). Differences between Americans and Chinese in the circumstances evoking pride, shame, and guilt. *Journal of Cross-Cultural Psychology, 29*(5), 616–629.
Strang, H. (2002). *Repair or revenge: Victims and restorative justice*. Oxford: Clarendon Press.
Tangney, J. P., Miller, R. S., Flicker, L., & Barlow, D. H. (1996). Are shame, guilt, and embarrassment distinct emotions? *Journal of Personality & Social Psychology, 70*(6), 1256–1269.
Tay, A. E.-S. (1968). Law in communist China-part 1. *Sydney Law Review, 6*, 153.
Taylor, J. G. (2004). The context for community participation in China. In J. Plummer & J. G. Taylor (Eds.), *Community Participation in China: Issues and processes for capacity building* (pp. 23–35). London and Sterling: Earthscan.
Triandis, H. C. (1995). *Individualism & collectivism*. Boulder: Westview Press.
Utter, R. F. (1987). Dispute resolution in China. *Washington Law Review, 62*, 383.
Walgrave, L. (2000). Extending the victim perspective towards a systematic restorative justice alternative. In A. Crawford & J. Goodey (Eds.), *Integrating a victim perspective within criminal justice: International dabates* (pp. 253–284). Aldershot: Ashgate Publishing.
Walgrave, L. (2008). *Restorative justice, Self-interest and Responsible Citizenship*. Cullompton: Willan Publishing.
Wall, J. A., & Blum, M. (1991). Community mediation in the People's Republic of China. *Journal of Conflict Resolution, 35*(1), 3–20.
Wang, J. (2013). To divorce or not to divorce: A critical discourse analysis of court-ordered divorce mediation in China. *International Journal of Law, Policy and the Family, 27*(1), 74–96.
Wong, D. S. W. (1999). Delinquency control and juvenile justice in China. *Australian & New Zealand Journal of Criminology, 32*(1), 27–41. doi:10.1177/000486589903200104.
Wong, D. S. W., & Mok, L. W. Y. (2013). Evolution of restorative justice practices for juvenile offenders in the People's Republic of China. In J. Liu, B. Hebenton, & S. Jou (Eds.), *Handbook of Asian criminology* (pp. 393–406). New York: Springer Science+Business Media.
Yu, Y., & Liu, Z. (2007). The system of People's mediation and its re-design in China: Subsidiary discussion on crime prevention of civil mediation [*woguo renmin tiaojie zhidu jiqi chonggou: jianlun minjian tiaojie dui fanzui de yufang*]. *Journal of Zhejiang University (Humanities and Social Sciences), 37*(2), 35–42.
Zehr, H. (1990). Changing Lenses: *A new focus for crime and justice*. Scottdale, PA: Herald Press.
Zhang, H. (2013a). Revisiting people's mediation in China: Practice, performance and challenges. *Restorative Justice: An International Journal, 1*(2), 244–267.
Zhang, J. (2013b). Ancient China's legal tradition and legal thought. *Social Sciences in China, 34*(2), 134–151.
Zhao, K. (1958). How people's mediation committee in Jurong country played its role [*jurong xian renmin tiaojie zuzhi shi zenyang fahui zuoyong de*]. *People's Judicature*, 2, 15–17.

Chapter 3
Criminal Mediation in the Chinese Criminal Justice Context

1 Introduction

As China advances its modernization process, the power to impose criminal penalties has become the monopoly of the state. Nevertheless, mediation, as a conflict resolution method, has not disappeared from the modern Chinese criminal justice system. In this chapter, we highlight the criminal justice system within which criminal mediation has been situated. This includes a general introduction of the criminal legislation concerning mediation, as well as the mediation practices that have been reported so far. Special attention will be given to the latter, calibrating the research and summarizing the pitfalls in practice, as well as the gaps in the literature.

2 Modern Criminal Law and Criminal Procedure Law in China

In the late 1970s, the Chinese Communist Party, under the leadership of Deng Xiaoping, put an end to the constant political campaigns and resolved to bring the country in line as a developing economy. The legal system was to be established in order to secure economic development and serve the modernization program. In 1978 and 1979, the National Congress passed the criminal law (CL) and the criminal procedure law (CPL), respectively. Borrowing the Western inquisitorial model, the legal system included proceedings such as investigations, prosecution, pretrial proceedings, court trial and sentencing, and post-sentence execution. Punishing offenders and protecting the people were the prioritized objectives. The ideology of the Communist Party was represented in both laws and was depicted by guiding principles such as upholding the Marxist-Leninist-Mao ideal, consolidating the People's Democratic Dictatorship and combating the enemies of socialism.

X. Yuan, *Restorative Justice in China*, Springer Series on Asian Criminology and Criminal Justice Research, DOI 10.1007/978-3-319-63922-2_3

Based on the political rhetoric of promoting the rule of law, as well as the progress toward modernization, both laws have undergone several changes in the past decades. The recent major revisions occurred, respectively, in 1996 and 2012 for the CPL and in 1997 for the CL. Notably, the CPL 1996 incorporated some cardinal principles of the adversarial system into the previous inquisitorial system (Liu and Situ 2001), which reflects the influence of both global norms and Western legal proceduralism (Leheny and Liu 2010). Nevertheless, the legal tradition still has a role to play, which is evident in some legal provisions (Liu and Palermo 2009). For example, Article 36 of the CL stipulates that "if a victim has suffered economic losses as a result of a crime, the criminal shall, in addition to receiving a criminal punishment according to law, be sentenced to making compensation for the economic losses according to the circumstances. If the criminal who is liable for civil compensation is also sentenced to a fine but his property is insufficient to pay both the compensation and the fine, or if he is sentenced to the confiscation of property, he shall, first of all, bear his liability for civil compensation to the victim" (National People's Congress 1997). All in all, with the revisions made to improve the two laws, it is more appropriate to consider the Chinese criminal justice system as a work in progress (Belkin 2000), yet there is a converging point at which the control of the Communist Party, the strong influence of Western culture, and Chinese traditional legal culture each have their places (Liu and Situ 2001).

3 The Place of Mediation in Criminal Legislation

The Chinese CPL, enacted in 1979, allows mediation between the offender and the victim for certain criminal offenses. For instance, Article 127 of CPL 1979 stipulated that the people's court can mediate in cases involving these offenses; the victims are permitted to settle the case with the offender and withdraw the case from the court at any time before a judgment is proclaimed by the court. It was unclear why the CPL 1979 did not specify which criminal offenses were applicable to Article 127; we can only infer a broad scope.

The CPL 1996 clearly stipulates that in certain criminal offenses, the victims can initiate the criminal proceedings. These offenses include (1) offenses for which the victims can choose to file an official claim or not (the "complaint offenses"), (2) minor criminal offenses which the victims have evidence to prove, and (3) offenses in which the victim has evidence to prove that his personal or property rights have been violated, although the police or the prosecutor decided not to pursue the case (Article 170). In all these cases, when the victims have initiated a prosecution, they are permitted to settle the case with the offender and to withdraw the case from the court at any time before a judgment is proclaimed by the court (Article 170, Article 172).

According to the criminal law (CL) , the offenses for which victims can choose not to initiate a prosecution, namely, the "complaint offenses," include insults and slander (Article 246 of CL), forced interference in the freedom of marriage (Article 257 of CL), abuse (Article 260 of CL), and occupying the properties of others

(Article 270 of CL). The "minor criminal offenses" are listed in the Supreme People's Court's judicial interpretation, and they include intentional minor harm against the person (Article 234 of CL), unlawfully intruding into another's residence (Article 245 of CL), infringing on freedom of communication (Article 252), bigamy (Article 258), abandonment (Article 261), manufacturing and selling fraudulent products (Chap. 3, Sect. 1, CL), infringing on intellectual property rights (Chap. 3, Sect. 7, CL), and crimes punishable by less than 3 years' imprisonment prescribed in Chaps. 4 and 5 of the CL. Notably, in both the "complaint offenses" and the "minor criminal offenses," the people's court can mediate between the victim and the offender (Article 170, Article 172). While the CPL 1996 also recognizes the right of victims to participate in a public prosecution (Zhang 2004), reconciliation with the offender is generally not permitted in the public proceeding.

The CPL 2012, in its revision, specifically allows the victim and the offender to reach an agreement during the course of the criminal proceedings even when the prosecution is brought by the public prosecutor. Article 277 allows a broad range of criminal offenses to end in an agreement: (1) criminal offenses against the person and against property as prescribed in Chaps. 4 and 5 of the CL arising out of civil disputes and punishable by less than 3 years' imprisonment and (2) negligent offenses that are punishable by less than 7 years' imprisonment, excluding the crime of dereliction. The agreement should be based on voluntariness and forgiveness on the victim's side, as well as sincere remorse and a degree of responsibility acknowledged by the offender's side (Article 277, CPL). Compared with the CPL 1996, this newly added provision expands the scope of the application of mediation: Victims and offenders are now allowed to reach reconciliation in cases in which the public prosecutor initiates the prosecution.

4 Criminal Mediation in Practice

In China, mediation in criminal matters has been termed as criminal mediation, penal mediation, criminal reconciliation, or *xingshi hejie*. It quickly spread across different provinces and regions of the country, although initially, its use was limited to cases of intentional harm against the person and traffic offenses. This practice did not gain official recognition until the 2012 CPL included a section on mediation. Previously, the development of criminal mediation largely relied on criminal policies, as well as initiatives taken by judicial practitioners. Local judicial authorities issued their own official documents concerning criminal mediation in order to standardize the practice (Berti 2011). For example, in 2006, the Hunan Provincial Procuratorate issued the Regulation on Applying the Criminal Mediation by Procuratorates to Handle Criminal Cases (trial implementation). The regulation requires that certain minimum standards be met for starting criminal mediation, that is, the evidence is sufficient and the offender has no dissenting opinion regarding the major criminal facts. In fact, the contents of the regulations on criminal mediation in different locations have more similarities than differences.

Reports on criminal mediation are not difficult to find in published books or journal articles. For instance, Feng and Cui (2008) reported on the practice of criminal mediation in the Chaoyang District prosecutor's office (Beijing). According to their report, the prosecutor first decides whether to initiate criminal mediation, and if so, he/she usually consults the victim to see if the victim is willing; the offender is informed only after the victim agrees.

Two systematic studies are cited below that supply abundant details with regard to the implementation of criminal mediation in the current criminal justice context.

4.1 An Edited Book on the Theory and Practice of **Xingshi Hejie** *in China*

Song and Yuan's edited book *Theory and Practice of Criminal Mediation in China* (2009) included the mediation practices reported by local judges and prosecutors. The criteria on which the cases were selected were not indicated in the book. According to the editors, the mediation practices reported basically reflect the status quo of criminal mediation in China. Among all 83 case reports collected, almost one-third (25) dealt with juvenile offending, and another one-third (26) reported on disputes among people who had relationships prior to the offense (family, neighbors, colleagues, acquaintances), while assaults by strangers, traffic offenses, and other property crimes accounted for more than one-third (32) (see Table 3.1).

The 83 case examples were supplied primarily by prosecutors from various local prosecutors' offices and judicial administrative organs across 11 provinces in China. Among these mediation cases, mediation was facilitated by either the prosecutors or the local people's mediation committees. Most of the cases succeeded in reaching an agreement, while very few failed. All the case reports followed a template that comprised three parts: the description of the criminal matter, the process of handling the criminal matter through mediation, and comments or remarks.

Despite the lack of academic rigor in these reports, they provide a view of whether these cases were properly handled from the reporters' perspective. In an analysis of these reports, several features stand out.

First, the analysis seems to suggest that the starting point for the prosecutors to initiate mediation lies with the gravity of the offense as defined in the law (the principle of legality). Yet consideration is also given to the relationship between

Table 3.1 Types of offenses in criminal mediation in Song and Yuan's study (2009)

Types	Family disputes (assault, theft, etc.)	Assault between strangers	Juvenile delinquency (including college students)	Disputes between neighbors, colleagues, acquaintances	Traffic offenses	Others (mostly property crimes)	In total
Numbers	12	14	25	14	8	10	83

the offender and the victim prior to the offense, i.e., whether they are relatives, friends, neighbors, acquaintances, etc. Some reports mention that the victims expressed an unwillingness for the offender to be punished. In addition, the reports show that the opinions of the offenders' work units (*danwei*) or neighbors were also collected.

Second, special concern was given to young offenders in compliance with the policy line of "education first and punishment second" in juvenile laws. The dangerousness of the offender toward society was assessed, taking into account facts such as a first-time offense, "turning oneself in" to the authority (*zishou*), being willing to cooperate, remorse, etc. Based on these reports, the prosecutors acted as coordinators (*xietiao yuan*) between the young offenders and the victims. The offenders were encouraged to repent by making reparation, and on that basis, judicial leniency was given. Some cases were referred to the local people's mediation committees, where dialogue and the exchange of views and emotions were said to be conducted, which led to restitution agreements. In other cases, it was reported that the prosecutors referred the case to the local community, where the community workers were responsible for helping and teaching (*bang jiao*) the young offenders. The school and other associated institutions were also asked to supervise the performance of the young offenders.

The third intriguing finding is associated with street crime, such as theft or assault among strangers. These reports suggested that the mediation procedure, particularly in these cases, is more beneficial to the victims, since the recovery of property loss directly from the offender occurs more easily compared to lengthy court procedures in which execution cannot be guaranteed even after the judgments are delivered. Certainly, pragmatism prevails here.

4.2 Professor Song Yinghui's Empirical Research

Professor Song Yinghui and his research team from Beijing Normal University have taken the lead in carrying out empirical studies on criminal mediation in China. Apart from a 2008 study (Xiang 2013), the most extensive research was conducted between September 2006 and December 2008, covering Beijing, Shandong, Hebei, Jiangsu, Zhejiang, Anhui, Guangdong, Xinjiang, Tibet, Gansu, Jilin, and Liaoning. The results of this study were presented in a symposium on Criminal Mediation and Improvement of the Criminal Procedural Law (in Beijing, 2009).[1]

Like Professor Song's previous studies, this study was quantitative. The researchers distributed questionnaires to the judicial staff (senior judges, prosecutors, and police officers) and to the general public in these geographic areas. A total of 2364/2750 (valid/completed) questionnaires were received, among which 1123 were collected from the judicial staff (police 262, prosecutors 545,

[1]The report is available at http://www.jcrb.com/zhuanti/fzzt/xshj/jj/200901/t20090120_128359.html?randid=0.07197336202,955,618.

judges 316) and 1241 from the general public (including teachers, students, civil servants, city residents, and farmers). In addition, the researchers selected eight local prosecutor's offices at three sites to observe criminal mediation (the number of cases observed is unknown) between June 2007 and June 2008.

The results are presented in several categories, and we provide a brief description below (Song et al. 2009).

(a) *The scope of mediation cases*. Over 90% of the respondents said there should be certain standards that limit the scope in terms of the severity of the crime. Among the successful mediation cases observed, intentional harm (light), theft, and traffic offenses accounted for 77.3% (see Fig. 3.1).

(b) *Mediators*. As observed, in most areas, the mediation was either performed solely by the state authority or jointly by the state authority and local community organizations; mediation was performed only by community-based organizations and their mediators in very few places. On the issue of who should be the mediator, the data collected through the questionnaires suggested that 72.4% of the general public preferred the involvement of the state authority in mediation, while only 9.5% favored societal organizations. Among the judicial staff who took part in the survey, almost half (46.9%) preferred for the state authority to preside over criminal mediation, and only 11.9% preferred societal organizations.

Among all 328 cases tracked in this study, those presided over by prosecutors accounted for 90.9% and by people's mediators, 7.6%; the remaining cases were settled by the parties themselves or others. However, the success rate, in terms of agreements being reached, of mediation conducted by the people's mediators was higher than that by prosecutors (see Fig. 3.2).

(c) *Participants in mediation*. Again, among the tracked 328 cases, the most common were mediations between only the perpetrator and the victim and mediations involving the perpetrator, victim, and their relatives and friends. Mediations attended by the local community or by people who were known to both parties were rare. However, the success rate in terms of agreements being reached was higher in the latter situation than the former ones.

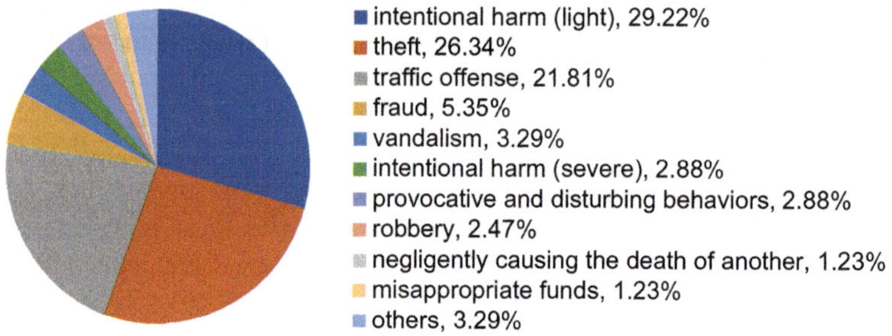

Fig. 3.1 Distribution of successful mediation cases according to type of offense in Song et al. (2009) study

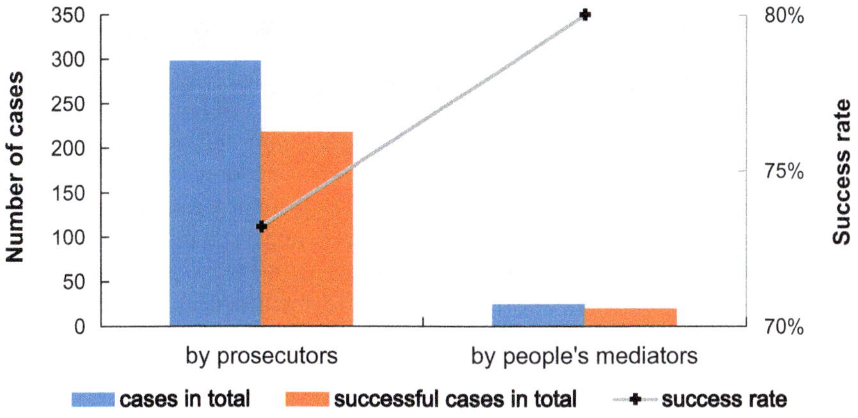

Fig. 3.2 Numbers and success rates of the cases in Song et al. (2009) study

(d) *Agreed measures through mediation.* Economic compensation and apologies were the two primary measures, while in some places, other measures were observed, such as a perpetrator being asked to support the victim's parents when the victim was killed.

(e) *Measures for successful mediation cases.* The questionnaire directed at the judicial staff showed that they placed great hope on the use of non-prosecution in successful mediation cases; however, as revealed in most regions, the application rate for non-prosecution was rather low, as opposed to the two other types of judicial decisions: returning the case to the police for dismissal or proposing sentences to the court.

(f) *Time required for mediation.* The average time spent on each mediation was 111 minutes. According to the researchers, this may suggest that mediation, to a considerable extent, may add to the workload of the judicial authority.

(g) *The factors influencing the likelihood of success.* The researchers identified certain scenarios that might affect the outcome of mediation, including the types of crimes, whether or not it was a joint crime, whether the perpetrator and the victim were known to each other, and whether the perpetrator came from the same geographic residence as the victim. In the meantime, 85 cases out of the tracked 328 failed to reach an agreement, mainly because the parties could not agree on the amount of compensation or the perpetrators were willing to compensate the victims but lacked the means.

(h) *Achieved effects.* As summarized in this study, mediation has achieved multiple benefits and effects. First, it restores social relationships and resolves conflicts. According to visits after the mediation, 90.9% of the perpetrators and 79% of the victims showed satisfaction with the mediation. Moreover, among the 33 cases in which the perpetrators and victims were known to each other before the offense, in 30 cases, both the perpetrators and the victims claimed that their relationships had been restored. No appeals or petitions arose after the cases were concluded in mediation. Second, mediation helps the offender to reintegrate into society and prevents him from reoffending. Among the 143 visited offenders, none had reoffended (only one was given an administrative penalty), and 88.8% of them went back to work or school or helped their families with their work. Third, mediation protects victims' rights by enabling victims to obtain the compensation due to them on time and by providing them with emotional comfort so as to alleviate the crime's impact. Finally, mediation has a positive influence on the criminal justice process by reducing the presentence custody, increasing the use of diversions, and minimizing the use of prison sentences.

(i) *Public concerns*. It was found that 48% of the public considered mediation to be a good way of handling criminal cases, because it was beneficial to the victims and offered a second chance to the offenders. However, over half of the public showed concern about letting offenders off, especially those who are rich and privileged. To illustrate, 80% of the public considered that mediation could lead to unfairness due to the different economic conditions of the offenders, whereas only 20% believed that it would not.

4.3 Pitfalls, Concerns, and Critiques

The practice of criminal mediation in China is not short of criticism. Despite the perceived benefits, criticisms have been raised mainly by legal scholars as well as by the public (*minyi*, 民意). Although there has been no poll surveying public opinion, questions about the fairness of the mediation practice have been continuous. The widest attention has been drawn to the cases of *Hangzhou Speeding* in 2009, *My Father is Li Gang* in 2010, and *Yao Jiaxin* in 2010, where efforts toward reconciliation with the victims were reported. However, the revelations of social inequality and the public outcry for equal justice swept away the individual attempts to reconcile. In the first two cases, the offenders, as disclosed, both came from rich or powerful families; in the third case, the offender confessed that his motive for killing the victim emerged from his concern that the villager could be a trouble-seeker.[2]

Public opinion aside, other concerns and worries voiced by scholars and practitioners are summed up as follows (Zhao 2008; Yang and Jin 2009; Wang and Liu 2009; Qian 2009).

Ambiguous role of the prosecutor The prosecutor is endowed with the responsibility to prosecute on behalf of the state, but this role is questioned when the prosecutor suggests criminal mediation to both sides. Moreover, when the prosecutor takes up the presiding role in the mediation, it is likely that both sides will feel pressured. For example, the offender would feel coerced into accepting the victim's requests in order to avoid an unfavorable judicial decision; the victim might take advantage of mediation to make the offender pay a high price.

[2] This information was mostly gathered online.

Greedy and punitive victims It remains a concern that victims may take advantage of this process, asking for overly high compensation that is disproportionate to the offender's culpability. Some victims may even repeal an agreement that has been settled with the offender, putting the latter in jeopardy. Frequently, the victims do not want any compensation but insist on a severe punishment for the offender.

Absent communication process Some scholars have contended that deliberation and negotiation are generally missing (Shi 2007; Di 2008), which reduces the mediation to what has been described as buying punishment for money (Trevaskes 2009).

Consistency in the treatment of the offender Another concern of both scholars and practitioners is the consistency in the sentences of offenders. Equal justice for offenders has been grounds for rejecting criminal mediation, although others who support criminal mediation have claimed that equal justice does not exclude specific treatment for different offenders under different circumstances.

Institutional constraints Two practical boundaries apply when the prosecutor decides to refer the case to the local mediation organization. First, the time limit with regard to the next step of judicial disposition makes the referral to a third organization nearly impractical. Second, the disclosure of information to a third party may impair confidentiality. Thus, one would guess that even when neutrality is ensured by entrusting the mediation work to a societal organization, its implementation may be unrealistic. It is also reported that any dismissal decision taken by the prosecutor has to be approved by the prosecution committee (Xiao and Zhang 2010), which entails a lengthy procedure that might further lessen the prosecutor's enthusiasm toward applying criminal mediation. These concerns specifically touch upon how restorative justice can be integrated into the Chinese criminal justice system (Liu and Xiao 2007), whose underlying ideology and principles revolve around achieving justice through punishing offenders. The contrast between the restoration of the victims and fairness for the offenders seems to be an eternal issue, because *xingshi hejie* is deeply entrenched and firmly controlled by the criminal justice system (Xiang 2013).

4.4 Gaps and Topics for Further Research

In recent years, studies of criminal mediation in China have increased in number; in particular, empirical research is gaining a market in legal research among Chinese academia. This may reveal a departure from the previous research based on the impression that it was "too much preoccupied with philosophical and general thinking" (Zhou and Cong 2001, p. 60). Clearly, scholars have begun to adopt particular methodologies and to devise instruments to examine specific questions or hypotheses. However, the research methods largely appear to be simple and rough and fall short of the minimum transparency standard, confirming that reliability remains a concern for any empirical study.

Criminal mediation clearly points at a beneficial outcome for the victim, the offender, and society at large, while the (restoring) process goes unreported. In particular, the rehabilitation of offenders is emphasized in that the individual circumstances around the offender and the offense are taken into consideration. The possibility of reintegrating the offender is assessed by the criminal justice authority via engaging with the community around the offender, such as his work unit, his family, the school, the neighborhood, etc.

The concern for the social order is addressed in mediation, not only through the effective rehabilitation of the offender but also by considering whether the conflict can be successfully resolved in society. The legislative purpose for having criminal mediation written into the CPL is clear: achieving better social effects (*shehui xiaoguo*, 社会效果) through resolving confrontations and conflicts.[3] Therefore, social harmony is arguably the real compass in practice. However, it remains unclear exactly how *xingshi hejie* produces interpersonal harmony and social harmony. Interestingly, there is seldom any discussion on meeting victims' needs in the use of *xingshi hejie*. Instead, considerable attention has been given to the offense and the societal interest in exerting effective control over the offender. Therefore, the question arises of whether harmony can be achieved without taking the victims' needs seriously. The place of the victim and his experience in *xingshi hejie* practice has rarely been examined or discussed.

While the position of the victim in *xingshi hejie* requires more research, an equally important issue relates to community participation, i.e., how and whether the community is engaged in resolving the conflict. These unanswered questions merit further theoretical and empirical investigation.

5 Conclusion

It is apparent that while the Chinese criminal justice system is predominantly punishment-oriented, as are many other jurisdictions, victim-offender mediation has enjoyed legislative standing. This support has been made firm, with the recent adoption of a specialized section in the criminal procedure law. A closer examination of the practice reveals some concerns, although we accept that there is no perfect practice. While there is a clear tendency reported toward effectively rehabilitating the offender and maintaining social order, the interaction between the victim, the offender, and the society in resolving the conflict is not as self-evident. In the next part of this book, we will use a grounded approach to scrutinize the phenomenon of criminal mediation in China.

---

[3] When the practice of *xingshi hejie* was codified into the criminal procedure law in 2012, the Legal Affairs Committee of the National People's Congress introduced this move as aiming "to achieve better social effects through peaceful settlement of the disputes." An unnamed official expressed that "[i]ncorporating *xingshi hejie* into handling cases that have been prosecuted by the state, and enlarging its application scope to a reasonable extent, is beneficial to resolving confrontations and conflicts...." See the report: http://www.cnr.cn/gundong/201203/t20120308_509261905_2.shtml, retrieved on 12 October 2013.

References

Belkin, I. (2000). China's criminal justice system: A work in progress. *Washington Journal of Modern China, 6*(2), 1–24.

Berti, R. (2011). The Xingshi Hejie: Criminal concliation in Mainland China and in Taiwan. Paper presented at *the ACS (Asian criminological society) third annual conference*, Taiwan.

Di, X. (2008). Justifying restorative juvenile justice [*huifuxing shaonian xingshi sifa de zhengyixing tanxi*]. *Issues on Juvenile Crimes and Delinquency, 2008*(2), 4–11.

Feng, L. Q., & Cui, Y. (2008). Experience and problems with victim-offender mediation: Investigation on victim-offender mediation status quo of Chaoyang District of Beijing [*xingshi hejie de jingyan yu wenti—dui Beijing shi chaoyang qu xingshi hejie xianzhuang de tiaocha*]. *China Criminal Justice Magazine, 2008*(1), 108–115.

Leheny, D., & Liu, S. (2010). The politics of crime, punishment, and social order in East Asia. *Annual Review of Law and Social Science, 6*(1), 239–258. doi:10.1146/annurev-lawsocsci-102209-152957.

Liu, J., & Palermo, G. B. (2009). Restorative justice and Chinese traditional legal culture in the context of contemporary Chinese criminal justice reform. *Asia Pacific Journal of Police and Criminal Justice, 7*(1), 49–68.

Liu, P., & Situ, Y. (2001). Mixing inquisitorial and adversarial models: Changes in criminal procedure in a changing China. In J. Liu, L. Zhang, & S. F. Messner (Eds.), *Crime and social control in a changing China* (pp. 133–150). Westport/London: Greenwood Press.

Liu, Z., & Xiao, H. (2007). Criminal reconciliation: Local construction of restorative justice [*xingshi hejie: huifuxing sifa de bentuhua goujian*]. *Journal of Liaoning Administrators' College of Police and Justice, 2007*, 20–23.

National People's Congress. (1997). Criminal Law of the People's Republic of China. Beijing: China Legal Publishing House.

Qian, C. (2009). Several urgent issues for the practices of criminal reconciliation [*xingshi hejie zai sifa shijian zhong jidai jiejue de jige wenti*]. In Y. H. Song & J. Yuan (Eds.), *Theory and practice of criminal reconciliation in China* (pp. 169–174). Beijing: Peking University Press.

Shi, L. (2007). Criminal reconciliation: The "third realm" of criminal dispute settlement [*xingshi hejie: xingshi jiufen jiejue de disan lingyu*]. *Tribune of Political Science and Law, 25*(6), 80–88.

Song, Y., Guo, Y., Li, Z., Luo, H., He, T., Xiang, Y., et al. (2009). Empirical study on criminal Mediaiton in public prosecution cases [*gongsu anjian xingshi hejie shizheng yanjiu*]. *Chinese Journal of Law, 3*, 3–22.

Song, Y., & Yuan, J. (Eds.). (2009). *Theory and practice of criminal reconciliation in China*. Peking: Peking University Press.

Trevaskes, S. (2009). Restorative justice or mcjustice with Chinese characteristics? In M. Farquhar (Ed.), *21st century China: Views from Australia* (pp. 77–96). Cambridge: Cambridge Scholars Publishing.

Wang, G., & Liu, H. (2009). The status quo, problems and solutions for the pilot work of criminal reconciliation [*xingshi hejie shidian gongzuo de xianzhuang, wenti ji duice*]. In Y. H. Song & J. Yuan (Eds.), *Theory and practice of criminal reconciliation in China*. Beijing: Peking University Press.

Xiang, Y. (2013). Criminal mediation in mainland China: A leap from judicial endeavor to legal norm. *Asian Journal of Criminology, 8*(4),247–256.

Xiao, W., & Zhang, G. (2010). The dilemma and the way out for criminal mediation [*xingshi hejie de kunjing yu chulu*]. *Journal of Law Application, 4*, 7–10.

Yang, B., & Jin, S. (2009). Constraints in the application of criminal mediation at the prosecution level and its solutions [*xingshi hejie zai jiancha huanjie shiyong zhong de zhiyue yinsu ji duice*]. In Y. Song & J. Yuan (Eds.), *Theory and practice of criminal reconciliation in China [woguo xingshi hejie de lilun yu shijian]* (pp. 158–168). Beijing: Peking University Press.

Zhang, X. (2004). *A restorative justice audit of the Chinese criminal justice system*. London: The London School of Economic and Political Science.

Zhao, G. (2008). Criminal reconciliation: Concerns, confusion and solutions [xingshi hejie zhidu de zhidu yinyou, shijian kunhuo ji jiejue lujin]. Paper presented at *the symposium on criminal reconciliation and procedural diversions [xingshi hejie yu chengxu fenliu yantaohui],* Beijing.
Zhou, L., & Cong, M. (2001). Criminology in China: Perspectives and development. In J. Liu, L. Zhang, & S. F. Messner (Eds.), *Crime and social control in a changing China* (pp. 57–63). Westport/London: Greenwood Press.

Part II
Discovering Realities: A Naturalistic Qualitative Inquiry

Chapter 4
Discovering Realities: A Naturalistic Qualitative Inquiry

1 Introduction

Engaging in fieldwork requires both deliberation and decision. Researchers must be able to justify why the methodology qualifies and to make clear how it is carried out. In the first place, we must explain to readers why this approach is adopted, instead of another one. In this chapter, we start by giving readers an overview of the status quo of criminological fieldwork in China. Then, we explain why we adhere to a naturalistic qualitative approach; more importantly, we describe how the issues of access and the researcher's identity in the field enterprise were handled. Furthermore, we discuss the issues of sampling, data collection, research ethics, as well as data analysis.

2 Existing Fieldwork of Criminology in China

What does fieldwork mean? Miller and Miller (2015) asserted that "[v]irtually all fieldwork entails original data collection through a time-consuming, stepwise, social interaction-oriented process of gaining entrée, developing rapport, and some combination of interviewing, observing and participating" (p. 88). Dissociating itself from other disciplines, thanks to the Chicago School of Social Ecology in the early twentieth century, criminology has become a major field of scientific inquiry. As witnessed by a flood of publications produced from excellent field investigation on crime and delinquency, criminology has a tradition in ethnographical fieldwork as well. The 1960s was dubbed as the "golden age" of crime fieldwork (Miller and Miller 2015). Although the notion of "fieldwork" in the social sciences derives from the natural history discipline (McCall 2006), today, the meaning of "fieldwork" is closely related to participant observation or refers to researchers performing data collection activities in a field setting vis-à-vis conventional and researcher-controlled settings. Below, a broad notion of "fieldwork" is adopted that comprises the

X. Yuan, *Restorative Justice in China*, Springer Series on Asian Criminology and Criminal Justice Research, DOI 10.1007/978-3-319-63922-2_4

normative activities from which the issues of access, data collection, and ethical concerns arise.

While fieldwork is a catchphrase in the Western world of social sciences, it is relatively new for Chinese social scientists based at various universities and research institutions. Although China has some great ethnographers, such as Fei Xiaotong (费孝通 1910–2005), who followed Malinowski and was trained at the London School of Economics during the 1930s, the development of the social sciences in general was severely curtailed in the New China (People's Republic of China) founded in 1949. During the 30 early years of political shifts, a number of social science disciplines, including sociology, were disbanded (Dirlik 2012), and those who spoke in favor of the revival of the social sciences were labeled as rightists (Thurston 1983). Social sciences heralded their spring under the leadership of Deng Xiaoping and were endowed with the political task of serving and modernizing the socialist state. The official exchange between Chinese and American scholarship following the establishment of diplomacy between the two nations has enriched the empirical work and contributed to international knowledge about the then relatively unknown society (Thurston and Pasternak 1983).

The academic pursuit of knowledge has not been limited to the temporary and sparse official-level exchanges. In fact, thanks to the openness and emancipation deepened by economic development in China, foreign researchers with their own research projects have now been able to enter this country and to collaborate with local social scientists. Criminologists in America, especially Chinese expats who were trained in the West, have devoted more attention to testing criminological theories in a Chinese cultural context over the past two decades. To name a few, Hong Lu et al. (2002) tested the key assumptions of Braithwaite's (1989) reintegrative shaming theory utilizing survey research in Shanghai. Zhuo et al. (2008) tested routine activities theory and social disorganization theory using a victimization survey in Tianjin. Some scholars, while acknowledging the valuable input from cross-cultural researchers, have also called for the development of new concepts and theories that capture the distinctive features of Chinese society (Zhang et al. 2008).

There seems to be a consensus on the limitations of empirical research in China, with the greatest difficulty posed by the lack of access to relevant data (Zhang et al. 2008; Yu 2008; Dai 2008; Lu and Kelly 2008; Liang and Wilson 2008). Additionally, while survey methods have been applied to the collection of data for social empirical investigations, there has been very little qualitative research done on China's crime and criminal justice. A more recent empirical study by McConville (2011) sought to examine the working practices and philosophies that underpin China's two-tier criminal courts. Performed by trained researchers, this large-scale study covered 13 courts in China, examining recently completed first instance cases, observing court trials, and conducting semi-structured interviews with judges, prosecutors, and defense lawyers. Adopting an empirical approach to a certain degree, this extensive study in the legal field did not touch on many distinctive criminological issues.

The domestic growth of criminology as a discipline in China has been delineated by Cao and Wu (2005), Kang (2002, 2008), and Wang and Zhao (2008). Broadly speaking, the destiny of criminology closely relates to the political and societal environment.

Earlier on, the Marxists believed that crime could be totally eradicated in socialist China; hence, there was no necessity to study crime. After realizing that research might be needed, criminology mainly followed the theory learned from the Soviet Union: The quality and the content were very limited (Cao and Wu 2005). Wang and Zhao (2008), in reviewing the Chinese criminology research in 2007, concluded that three themes were prominent in the literature: general criminology and criminal justice, criminal policy of harshness and leniency, and state compensation schemes for crime victims. So far, these themes have not been sufficiently examined; moreover, the themes that are studied in criminology tend to fall into the legal sphere. For example, the discussion on the state compensation schemes for crime victims heavily revolves around the protection of victims' rights within the legal framework. Due to the constraints imposed by the political and societal environment, e.g., crime data still being considered a "state secret" (Liu 2007), Chinese academics generally lack skills and experience in conducting empirical research (Xu et al. 2013; Zhou and Cong 2001). Hence, the study of crime and criminal justice in China usually falls into "general discussions or speculations without a sound theoretical framework and empirical analysis" (Zhang 2011, p. 83, as cited in Xu et al. 2013).

3 A Naturalistic Qualitative Approach

For a long time, qualitative and quantitative methodologies have represented different lines of thinking, with polar research techniques and methods. The qualitative methodology fits with the theoretical tradition of interactionalism (Becker 1963, 1970; Blumer 1969; Hughes 1971), with an emphasis on understanding the actions of participants. Quantitative methodology, by contrast, focuses more on the statistical representation of social realities and claims to be more scientific and objective than the possibly subjective interpretations of qualitative research. It is noted that these two methodological approaches not only entail a distinctive set of techniques but are also driven by contrasting theoretical orientations. This could explain why the use of interviews in qualitative studies and quantitative research denotes different ideas. But overall, the selection of a particular research method hinges on the need to deal with specific research questions or puzzles.

The purpose of the current inquiry is to gain knowledge of the perspectives and attitudes of those involved in mediation programs in their natural settings. It requires a detailed documentation of what is said and how people behave in certain settings, as well as their opinions toward the process. Unfolding the social realities from the perspectives of the participants gives this research an ethnographic edge.

Ethnography and qualitative research share some research techniques, such as participant observation, and Bryman (2008) suggested that the difference between them may be a matter of degree. While ethnography means a full description of an entire setting (Charmaz and Mitchell 2010), qualitative research may only focus on a segment or an aspect of it; moreover, ethnography requires the researcher to be immersed in the field for a relatively longer time.

While academic questions regarding the choice of methodology seem very pertinent, and the solutions offered by academics sound quite appealing, a practical question facing the researcher is: How can we get there? This is followed by the question of how much we know about the "inside." The relatively closed door to foreign investigators and the political surveillance of activities in relation to sensitive topics have brought uncertainty and concern to fieldwork in China. Foreign scholars that bring elaborate and scientific instruments to China may either end up discarding them and adopting a new research design (O'Brien 2006) or encountering the "serendipity" that beckons a new mission (Pieke 2000). Like many of my predecessors, I devised a set of research questions to guide the exploration; however, they proved to be out of touch with reality after I arrived in the field. I will return to this issue in the section on data collection.

Similarly, the ethical committee of the university generally requires that the process of recruiting research participants should at least have a clear and transparent guide with regard to involving human beings in the research; it would have been a problem if we had had to explain this to the ethical committee. Initially, the only solution I could provide was perhaps that after I reached the field, I would conduct negotiations with the gatekeepers to facilitate access to potential respondents. My KU Leuven supervisor proposed writing a letter on behalf of the university to the relevant ministry in China in order to gain its permission and assistance. Early foreign ethnographers who entered China were usually affiliated with research institutions or universities under an official arrangement (Thurston 1983). However, in our case, the degree to which the envisaged inquiry could attract its attention and result in cooperation was doubtful. The official channel through bureaucratic procedures entails effort, energy, and time from the government officials. Given the complexity involved and the anticipated complications it could attract, I did not proceed with this idea.

Thus, what was the key to the research field in this study? We contacted a local professor in Nanjing through e-mail. This professor agreed via e-mail to help connect me to a criminal justice institution. He did not explain how the steps would be taken but only told me to be present. It was a genuine concern, indeed, that there was no form or agreement in writing from any institution to secure my access. Perhaps this early negotiation process already suggests a point of difference in the ways of thinking and behaviors between the West and China. Nevertheless, these apparent uncertainties occupied this study and seemed to suggest that I had to "go with the flow," or in the Chinese expression, *shun qi ziran*.

Being present and trying to understand social realities which are "multiple, constructed and holistic" (Lincoln and Guba 1985, p. 37) are the aims of a field investigation. Looking back on the whole process upon writing, this study is more of a naturalistic qualitative inquiry than a purely ethnographic study. Indeed, "naturalistic" describes a paradigm for inquiry including the very first steps of the project (Guba 1981). Nevertheless, this study has employed concepts and approaches from ethnography that have enriched it in many ways.

This small case study is aimed at gaining an in-depth understanding of the practices of criminal mediation conducted in China. The research was "small" in that it was only based on one district of Nanjing (the capital city of Jiangsu Province), in particular, on the criminal justice institutions that implement criminal mediation. The choice was primarily made based on convenience – the access facilitated by the professor at the local university. Additionally, the city of Nanjing[1] is a city neighboring my hometown, and therefore, the geographic proximity and familiarity were added values with respect to the daily interactions with the people in the field.

4 Accessing Institutions, Documents, and People

4.1 Entrée

China has traditionally been portrayed by criminologists as being suspicious of any crime-related investigation, because this type of research is usually conceived as an exposure of the "dark side" of society (Broadhurst and Liu 2004). Moreover, China has been criticized by human rights organizations because the exact number of death penalty executions each year is never made public; however, there has been some speculation (e.g., based on the number of death penalty reports in the newspapers). The entry into its formal and closed criminal justice institutions colors this research enterprise with political sensitivity and scrupulousness.

These considerations persuaded me to accept and to maintain the access I was given, because it provided a good (and perhaps the only) opportunity to enter into the field. Here, I cannot agree more with Blaxter et al. (1996, p. 145, as cited in Noaks and Wincup 2004, p. 72) that "ultimately, therefore, research comes down to focusing on what is practically accessible. Research is the art of the feasible." However, the actual experience will enable me to eventually offer some reflections on it.

Gatekeepers of the field are defined as "those individuals…that have the power to grant or withhold access to people or situations for the purpose of research" (Burgess 1984, p. 48, as cited in Noaks and Wincup 2004, p. 56).

Initially, the local criminology professor brought me into contact with a local juvenile prosecutor's office (hereby JPO) and, later, a juvenile court in Nanjing. There was no formal (official) permit, except with the juvenile court, where I, as "an intern," had to register in the office according to the standard practice. The prosecutor and the judge acted as individual gatekeepers during the course of my study. They both had the power to close the door to me if they pleased; but they did not, as I will explain later.

My first contact with the JPO was in the midst of a project initiated by the criminology professor in cooperation with the JPO. They agreed that I was to act as an external evaluation researcher following the criminal mediation they handled. Upon the end of the project, as planned, they would hold a national conference to deliver the final evaluation report. To achieve this purpose, the prosecutor from the JPO felt

[1] In China, the first-tier cities are those megacities occupying national significance in terms of economy and politics, such as Beijing, Shanghai, Guangzhou, Shenzhen, and Tianjin. The other cities are listed as second-tier or third-tier. Nanjing has a population of roughly six million.

a duty (and perhaps pressure) to provide enough cases for the study. In particular, the prosecutor was obliged to meet this requirement because the guidelines adopted for the project[2] required a neutral third party to perform the mediation.

To maximize the scope of the information and the data for my PhD project, the Chinese professor introduced me to a juvenile court (hereafter JC), because he considered juvenile offending suitable for gaining an understanding of criminal mediation. Then, for the benefit of the project, the prosecutor at the JPO also introduced me to a mediation room (hereafter MR) at a local police station.

4.2 Ongoing Access

After gaining entry, my access to court trials, case files, and mediation sessions was virtually secured. The negotiations were again conducted orally. The JPO made it explicit that I could consult the dossiers, contact the mediation participants for interviews, and observe any mediation sessions available. The collected data would be used for their project and for my PhD project.[3] At JC and MR, the staff agreed that I could consult these case files and use them for this project. Concerning my access to the offenders and victims (or disputing parties), while the prosecutors and judges all collaborated in different manners, the mediator in the MR was not congruent with this idea, and thus, no interviews with participants were obtained there.

In general, my experience was different from that of Noaks and Wincup's (2004, p. 56) research conducted within the criminal courts: "(in our experience) courts sometimes object to researchers taking notes during court proceedings without prior permission. Should the researcher wish to look at court files or interview court staff, defendants, victims, witnesses, judges, magistrates or legal professionals they need to secure permission from the Lord Chancellor's Department. Even if this access is agreed this precludes researchers having access to particular groups and to particular settings."

Based on the principle of reciprocity, I provided help and assistance in writing a note for the newsletter release, distributing cases to judges according to the assigned number, typewriting for the court trial when the judicial assistant was unavailable, etc.

It would be useful to make a distinction between "entry to the institution" and "entry to the sector." I can only say that I remained in one or another sector within JPO or JC, rather than in a prosecutor's office or in a court as a whole, albeit they represented the whole institution from an outsider's perspective. The reason for this was that I was perceived as a person under the supervision of or in collaboration with certain prosecutors or judges inside the institution; in other words, I "belonged to" a specific individual. However, on most occasions, my scope of movement was confined to what was expected of me implicitly by that individual. For example, because I worked with a specific judge in her sector, I could not move freely to

[2] In the appendix, readers can find the excerpt of the guideline.

[3] The use of "their" and "my" here is to distinguish two projects in parallel.

another sector, even within the same court. Such movement would appear to be an act of betrayal (of her trust).

However, this confinement was dynamic rather than static. This became clear on the first day, when I went to visit the juvenile judge. After I explained my research project and purpose, she also introduced me to the head of the criminal court (for adults) (hereafter CC), although it was only a brief greeting. The consent was never written but was oral, and I never needed permission from other judges to observe their trials or mediations. In most cases, the judge told me the time of the next mediation session or trial face-to-face in a casual manner. When there were no errands at hand, I could consult the case files, normally during the lunch break or late in the afternoon.

Being dynamic also means that it involves a high level of negotiation between the researcher and the officials in the institutions. Sometimes, I had to inform the judge that I had to go to the JPO because of an awaiting case. I also had to ask the prosecutor if I could go upstream to the police stage, because I had learned that a number of cases had actually been mediated there. No problems emerged in either situation. I appreciated the smooth cooperation they granted to this project. However, when I began writing, I was expected to provide a theoretical reflection on this.

4.3 Relationship or Connection: Quanxi *and* Renqing

While we accept that there are always strategies to consider if access is denied (Blaxter et al. 1996, cited in Noaks and Wincup 2004), we must also acknowledge or concede that, in this study, relationships played a key role in obtaining and securing access.

As explained above, my entry into the field depended entirely upon the connection with this criminology professor in China and his personal connection with the staff from the criminal justice institutions. The JC, the second site in this study, shared this characteristic. My connection with the people in the field was facilitated because of the perceived affinity with the professor and his university, notwithstanding my overseas research background and the current research project. I immediately shared a common language with the people there, e.g., by commenting on another professor we both knew. Another judge who contributed to this study by agreeing to be interviewed and facilitating other interviews was found to have had contact with the same university for work-related reasons, e.g., occasionally attending a lecture, a training, etc.

Here, I should refer to two previous studies that revealed the permeation of interpersonal relationships (*guanxi*, 关系) and human feelings (*renqing*, 人情) in Chinese society. Yang (1994) found that *guanxi* can be relied upon to provide any benefits that are requested, while Kipnis (1997) revealed that harmonious interpersonal relationships maintained through favors and gifts are greatly valued and socially encouraged. My experience conducting research within the criminal justice institutions concurs with the findings of the two ethnographers.

Notwithstanding the seemingly "cold" image that state agencies usually represent, inside the institutions, the human relationships, reinforced by gifts and favors, sustain ongoing networks among colleagues or friends. In the daily interactions at the court, sharing a box of snacks, a juice drink, or a watermelon was commonplace. These little gestures, barely counted as gifts per se, were simply supplements that reinforced relationships. Not only these "gifts" but also small "favors," such as providing an English translation, finding an audio lecture, etc., were provided as an exchange for the "favors" people had granted to me.

As previously mentioned, I interned at the juvenile court (JC), providing assistance to the judge and her assistant while collecting data for my own research. The workload there was beyond my expectation and took up much of my time during the initial weeks. The judge understood, and she also did favors for me, such as facilitating contact with a lawyer for my interview or asking her assistant to find some relevant statistical materials.

My first contact with the prosecutor from the juvenile prosecutor's office (JPO) was a bit distant, but the following months proved to be a period in which the relationship was solidified. Similarities in our legal background and age range also facilitated our communication in many ways. Although this project was assisted by many people, the prosecutor at the JPO was a key figure in my empirical inquiry. Moreover, I have no hesitation in stating that she introduced me to the third site for this study, the mediation room (MR), where a substantial part of my observations in mediation sessions at the very local level were ultimately done. Overall, there seemed to be no boundary for the favors; arguably, they relied on human feelings people developed and expressed.

5 The Identity of the Researcher

5.1 The Researcher: Chinese or a Foreigner?

Obviously enough, I am a native Chinese speaker and had received almost 20 years of education prior to the 4 years of study abroad. My return to Chinese society to carry out a study may have been experienced differently compared to foreign anthropologists who are not members of it (Pieke 2000; Sæther 2006). In addition, I have a legal background and had previously interned in criminal justice institutions as a law student.

One may wonder whether any "taken-for-granted" perceptions arising from familiarity with the settings might have blinded me to certain things that a foreigner would usually be able to identify. I am not sure what would constitute those "certain things." If they refer to the hierarchical setting, certainly I felt uneasiness when I walked in the hallway of the official building, which differs from the open and equal academic surroundings in Leuven. To be honest, the internal structure of the court building in Leuven did not cause much pressure. The court building in China was as busy as a morning market, although there were security guards checking on those who were engaged in matters and keeping away those who did not have a permit from the judge. The people who were coming and going caused the already crowded building to become even more packed. Are all these factors included in the "certain things" mentioned above? I will provide a more detailed description of my observations in Chap. 5.

When people were aware of my overseas background, did they then perceive me differently from when I did not have a foreign background? People did sometimes ask me about my life and study abroad in personal chats; more often, people wondered how and why I decided to go there, as I was studying abroad. Such curiosity was easily answered by my explanation of my situation; their curiosity was just curiosity, and I saw that they all understood and were used to students becoming interns. There was a local law student in the same court examining the implementation of shared guardianship in court cases involving divorce. Also, when I followed a judge to the sector of community corrections in a local justice bureau, one official asked me if I was the one from America. Apparently, a few days earlier, they had received visitors from America accompanied by a professor from a local university.

Perhaps the question of being Chinese or foreign is more a sign of a researcher's reflexivity than of fact. I did feel that I was a bit foreign to the settings, even in my own land, especially at the beginning. As I said, there were no explicit standards/rules upon which I could rely to learn the proper conduct. To illustrate, one afternoon, all the staff attended an assembly meeting, leaving me alone in an office. The policemen came in to bring new case files. I was very distressed when I later understood that I should not have allowed the policemen to leave any files: One of the new cases was not accepted by the prosecutor. After that occurrence, I learned to be careful, aware that stepping on another landmine might bring my stay to an end. I also felt uneasy when I had to cooperate with the institution by accepting interviews from the local media – partially as propaganda for their work. It is true that, for a novice researcher who has no similar research experience, the process of conducting research also involves coping and learning.

5.2 An Insider or an Outsider?

This question occurred to me when I was writing about the study. Perhaps the process of writing stimulates the reflections of researchers once they are at a distance from their fieldwork.

A researcher's insider or semi-insider status arises from the nature of "their indigenous, native, or bicultural status," whereas being an outsider is often "equated with being a stranger or foreigner" (Ergun and Erdemir 2010, p. 17). It has sometimes been pointed out that the pitfall of a static understanding of insider and outsider statuses is that it can lead to a simplistic binary divide between the two statuses (Kusow 2003, as cited in Ergun and Erdemir 2010).

From a retrospective perspective, I must say that I was collecting data as an insider. I was not blind to the disadvantages of being an insider, and I enjoyed the advantages potentially associated with it.

I saw the judges and the mediators almost every day, and I saw the prosecutor quite often. They were definitely key actors in my study. I also saw the attending victims, offenders (or perhaps disputing parties), their lawyers, their relatives, etc. I was definitely part of them and part of the context I was examining. The tacit knowledge (Glaser and Strauss 1974; Lincoln and Guba 1985) I gained derived not only from the context but also from an understanding of the culture.

Being part of the group I was studying limited the need to probe about information I already possessed. The message that the occasional silence during the mediation conveyed to me – the looks in people's faces and their gestures – did not cause difficulty for me as an insider, a person from the culture. I found that when I was literally transcribing the interviews, there were many moments that I did not require the respondents to complete their sentences, thoughts, descriptions, etc. "You know, right? Xiao Yuan." Such a term, or similar ones, which are not uncommon, represent "feelings of empathy and emotions which insiders share from knowing their subjects on a deep, subtle level" (Hayano 1979, p. 101, as cited in Kanuha 2000, p. 443).

As suggested by Ohnuki-Tierney (1984, cited in Kanuha 2000), native researchers have the task of distancing themselves, both intellectually and emotionally. The distance in my study is mingled with and more evident in my reflection on research ethics, which I will explain in Sect. 9 of this chapter.

5.3 *Researcher's Bias: Knowing and Coping*

It may be advisable to be aware of a researcher's judgments and values so that any inherent bias can surface during the research process. To be honest, my immersion in the freedom I enjoyed at Leuven distanced me from the institutions in which I was embedded almost every day. My unspoken position – siding with those participants, those victims or offenders who came to seek justice – probably arose from my previous experience of interning at the Supreme People's Court and seeing countless people sleeping on the streets, hoping that their injustice would be addressed by officials at the highest level.

My bias also stemmed from the knowledge of mediation practices (described as "restorative justice") I received from Leuven. An open and communicative dialogue is supposed to be inherent in restorative justice; from this lens, I could not agree with some of the practices I saw in the field. However, there was no intervention on my side.

I probably was not a value-free/neutral researcher, by which I mean that I have my own values and judgments, which are shaped by my past. I was aware of this when I was in the field; hence, I always avoided judging people and actions on the basis of what I believed and felt. I recorded my personal/subjective reactions on a form that was separate from the observation or interview notes. I agree with Hammersley (2000), who drew on Weber, that "researchers should be committed primarily to the pursuit of knowledge, and therefore should be as neutral as they can towards other values and interests in their work, in an attempt to maximise the chances of producing sound knowledge of the social world" (p. 12).

6 Doing Research: Dialogue and Power

To the extent that the start of my fieldwork was amidst the local project initiated in collaboration between the Chinese university and the JPO, I was probably not the only person who was conducting research. Collaboration research, as a form of engaged anthropology (Low and Merry 2010), "ranges from participation in the research site to collaborative leadership through action research" (p. S209). On behalf of the university and the professor (with a personal overseas research background), I was to bring an independent perspective into the local project as both sides had designated. There was an overlap between this PhD project and the local evaluation project at the time. The data obtained for the latter could be used for my PhD project; however, perhaps collaboration does not accurately capture the relationships involved. I had a continuing dialogue with the professor and the criminal justice actors.

The power relationships arising from the particularity of the context deserve analysis. Here, I focus on my relationship with all the research participants, although I do not ignore the fact that criminal justice institutions can have domination over everyone outside the institutions. Nevertheless, the judges and prosecutors as individuals are also subject to the powers above them.

I would rather use power, to use Foucault's term, as an analytical tool to describe my relationships with the prosecutors, judges, and mediators. For Foucault, power is "a mode of action which does not act directly and immediately on others. Instead, it acts upon their actions: an action upon an action, on existing actions or on those which may arise in the present or the future… it incites, it seduces, it makes easier or more difficult; in the extreme it constrains or forbids absolutely" (Foucault 1983, p. 220, as cited in Gallagher 2008, p. 297).

The power issue permeates every aspect of research relationships (Etherington 2007). The prosecutors certainly had power over me. For instance, whether I could remain in their office, and the length and frequency of my stays, depended on their actions upon my request. But I also had power. I sometimes called them, telling them I awaited new cases before appearing. The consensus was to complete the evaluation project together. My power perhaps also came from their perception of me as a doctoral student who already had gone far in the pursuit of knowledge along the academic path. Compared with the interning students, I probably looked more mature. I also found that people had a sense of pride when someone from abroad sought to learn from their experiences.

Dealing with my relationship with the nonprofessionals who were brought into contact with the criminal justice institutions was trickier. Would they feel pressured to consent to the interview because of a perceived affiliation with the criminal justice institutions? Could this perception influence the respondents' choices and the content of their answers? While these issues will be addressed further in the data collection section of this chapter, acknowledging the power issue in the research process might lead to caution and efforts to do justice and no harm to the respondents (Ellis 2007).

7 Sampling

There is no general or fixed rule in fieldwork with regard to the selection of research locations, informants, research participants, etc. The researcher must make his/her decisions based on both theoretical interests and practical constraints. While methodology handbooks (Emmel 2013; Bryman 2008; Denzin and Lincoln 2011) always list several typical sampling strategies, such as opportunistic sampling, purposeful sampling, snowball sampling, theoretical sampling, etc., they provide no direct guidance about where and how the researcher should proceed in choosing a method of sampling. The sampling approach adopted in this study could be seen as a combination of snowball and purposeful sampling.

Snowball sampling involves the use of a small group of informants who can connect the researcher with a wider group of respondents who can be interviewed later. Like snowballing, a chain of new informants is formed in this way. This reliance on one's social relationships is sometimes very effective in recruiting participants and is widely used in research, revealing "hidden" populations or groups of people who engage in stigmatized behavior. In this study, snowballing is closely related to the issue of access. Once the professor introduced me to his social connections who could provide me with access to their respective institutions, these people then introduced me to other individuals who might be needed in my work. The fieldwork, although facilitated by a snowballing process in terms of my access to key institutions, was, to a greater extent, guided by the theoretical perspective.

Theoretical sampling has been defined by Glaser and Strauss (1974, p. 45) as "the process of data collection for generating theory whereby the analyst jointly collects, codes and analyzes his data and decides what data to collect next and where to find them, in order to develop his theory as it emerges." They also noted that this process of data collection is controlled by the emerging theory, rather than based on a preconceived theoretical framework. Their discussion of theoretical sampling, however, corresponds with that on purposeful sampling in a naturalist inquiry (Lincoln and Guba 1985), which also focuses on "emergent" instead of "a priori" theory.

The current research has aimed to examine mediation in its three criminal justice phases within the criminal justice context. Mere investigation at the prosecution phase was not enough to capture the social realities of this phenomenon. Furthermore, the amount of data collected from the seven cases available at the local prosecutor's office was far from enough. The professor was aware that the local court, given its application of victim-offender mediation, was likely to provide rich information. After two stages of exploration, I also learned that many criminal cases had been resolved at the police stage without any intervention from the prosecutors or had been mediated, although no agreement had been reached. It became pressing for

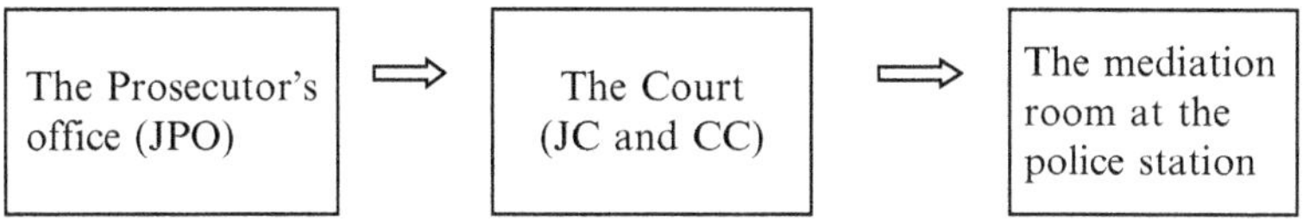

Fig. 4.1 Sampling steps

me, after examining mediation at the prosecution and court phases, to examine exactly how mediation was performed by the people's mediators at the police level. Hence, the information collection occurred in three stages (see Fig. 4.1).

Theoretical saturation means that no additional data can be found that will contribute to the categories developed by the researcher (Glaser and Strauss 1974). The researcher must make the decision in the field about whether and when a category is saturated. The criteria for determining saturation, according to Glaser and Strauss (1974, p. 62), "are a combination of the empirical limits of the data, the integration and density of the theory, and the analyst's theoretical sensitivity." In dealing with this, we started with the data collected at the prosecutor's office as a pilot study. Emerging themes were categorized at this phase. They were supplemented by new data collected at the later phases. Because the situations and observed groups were different, it would be naïve to neglect the differences across the different stages. However, when the themes began to reoccur, with no new themes emerging, it became apparent to me that there was no need to continue immersing myself in the settings. It is worth mentioning that there were "slices of data" – "different views or vantage points from which to understand a category and to develop its properties" (Glaser and Strauss 1974, p. 65) – that merited a later comparative analysis.

8 Data Collection

Previously, we set out to disentangle my identity from the research process, drawing on some concepts from anthropology. In this section, our focus will be on the data collection itself. Some of the themes that we have previously touched upon will become even more salient in this section.

8.1 Interviewing

The conventional rules require researchers to prepare the research instruments before entering the research settings. By contrast, a naturalistic qualitative approach emphasizes the "context," as well as humans as research instruments. Although attempts were made to devise a list of topics that were to be covered, it was not until I was in the field that I found that it was nearly impossible to contact the respondents before any mediation was arranged. Therefore, there was no point in retaining the prepared separate lists of questions regarding pre- and post-mediation. Thus, I made corresponding changes and included the themes as follows:

- Whether the victim and the offender had previous contact; if so, what type
- Why both sides decided to attend mediation and how they were informed
- Whether they had knowledge of what would happen during the meeting
- Whether they were aware that a mediation arrangement could have an impact on judicial decisions
- What kinds of needs and expectations had or had not been met
- How they had experienced the process of mediation, in general
- Whether the mediation led to any changes in their perceptions about their own behaviors or those of others
- Whether there was any aspect of mediation they would like to see improved

The last question in the interview asked whether the respondents had anything to add besides the questions addressed and whether they had questions for me. In some cases, the respondents consulted me with their specific questions. For example, an offender wanted to know what the official decision awaiting him/her would be, as did the victim. I felt that I should provide no more information than what was specified as the possible procedures and outcomes in the criminal law and criminal procedure law, based on what I knew from my previous legal background. The ethical issues involved will be addressed later.

The interviews lasted between half an hour and 1 h. The questions had to be asked in plain language rather than the formal questions listed above. While the majority of the respondents were approached by phone in their spare time, a number of them were interviewed face-to-face in offices, meeting rooms, the yard outside the court, or the detention center. With permission, some interviews were tape recorded and transcribed the same day or, at most, 3 days after the recording. Notes were sometimes taken by hand, when the respondents refused to allow their interview to be taped, and were reviewed shortly afterward on the same day; they were entered on the computer to ensure that memory loss did not lessen the accuracy of the data. At some point, I approached the respondents again for a short interview in order to supplement the previous interviews. This also offered an opportunity to check whether my interpretation as an interviewer and observer also made sense to them – a "hermeneutic" process (Giddens 1993).

For some respondents who were not available at the scene and lived outside Nanjing, I had to reach them by telephone later, instead of directly using an office line from JPO or JC. The respondents were usually contacted during the evening after they had dinner at home. Many of the interviews had to be conducted in this way, as I found that the respondents had to work during the day, and setting up a meeting in Nanjing would have cost time and money for both sides. The respondents did not receive any subsidy for their time from me or the research project.

The strengths and disadvantages of interviewing over the phone are discussed here. Face-to-face is a favored form of interview in many circumstances, because it can initiate an open, honest, and direct exchange between the researcher and the interviewee. This personal, one-on-one setting also enables the researcher to capture the respondents' facial expressions, body gestures, pauses, etc. Yet for practical constraints, I had to rely on telephone interviews to approach one-third of the respondents instead of interviewing them face-to-face. Aware of the advantages involved in face-to-face interviewing, we noticed that telephone interviewing was not as disadvantaged as we assumed. First, the respondents had already met me when they agreed to be interviewed; thus, when they were contacted, they did not feel that I was intruding upon them. I also made use of the first contact to leave a good and honest impression on the respondents. Second, the respondents felt more relaxed in their own homes than in the solemn criminal justice settings and tended to be more open in expressing their opinions and comments. Third, ordinary Chinese citizens are more accustomed to telephone calls than to Skype meetings or e-mails. Mobile phones are so widely used in China that some local justice bureaus are now issuing customized phones to offenders-in-release to monitor them, similar to the monitoring devices used in the Western world. A study of the research methodology found that there were no noticeable differences between the responses given on the telephone and those provided face-to-face in that there were "similarities in the quantity, nature and depth of responses" (Sturges and Hanrahan 2004, p. 113, as cited in Bryman 2008, p. 457).

While the standard practice, after obtaining the respondents' consent, is to allow the respondents to fill in the general demographic information sheet themselves or with the help of the researcher, we found that this procedure became problematic in the specific context. First, in the criminal justice milieu, any investigative tone as such would create psychological uneasiness in the respondents, especially the offenders. Second, during the telephone interviews, we found that the respondents lost patience while providing this information. We specifically decided not to ask them to provide this information. Instead, the information flowed out when the respondents described the events, when they were addressed during the mediation sessions or the court trials, or when the data were found in the case files.

8.2 *Observing*

Observing is regarded as effective in capturing social realities from the perspective of those being studied. The role of the researcher in the examined settings, according to the degree of the researcher's engagement in the activity of the observed, has been distinguished as: a complete participant, a participant-as-observer, an observer-as-participant, and a complete observer (Gold 1958, as cited in Burgess 2000). I adopted the role of participant-as-observer, which meant that I "participated as well as observed by developing relationships with informants" (Burgess 2000, p. 81). In the three settings, I made it known that research was my overriding interest and the purpose of my observation. Spending a period of immersion in the research settings enabled me to observe the natural behaviors that were essential to the data collection. As recorded, overall, I spent the first and second month mainly at the prosecutor's office, the third and fourth months at the court, and the last month in the mediation room within the police station.

While I was embedded in the criminal justice institutions, as a doctoral student and as an intern, I refrained from taking part directly in any discussion or conversation – the key activities revolving around mediation. However, a judge once entrusted the mediation with me because he was too busy to do it himself. Caught between the trust of the judge and the researcher's role, I chose to help him, but the consequences of this will be addressed later in the ethics section as well as in the data analysis.

In these criminal justice institutions, to what extent did my presence influence the behaviors of those who were being observed? It is widely believed that under observation, people tend to perform according to their perceived "ideal image." The actors in the criminal justice institutions were probably more aware of my presence due to the relatively intense interactions on a daily basis. After a period of assimilation, however, I became less visible. For example, after some time, people began to address me by my nickname or to engage in frequent chats in private. In the local mediation room, all those (policemen, cleaning ladies, security guards, etc.) who walked in and out started to accept that Mediator G had a new "apprentice," because I addressed him as *shifu* in Chinese (meaning: teacher). While at the very beginning, someone would ask who I was, and Mediator G would give an introduction; later on, no one would ask this question. Gradually, the staff started to perceive me as being "in their group," e.g., greeting me when I arrived in the morning, sharing their snacks with me, etc. I discovered that while the policemen definitely had an official rank, the mediators, the cleaning personnel, and the security guards had a lower status and work-related benefits. As a student with a clear eagerness to pursue knowledge, I could easily be distinguished as a member of the latter.

My observational notes consisted of two parts. One part related to the observation of the research settings and daily routines, and the other concerned certain mediation sessions and court trials. The former could be retrieved from the diary that I kept each day (for one example, see below), and the latter followed the clear guidelines of the observation list.

Field diary, 19 March 2014

Today, I visited the juvenile court located in the X district. W is acting as the chief judge. As I saw that she was very busy, I did not talk much and just sat there examining the case file she gave to me. I briefly introduced myself and what I was planning to do there. She was nice enough to introduce me to the criminal court staff so that later on, I could follow adult cases as well. I found that she was really focused on her work and seemed not to have time to chat with me. Only at noon, she asked me about which university and in which country I am now studying, which I guess Prof. xxx had already mentioned. I promised to bring the introduction letter next week when I come in. W asked me to come again next Tuesday because she would go on business later this week and only would come back next Monday.

Observation list for mediation

1. What is the general setting of the place of the mediation?
2. How does the mediation start? Who are the participants?
3. What does everyone say, and how does everyone behave? What are their expressions, postures, and emotions?

4. What are the topics that are addressed during the mediation?
5. How does the mediation go in general? What is the atmosphere?

The participants, except the actors in the criminal justice institutions, were not sensitive to the presence of an unfamiliar and perhaps irrelevant person. Culturally, it would be very impolite for me to call for everyone's attention to introduce myself before each mediation/trial started. In the mediation room, it was Mediator G who usually briefly mentioned who I was and why I was sitting there, and then, the disputants would nod. During the mediation process, no one turned around to look at me. The inattention to my presence was mostly due to the tension of the scene, as the participants were very focused on their own roles. Also, the presence of a student was perceived as unimportant and unthreatening. No one conceived of or raised the issue of privacy; the concept as such was virtually nonexistent among our respondents. We noticed that, in the mediation room, the door was almost always open, and the cleaning ladies or security guards sometimes appeared and stayed to listen. Mediator G was sometimes unhappy with this situation because he was afraid that they would disperse the collected stories among their circles.

8.3 *Between Interviewing and Observing*

Interviews and observations are key to qualitative research, and depending on the context, they can be combined in the data collection process. In the field investigation, which was aimed at understanding the social realities from the perspective of the research participants, observations and interviews can supplement each other to verify what has been understood. For example, the atmosphere, as well as the emotions that I captured in my observations, could later be demonstrated in the respondents' answers. Further, the interviews may not necessarily happen before or after the observations; they can be conducted during the process of observing. Again, this relates to the particular context. For example, in one case, both parties were called to the judge's office: When one party arrived first, the judge chose to hear this party's opinion while waiting for the other party to arrive. The judge was then asked to attend an assembly meeting but promised to return soon. Then, I, also being positioned there, could use this time interval to address a few questions with the respondents' permission. In the local mediation room, one party occasionally arrived first, giving me an opportunity for conversation. This was especially useful when the mediator did not allow me to contact the participants after the mediation session had finished.

8.4 *Diaries and Field Notes*

Keeping a journal in the field is a "biblical" practice for ethnographies, lest the researcher's memory fades with the passage of time and the accumulation of data. It is not very clear what a journal entails; for instance, the field journals mentioned by Rodwell (1998) include a *personal log* or *reflexive journal*, a *methodological log*, a *field journal*, an *expanded field journal*, and a *log of day-to-day activities* (original italics, p. 104–106). To creating conceptual confusion, the focus below is only on my main activities: the diaries and the field notes.

I made entries in the diary every day, recording the events, interactions, impressions, etc. I witnessed. It also documented my own feelings, emotions, or reflections and thoughts on the research questions, methodologies, themes, and topics.

While the interview transcripts and observational notes generally captured what was experienced by the research respondents, some of them were completed by my notes – personal reflections upon or analysis of the methodological issues, conceptual categories, etc. As we provided an example of the field diary above, an example of my notes is supplied below:

> *My notes on the interview*:
>
> The mediation procedure did not give any peace to the victim. Dissatisfaction with the reparation, as well as his "victimization" experience throughout the event, led to a deeper sense of unfairness about the law and society. "The mediation was coerced," he said, "if I didn't accept, the case was simply stranded, since the judge would never decide as I intended. As for whether he (the offender) has the capability to compensate, there is difficulty with the execution." "What if I don't accept? Can I sue him, or can I appeal? The judge called me yesterday persuading me to get over it. I don't want to make things difficult for him, and I don't want to come to court again."

The court does not care whether the relations are restored in the mediation; instead, it aims at ending disputes arising in society, so that the offender will not become an "unstable element" in society by being sent to prison, and the victim can accept the outcome and obtain the compensation. This, in the eye of the judge, is *xi shi ning ren* 息事宁人 (bringing an end to a dispute and bring peace to people).

Maintaining field notes and diaries are not only considered a way of collecting data, they also represent the researcher's preliminary analysis as themes emerge from the data. They can constitute, or contribute to, the analytic "memos" that are essential to the comprehensive data analysis stage (Glaser and Strauss 1974).

Because I did not create special categories regarding the types of notes or diaries at the time, it later took a bit more time to retrieve them and process them together with other data. However, there did not seem to be a best practice for indexing the field notes. Because all the notes or diaries were taken in chronological order, it was not difficult to make the link between them and the other data.

8.5 Case File Analysis

For many Western social science researchers, case files are kept strictly within the criminal justice apparatuses, and access to them usually requires a lengthy approval procedure from the state authority. To a large extent, this study focused on "live" cases that were currently in progress or had recently been closed.

Scholars have warned about the danger that researched institutions may attempt to hide or alter materials that are considered detrimental to their reputation. While this may exist in extreme conditions, this possibility can generally be eliminated in our case study. None of the cases were considered to be politically sensitive; and if the institution had sensed any potential threat, the research would have been halted in any case. Further, no staff would risk her/his career and integrity to alter official documents that would be checked by other criminal justice staff or lawyers. In fact, our researched institutions were so busy that no one would have bothered to think about this issue. Notwithstanding that the information collected from these case files was only for my familiarization with the facts and circumstances related to the conflicts, I was bound by the obligation to maintain the confidentiality of the information in the files.

9 Research Ethics

Traditionally, ethical researchers are expected to think about "informed consent, the right to information concerning the purposes, processes, and outcomes of the study (related to fairness), the right to withdraw at any stage (related to autonomy), and confidentiality (to protect the right to privacy and do no harm)" (Etherington 2007, p. 601). While these ideas are upheld within the guidelines or codes of ethical practice, we may wonder whether they are sufficiently sensitive to all cultural and societal contexts and to what extent they are useful in addressing the practical constraints or dilemmas raised by this study. In other words, an awareness of both the ethics and the context are highlighted in this study. Ethics and practicalities can sometimes be inextricably interwoven, as shown in studies involving refugees (Hugman et al. 2011) or other vulnerable groups.

9.1 The Issue of Informed Consent

The concept of informed consent, derived from biomedical research (Burgess 2000), is grounded in the Kantian moral philosophy that all human beings must be recognized as moral beings, derived from their capacity to reason (Hugman et al. 2011; Dennis 2009). It is required for investigations involving human subjects, to protect the research participants' anonymity, rights, privacy, and autonomy as individuals (Bin Liang and Lu 2006). To ensure ethical compliance by researchers, a peer review process undertaken by ethical committees is the well-established practice to scrutinize research proposals. In the current study, the ethical committee for social sciences and humanities at KU Leuven (the name: SMEC) had not been established when the fieldwork was carried out (starting in February 2014).

Notwithstanding the popularity of recording participants' consent by securing a form of "contract" from them, what exactly does "informed consent" mean for the participants, or how is it understood by them (Hugman et al. 2011)? How is this experienced by those coming from a different culture and getting involved in an unusual setting? Perhaps respect and protection for the participants are more important than simply asking the participants to sign a consent form. This might be true not only to protect our respondents' anonymity (Bin Liang and Lu 2006) but also to avoid increasing the inherent imbalance of power that may exist in the relationships (Etherington 2007). For these reasons, I did not ask our research participants to sign a written consent form.

The obligation to give the respondents relevant information and obtain their oral consent was more pressing in this study, because in many cases, I was recommended by the criminal justice staff to the potential respondents (offenders, victims, and lawyers). This seemed inevitable, as my contact with these respondents could only be obtained through the criminal justice institutions. The general tone used by these staff was by no means an order: "This is our doctoral researcher, affiliated to xxx University. She wants to talk to you about some issues related to mediation, the subject of her doctoral research. You could have a chat with her, if you wish." One may wonder whether the voluntariness of the respondents' consent became questionable upon such a request from the officials. Below, we will address this reasonable concern using real examples from this study.

In one case, both parties were asked to cooperate with the study upon receiving the mediation agreement from the judge. Walking out of the judge's office, the offender refused, saying that he was running out of time, but that he could be contacted later by phone. However, I found that the phone was powered off, and days later, I learned indirectly from the judge that he had returned to his hometown. The victim in this case agreed to stay for the interview and spoke of his feelings and opinions. In a second case, the offender was asked to cooperate with the interview. Although he did not refuse directly, he also chose not to respond to my phone/text messages later. In these two situations, I respected their decisions.

To respect the human autonomy of our respondents during face-to-face or telephone interviews with them, I usually repeated my explanation of the purpose of my research. I told them that they could choose not to answer the questions if they so desired. I also told them that everything they said would be kept confidential, and that it would only be used for study purposes, with their identities anonymized. The respondents were generally willing to help with my study, and some even said that I could contact them again later if I had more questions.

While the practice of building rapport and trust with the people in the field is normally justified so that they will behave naturally, Ferdinand et al. (2007) questioned whether this is "a mild form of deceit and exploitation" (p. 533). Indeed, the key actors in our study might not have realized that they were being studied, e.g., the judges might have had no awareness that I was studying them when I was sitting with or having a talk with them. Moreover, even when people agreed to participate, they may not have fully understood what "research" entails. In the Chinese understanding, any doctoral student who comes to the field seeks to "learn" from the practice. This was evident when the local mediator introduced me to the disputants as "a doctoral student coming here to learn."

9.2 The Issue of Confidentiality

Ferdinand et al. (2007) captured a schism in the research ethics literature between those who support the mainstream codes of ethics and those who offer alternative counterarguments. Drawing on their own field studies, Ferdinand et al. (2007) argued that ethical researchers should have the responsibility to find solutions to situated dilemmas throughout the course of their research. "In the end how researchers deal with ethical dilemmas ultimately comes down to personal choice, and the responsibility that goes with this…" (p. 540). I consider that there were two levels of confidentiality in this study: one for my relationship with the criminal justice staff and one for the nonprofessionals.

To protect the safety and dignity of the nonprofessional participants, I tried to ensure that the interview setting and the content of the interviews were sufficiently confidential.

Ethnographers who have previously conducted research in China have found it very difficult to arrange confidential interview settings (Pasternak 1983; Whyte 1983), particularly when the interviewees were identified by officials and the interviews were located in certain places. The beginning of my research study was no exception. When the prosecutor introduced me to the respondents, she also took it for granted that the interviews would be conducted in her office. The first interview was indeed in the prosecutor's office, with the door open and others coming in and out. To protect the respondent's anonymity and his personal security, I had to terminate the interview. Based on the same concern, I also politely refused the invitation to conduct telephone interviews in the prosecutor's office. Instead, I requested a meeting room to use to conduct the interviews, which the prosecutor kindly provided. Although it was still within the building, it minimized any interference during the interviews and secured confidentiality. There was one interview that had to be conducted in the detention center without the presence of any third persons.

Despite my opening statement that their information would be kept confidential, no one posed any questions regarding how their privacy and anonymity would be protected. Instead, they directly said: "That's OK! That's OK. Just tell me what you want to know." In some cases, they asked me to skip the statement and ask the questions immediately. At any rate, I had to keep their answers confidential, inter alia, from the criminal justice staff. But in reality, the latter did not show any desire to pry, and when they displayed any interest, they only wanted to know whether my opinion concurred with theirs in terms of e.g., assessing a young offender's remorse.

Confidentiality could have been compromised when I presented the seven cases for the local evaluation project. If she so desired, the prosecutor could have pieced together "who is who" based on her thorough knowledge of the cases. Notwithstanding this real circumstance, all the cases had been closed prior to the production of this report; it seemed that the criminal justice staff cared more about the general "achieved effects" from the experience of handling juvenile offending in order to produce a news release, for example. However, I also did not bring about any immediate positive change, although a claimed critical ethnographer is expected to leave a site better (Dennis 2009). Indeed, I was told that "everything stays the same." But "the same" does not mean bad, as I will show in the findings.

9.3 "No Harm" and Responsibility: The Relationship Between the Researcher and Respondents

I have briefly mentioned the power issue between myself and the respondents, who were ordinary Chinese people. Although I have addressed how my awareness of the perceived power imbalance led me to handle practical constraints throughout the course of the fieldwork, the mere principles of informed consent and confidentiality could not embrace the entire content of the research relationship. Indeed, the researcher-respondent and researcher-institution relationships were the key themes permeating all the data collection activities, including the interviews, the observations, and the case file analysis. Below, I would like to dwell a bit more upon the complexity of this issue.

Trust underlies all proposed relationships. It is not only gained through daily interactions but can depend heavily on a third person to connect both sides. For example, when I was introduced to the potential respondents by the criminal justice staff, or introduced by the professor to the institutions, or when the potential respondents perceived my presence in the institutions, they recognized me as genuine and trustworthy. An introduction by a third person overcomes the "alienation" that may be felt by the respondents when they have no idea or way to verify the authenticity of a researcher's good intentions.

The responsibility required of an ethical researcher determines that a blind eye should not be turned to the vulnerability of the respondents. Some confessed that they had refrained from telling their family members about the information they had disclosed to me. Victims also shared their feelings of anger and helplessness with me. I could not interrupt but only listen. There were also six young offenders interviewed for this study. Although they appreciated the opportunity to have someone listen to them, upon closing the interview, I faced the moral question of whether I, in addition to expressing my appreciation for their time and input, should offer some personal encouragement. The offenders showed different degrees of anxiety about their future, due to the situations in which they were currently involved. I felt that while such encouragement was not part of the data collection, it was part of the researcher's obligation to the respondents' well-being – an ethic of care (Ellis 2007). I spent some time just listening to what they wanted to share and offering encouraging words to them.

Although I generally agree with Ferdinand et al. (2007) that an ethical researcher has to find her own solutions to dilemmas, the above discussion by no means demonstrates that every aspect was perfectly handled. In fact, such a claim would be nothing but a fantasy. After the court trial of one case, the victim refused an invitation to be interviewed afterwards, saying: "you are belonging to the *gong jiaren* 公家人 (officials). I don't want to have any contact with you anymore." This perception, although arising from the feeling of anger from the court trial that had just concluded, may also have stemmed from a previous circumstance in which I was asked by the judge to perform the mediation. Given the complexity of the context, I can only reflect on the situation. I was also part of the context, remaining there with all my participants.

9.4 A Note on the Representativeness and Trustworthiness of the Sample

In contrast to large-scale samples across the whole country, the sample formed in this study was solely from the city of Nanjing. Its representativeness of China is limited, given China's vast geographic landscape and the associated varying features. Nevertheless, representativeness was not a goal I pursued; rather, the trustworthiness of this study, which falls under a naturalistic paradigm, carries significance just as reliability does for any research within a conventional paradigm (Guba 1981; Lincoln and Guba 1985).

Methodological weaknesses must always be exposed to and tested against the trustworthiness demonstrated by validity, reliability, and objectivity. Validity may have varying significance in the qualitative research tradition and the quantitative tradition. As Hammersley (1990, p. 57, cited in Silverman 2010) stated, it means truth, "interpreted as the extent to which an account accurately represents the social phenomena to which it refers." Reliability may have different illustrations, but we could not agree more with Silverman (2010, p. 290), who asserted that it simply indicates "you can show your audience the procedure you used to ensure that your methods were reliable and your conclusions valid." Again, objectivity, pursued by a qualitative researcher, can be understood to mean that the researcher presents the data as it is, instead of manipulating it to fit the researcher's own expectations or ideas.

Guba (1981) and Lincoln and Guba (1985) suggested, however, that the trustworthiness built within a conventional paradigm should be replaced by credibility, transferability, dependability, and confirmability in a naturalist paradigm. Credibility involves activities that enhance the probability that the findings will be found credible; transferability is determined by whether the decisions that were made based on the context under investigation can have meaning and usefulness in other contexts; dependability takes into account the instability and design-induced change in emergent research; and confirmability places the emphasis on the data, which indicates that the results are linked to the data themselves. These four terms are the naturalist's equivalents to the conventional terms "internal validity," "external validity," "reliability," and "objectivity" (Lincoln and Guba 1985).

To ensure that this study reached the acceptable standard of trustworthiness, I relied on techniques such as triangulation and peer debriefing.

(a) Triangulation. In this study, triangulation referred to a combination of different data sources, e.g., participation, interviews, and case files, which can bring different kinds of evidence to bear on a problem (Denzin 1989, cited in Esterberg 2002).
(b) Peer debriefing. I sought debriefing with a professor in another faculty at KU Leuven on a regular basis for her feedback and advice. I could not do member checks on the data analysis after leaving the field, simply because it was almost impossible for me to allow the research respondents to check whether the deconstruction and reconstruction of the data matched how they interpreted their experiences.

Furthermore, there might be a presumption that the political entity of mainland China, which imposes a restriction on people's freedom of expression (Lai et al. 2010; Hsieh and Boateng 2015), may counteract the truth told by the participants. Although this possibility is not excluded, there might be an alternative perspective regarding this issue. That is, there is a demarcation between the "official rhetoric" and "ordinary common sense": On open platforms and stages, only the rhetoric conforming to the official line is permitted and, therefore, channeled to the public, but on a daily basis, another type of language is used among friends, acquaintances, and so on. In this study, the participants were given opportunities to talk about how they felt and what they thought. They generally spoke out about what they wanted to convey, both praises and criticisms.

Overall, we cannot ignore the shortcomings and limitations involved in the approach adopted here. Unlike lab experiments, in which the variables can be carefully monitored, our field exploration deals with human beings, which means uncertainty and unpredictability cannot be avoided in most cases. There are some aspects that we consider could have been done better, despite the efforts that were made.

Firstly, the access, in terms of the interviews, was constrained by the "word" from our gatekeepers. I was not able to conduct interviews with the parties at dispute in the local mediation room, not because they refused to agree to them but because I was not allowed to contact them. I speculated, on the basis of working closely with the mediator each day, that this was primarily due to the concern of the mediator that the interviews would disturb the parties and once again stir up their conflicting sentiments. He was clearer than anyone else that the conflict had, for the moment, been appeased through multiple mediation techniques. The same thing happened regarding a potential respondent who worked in a justice bureau other than where the gatekeeper worked. The interview was considered as "one department granting a favor to another department." Later, the gatekeeper informed me that the head of the justice bureau had implicitly refused the request to conduct interviews with their mediator staff, without giving any reason. Although they were the only two such instances occurring in the field, they determined that I was only able to rely on other sources, such as observations, to maximize the information I could obtain.

Secondly, the major limitation lay in the reliance on telephone interviews rather than face-to-face interviews. As stated in the data collection section, telephone interviews were conducted with some offenders and victims when they had left the scene and a face-to-face meeting would have been very difficult to arrange. Although I argue that the interviews still reached an acceptable standard in terms of quality, I must concede that I definitely felt that the interviews could have gone deeper if a face-to-face meeting could have been arranged without difficulty. In the future, researchers may be able to overcome this shortcoming by becoming closer to the offenders and victims in order to dig deeper into their personal beliefs and stories.

Thirdly, as a developing country, China is constantly changing, as are the lives of the people who live there. It would be very interesting to discover our respondents' opinions and perceptions during the period after they experienced the mediation. A comparison of the different responses, if there are such differences, might have added to our understanding of key concepts in restorative justice, such as reconciliation and satisfaction. This limitation resulted from the very "context" that this study examined; in other words, I explored "what was happening now," the phenomenon in its real context, rather than something beyond the context.

10 Data Analysis

Data analysis was the most difficult phase in this study. While all the findings will be presented in the next chapter, below, I explain how the analysis was conducted. While the qualitative analysis software NVivo was employed, the focus will be on how the codes were identified and categorized.

10.1 Working with NVivo

One of the most significant developments in qualitative research over the last two decades was the emergence of computer software as a tool to assist in the analysis of qualitative data (Bryman 2008). Notably, several research methods handbooks began to introduce NVivo. In June 2013, I received two half-days of training in NVivo, consisting of theoretical and practical sessions, which was organized by the Doctoral School for the Humanities and Social Sciences of KU Leuven. While immersed in the field to collect data, I gained practical experience by using this software. The systematic processing of data with this software did not begin until I returned to desk research. With the help of colleagues through various discussions and guidance, I was able to use NVivo effectively.

10.2 Coding

Coffey and Atkinson (1996, p. 29) suggested that qualitative coding entails three basic procedures: "a) noticing relevant phenomena, b) collecting examples of those phenomena, and c) analysing those phenomena in order to find commonalities, differences, patterns and structures." I started by open coding the interview transcripts, the interview notes, and the observational notes that were entered into NVivo. The codes initially formed were based on a piece of information, a term, a sentence, etc., retrieved from the above sources. A comprehensive list of codes was accumulated. I constantly checked what had been coded and the relationship between the new codes and the old codes. To make sure that each code was identifiable and accurately conveyed the message, I also repeatedly read the texts and documents. When the same code is continually loaded with information, the category and subcategory and, finally, the theme can be identified.

At the outset, I coded people's emotions according to what they explicitly expressed. It was noted that translating emotional terms from Chinese to English was not easy, because some meanings might be slightly changed or even lost. In dealing with these problems, I first identified some typical Chinese terms and spoke with a colleague who is an English speaker to determine whether the meaning of these translations was correctly conveyed; second, I put the original quotes in brackets following the English translations so that readers can see clearly whether they make sense in that context.

I now document some attempts to make the coding process transparent to readers. When the respondents explicitly voiced their feelings, I coded them as such. For example, when the respondent answered "*you dian xiu kui ba* (有点害羞吧)," I coded it as "feeling ashamed," or when the respondent said "*hou hui* (后悔)," I coded it as "regret." I did not explore the implications of these psychological terms in depth, because it was beyond the scope of this study. Experts might say the feeling of "regret" might be an indication of "feeling ashamed." This is an interesting argument, but I used the respondents' original words.

Next, I examined the context of what people said and how they behaved when I coded their emotions. In other words, their verbal and nonverbal expressions were interpreted in relation to what they had revealed before and after the expressions. For example, when the offender said he did not want to meet the victim and further stated, "I felt I lost face when all the classmates and teachers knew I did it," confronting the victim was more shame-related than fear-related. I coded it as "feeling ashamed."

Again, the connotations behind the words became very important, and hence, I needed to constantly cross check them. For example, when two people used the same word, regret (*hou hui*), while coding, I noticed that what the people had meant was totally different. In one case, regret meant the respondent felt an apology was owed to the victim. In the second case, regret meant the respondent simply regretted his own losses rather than the victim's. Constant comparison was required in deciding the code under which a piece of information should be entered.

10.3 *Constant Comparison and Writing Memos*

I strictly followed the steps of constant comparison proposed by Glaser and Strauss (1974, p. 105), which are "(1) comparing incidents applicable to each category, (2) integrating categories and their properties, (3) delimiting the theory, and (4) writing the theory." In my analysis, I compared different incidents for a category (e.g., feeling ashamed) with the previous incidents coded in the same category; different perspectives from the offenders, victims, criminal justice actors, and lawyers; and different conditions, situations, relationships, and outcomes across different categories. I constantly wrote memos about the comparisons (Charmaz and Mitchell 2010) to document fresh ideas emerging from the analytic process; in writing memos, the literature was also consulted in relation to the emerging categories and codes. The memo-writing practice is virtually the start of the writing process, whereby material is constantly absorbed. I provide a summary in the next chapter of all the cases I collected, including as many details as possible to provide a clear picture.

References

Becker, H. S. (1963). *The outsiders*. New York: The Free Press.

Becker, H. S. (Ed.). (1970). *Sociological work*. Chicago: Aldine.

Blumer, H. (1969). *Symbolic interactionism: Perspective and method*. Englewood Cliffs: Prentice-Hall.

Braithwaite, J. (1989). *Crime, shame and reintegration*. Cambridge: Cambridge University Press.

Broadhurst, R., & Liu, J. (2004). Introduction: Crime, law and criminology in China. *Australian & New Zealand Journal of Criminology, 37*(1 suppl), 1–12. doi:10.1177/00048658040370s101.

Bryman, A. (2008). *Social research methods*. Oxford: Oxford University Press.

Burgess, R. G. (2000). *In the field: An introduction to field research*. New York: Routledge.

Cao, L., & Wu, Z. (2005). A third view on Chinese criminology. *Journal of Fujian Public Safety College, 2005*(1), 27–30.

Charmaz, K., & Mitchell, R. G. (2010). Grounded theory in ethnography. In P. Atkinson, A. Coffey, S. Delamont, J. Lofland, & L. Lofland (Eds.), *Handbook of Ethnography* (pp. 160–174). London, Thousand Oaks, New Delhi: Sage Publications.

Coffey, A., & Atkinson, P. (1996). *Making sense of qualitative data: complementary research strategies*. London, Thousand Oaks, New Delhi: Sage Publications.

Dai, M. Y. (2008). Policing in the People's Republic of China: A review of recent literature. *Crime Law and Social Change, 50*(3), 211–227. doi:10.1007/s10611-008-9131-7.

Dennis, B. (2009). What does it mean when an ethnographer intervenes? *Ethnography and Education, 4*(2), 131–146.

Denzin, N. K., & Lincoln, Y. S. (2011). *The SAGE handbook of qualitative research*. London, Thousand Oaks, New Delhi: Sage Publications.

Dirlik, A. (2012). Zhongguohua: Worlding China. The case of sociology and anthropology in 20th-century China. In A. Dirlik, G. Li, & H.-P. Yen (Eds.), *Sociology and anthropology in twentieth century China: Between universalism and indigenism* (pp. 1–40). Hong Kong: The Chinese University Press.

Ellis, C. (2007). Telling secrets, revealing lives relational ethics in research with intimate others. *Qualitative Inquiry, 13*(1), 3–29.

Emmel, N. (2013). *Sampling and choosing cases in qualitative research: A realist approach*. London: Sage.
Ergun, A., & Erdemir, A. (2010). Negotiating insider and outsider identities in the field: "insider" in a foreign land; "outsider" in One's own land. *Field Methods, 22*(1), 16–38. doi:10.1177/1525822x09349919.
Esterberg, K. G. (2002). *Qualitative methods in social research*. Boston: McGraw-Hill.
Etherington, K. (2007). Ethical research in reflexive relationships. *Qualitative Inquiry, 13*(5), 599–616. doi:10.1177/1077800407301175.
Ferdinand, J., Pearson, G., Rowe, M., & Worthington, F. (2007). A different kind of ethics. *Ethnography, 8*(4), 519–543.
Gallagher, M. (2008). Foucault, power and participation. *The International Journal of Children's Rights, 16*(3), 395–406.
Giddens, A. (1993). *New rules of sociological method: a positive critique of interpretative sociologies* (2nd ed. With a new introduction). Cambridge: Polity press.
Glaser, B., & Strauss, A. L. (1974). *The discovery of grounded theory: Strategies for qualitative research*. Chicago: Aldine.
Guba, E. (1981). Criteria for assessing the trustworthiness of naturalistic inquiries. *ECTJ, 29*(2), 75–91. doi:10.1007/BF02766777.
Hammersley, M. (2000). *Taking sides in social research: Essays on partisanship and bias*. London and New York: Routledge.
Hsieh, M. L., & Boateng, F. D. (2015). Perceptions of Democracy and Trust in the Criminal Justice System: A Comparison Between Mainland China and Taiwan. *International Criminal Justice Review, 25*(2), 153–173, doi:10.1177/1057567715570050.
Hughes, E. C. (1971). *The sociological eye*. Chicago: Aldine.
Hugman, R., Bartolomei, L., & Pittaway, E. (2011). Human agency and the meaning of informed consent: Reflections on research with refugees. *Journal of Refugee Studies, 24*(4), 655–671.
Kang, S. (2002). The status quo and development of Chinese criminological studies. *Journal of Fujian Public Safety College (Pulic Security Edition), 16*(4), 3–10.
Kang, S. (2008). Background, development stages, features and main task of criminology in new China. *Academic Forum of Nandu (Journal of the Humanities and Social Sciences), 28*(3), 72–77.
Kanuha, V. K. (2000). "being" native versus "going native": Conducting social work research as an insider. *Social Work, 45*(5), 439–447. doi:10.1093/sw/45.5.439.
Kipnis, A. B. (1997). *Producing guanxi: Sentiment, self, and subculture in a north China village*. Durham and London: Duke University Press.
Lai, Y. L., Cao, L., & Zhao, J. S. (2010). The impact of political entity on confidence in legal authorities: A comparison between China and Taiwan. *Journal of Criminal Justice, 38*(5), 934–941.
Liang, B., & Lu, H. (2006). Conducting fieldwork in China: Observations on collecting primary data regarding crime, law, and the criminal justice system. *Journal of Contemporary Criminal Justice, 22*(2), 157–172. doi:10.1177/1043986206286918.
Liang, B., & Wilson, C. (2008). A critical review of past studies on China's corrections and recidivism. *Crime Law and Social Change, 50*(3), 245–262. doi:10.1007/s10611-008-9130-8.
Lincoln, Y. S., & Guba, E. G. (1985). *Naturalistic inquiry*. Newbury Park, London and New Delhi: Sage Publications.
Liu, J. (2007). Developing comparative criminology and the case of China: An introduction. *International Journal of Offender Therapy and Comparative Criminology, 51*(1), 3–8. doi:10.1177/0306624x06295774.
Low, S. M., & Merry, S. E. (2010). Engaged anthropology: Diversity and dilemmas. *Current Anthropology, 51*(S2), S203–S226.
Lu, H., & Kelly, B. (2008). Courts and sentencing research on contemporary China. *Crime Law and Social Change, 50*(3), 229–243. doi:10.1007/s10611-008-9132-6.
Lu, H., Zhang, L., & Miethe, T. D. (2002). Interdependency, communitarianism and Reintegrative shaming in China. *The Social Science Journal, 2002*(39), 189–201.

McCall, G. J. (2006). The fieldwork tradition. In D. Hobbs & R. Wright (Eds.), *The Sage handbook of fieldwork* (pp. 3–21). London, Thousand Oaks, New Delhi: Sage.
McConville, M. (2011). *Criminal justice in China: An empirical enquiry*. Cheltenham: Edward Elgar.
Miller, J. M., & Miller, H. V. (2015). Edge ethnography and naturalistic inquiry in criminology. In H. Copes & J.M.Miller (eds.), *The Routledge handbook of qualitative criminology* (pp.88–102). Oxon and New York: Routledge.
Noaks, L., & Wincup, E. (2004). *Criminological research: Understanding qualitative methods*. London, Thousand Oaks and New Delhi: Sage Publications.
O'Brien, K. J. (2006). Discovery, research (re)design and theory Buidling. In M. Heimer & S. ThØgersen (Eds.), *Doing fieldwork in China* (pp. 27–41). Copenhagen: NIAS Press.
Pasternak, B. (1983). Sociology and anthropology in China: Revitalization and its constraints. In A. F. Thurston & B. Pasternak (Eds.), *The social sciences and fieldwork in China: Views from the field* (pp. 37–62). United States of America: Westview Press.
Pieke, F. (2000). Serendipity: Reflections on fieldwork in China. In P. Dresch, W. James, & D. Parkin (Eds.), *Anthropologists in a wider world: Essays on field research* (pp. 129–150). New York and Oxford: Berghahn Books.
Rodwell, M. K. (1998). *Social work constructivist research*. New York & London: Taylor & Francis.
Sæther, E. (2006). Fieldwork as coping and learning. In M. Heimer & S. ThØgersen (Eds.), *Doing fieldwork in China* (pp. 42–57). Copenhagen: NIAS Press.
Silverman, D. (2010). *Doing qualitative research: a practical handbook*. London, Thousand Oaks, New Delhi and Singapore: Sage Publications.
Sturges, J. E., & Hanrahan, K. J. (2004). Comparing telephone and face-to-face qualitative interviewing: A research note. *Qualitative Research, 4*(1), 107–118.
Thurston, A. F. (1983). The social sciences and fieldwork in China: An overview. In A. F. Thurston & B. Pasternak (Eds.), *The social sciences and fieldwork in China: Views from the field* (pp. 3–36). Colorado: Westview Press.
Thurston, A. F., & Pasternak, B. (Eds.). (1983). *The social sciences and fieldwork in China: Views from the field (AAAS selected symposia series)*. Boulder: Westview Press.
Wang, M., & Zhao, B. (2008). Building harmonious society: New developments of Chinese criminological studies [*goujian hexie shehui: zhongguo fanzui xue yanjiu de xin fazhan*]. *China Legal Science, 2*, 181–191.
Whyte, M. K. (1983). On studying China at a distance. In A. F. Thurston & B. Pasternak (Eds.), *The social sciences and fieldwork in China: Views from the field* (pp. 63–80). Boulder: Westview Press.
Xu, J., Laidler, K. J., & Lee, M. (2013). Doing criminological ethnography in China: Opportunities and challenges. *Theoretical Criminology, 17*(2), 271–279.
Yang, M. M. H. (1994). *Gifts, favors, and banquets: The art of social relationships in China*. Ithaca, NY: Cornell University Press.
Yu, O. (2008). Corruption in China's economic reform: A review of recent observations and explanations. *Crime Law and Social Change, 50*(3), 161–176. doi:10.1007/s10611-008-9133-5.
Zhang, L., Messner, S., & Liu, J. (2008). A critical review of recent literature on crime and criminal justice in China: Research findings, challenges, and prospects (introduction). *Crime, Law and Social Change, 50*(3), 125–130. doi:10.1007/s10611-008-9134-4.
Zhou, L., & Cong, M. (2001). Criminology in China: Perspectives and development. In J. Liu, L. Zhang, & S. F. Messner (Eds.), *Crime and social control in a changing China* (pp. 57–63). Westport & London: Greenwood Press.
Zhuo, Y., Messner, S. F., & Zhang, L. N. (2008). Criminal victimization in contemporary China: A review of the evidence and challenges for future research. *Crime Law and Social Change, 50*(3), 197–209. doi:10.1007/s10611-008-9138-0.

Part III
Empirical Findings

Chapter 5
Case Summary and Description-Based Case Studies

This chapter consists of two sections. While the first section sketches the outline of the sample that was collected, the second section provides in-depth information regarding the facts and details of each case that was collected.

1 Case Summary

From February to June 2014, we collected 32 mediation cases and conducted 14 interviews with 12 participants on the offender side (including the families and the employers) and 17 interviews with 14 participants from the victim side (including the families). We also successfully approached three judges, three prosecutors, two mediators, and five lawyers for in-depth interviews. Additionally, we observed 29 mediation sessions performed by mediators, prosecutors, and judges.

1.1 Type of Cases

Assigning one type for each dispute may run the risk of over-simplicity, because each dispute may have a cause of one type and a consequence of another. I would still be attempting to categorize each case on the basis of its major features. Thus, here, I summarize the types and determine the type into which each dispute best falls. I found the following: 19 cases involved physical assault; six cases dealt with stealing, causing property losses; two cases involved involuntary manslaughter; one case related to sexual assault; and only four cases were of a purely civil nature, involving a house purchasing contract, a money lending, a garage use contract, and a business contract of a small amount. These four civil cases were not excluded from the thematic analysis.

X. Yuan, *Restorative Justice in China*, Springer Series on Asian Criminology and Criminal Justice Research, DOI 10.1007/978-3-319-63922-2_5

Table 5.1 Types of cases

Types	Total number
Assault	19
Sexual assault	1
Theft	6
Involuntary manslaughter	2
Debt and contract dispute	4
	In total: 32

Although all the theft cases were collected at the prosecutor's office, assault and involuntary manslaughter accounted for most of the cases collected at the court and police stages. The disputes mediated at the police stage were diverse, involving both civil and criminal cases. Perhaps the latter is related to the role of the police in both investigating offenses and maintaining societal order by resolving the conflicts that are reported to them (Table 5.1).

1.2 Adult and Juvenile Offending

Among these 32 cases, ten cases fell into the category of juvenile offending; they were prosecuted and tried, respectively, by the juvenile prosecution offense (JPO in short) and the juvenile court (JC in short). At the criminal court (CC in short), almost all the mediation was performed by the judge; at the police and prosecution phases, the mediation was performed by the mediators, the police, or the prosecutors.

Clearly, juvenile offending accounted for one-third of the cases collected. A typical question is whether and how this fact impacted the overall results of this study. In other words, how and to what extent did the particularities of these juvenile cases change the nature of the mediation practices, which were reported primarily on adult offenses? It is worthwhile to provide some clarity on the juvenile justice system in China and the nature of the juvenile court mentioned in this study.

The juvenile justice system usually refers to a set of separate rules and justice organizations that deal with juvenile crimes. In China, the birth of the juvenile justice system has been attributed to the establishment of the first juvenile court[1] in the year 1984 in the Changning district of Shanghai (Zhao and Chang 2010). Since then, a large number of courts in China have adopted a juvenile division in two ways: a fixed panel under the criminal court or a juvenile division equal to

[1] This "juvenile court" (*shaonian fating*, 少年法庭) was not equivalent to the juvenile courts (*shaonian fayuan*, 少年法院) as we understand them from Western experiences. For more details about the development of juvenile courts in the USA, please refer to Tanenhaus (2012).

other courts (including the criminal court) (Zhao and Chang 2010). However, the specialization of these juvenile justice organs and the professionalization of the personnel are a far cry from that in the West (Liao and Shi 2014). Currently, the juvenile justice system in China is attached to the adult justice system (Yao 2004) – the prosecution and trial of juveniles cite the same criminal code (criminal law for adults), with minor adjustments with respect to the age and personal character of the juveniles. Yao (2004) considered the juvenile justice system as equivalent to the rigid adult justice system, i.e., it decides culpability and criminal responsibility based on the criminal facts.

Although the present arrangement appears severe for juveniles, this study observes that there are higher expectations that juveniles will repent and avoid more serious mistakes. It can be said that there are more efforts to help young offenders in comparison with cases involving adult offenders. Consequently, there is no further need to explain why victims are expected to extend forgiveness in cases involving young offenders.

1.3 Success Rate

All the reparations included in the mediation agreements involved financial payments with apologies witnessed in the mediation session or recorded in the final agreement. The success rate of mediation, in terms of an agreement being reached, was very high. At court, only one out of 10 cases failed because the offender could not financially compensate the victims. At the prosecution phase, only one case failed in that no mediation was arranged because the offender could not offer reparations to the victim. In the mediation room (MR in short) at the police stage, we observed that no agreement was reached in three cases, but the remaining 12 cases were closed based on an agreement.

1.4 Participants and Characteristics

In 28 out of the 32 cases, face-to-face mediation was either directly observed or found in the case records. The number of participants varied, ranging from only the perpetrator and the victim, to a range of family members, relatives, neighbors, and employers who accompanied the offenders or victims.

The dynamics also varied, depending on whether a judicial authority or a mediator presided over the victim-offender encounter. A range of related factors were assumed, including the nature of the disputes, the character of the disputants themselves, the institutional surroundings, the attitudes from their "community of care," etc. Certainly, the macro-societal context in China may also have a hand in shaping individuals' minds and behaviors.

1.5 The Case

The case under study refers to a mediation case without specifying the direct or indirect character of the victim-offender encounter. For each case, we included interviews with both sides, observations of the encounter(s), and case file analysis. For varying reasons, not all the cases were as complete as I had expected. All the cases we collected involved mediation, and there were cases that included more than one mediation session.

Each case was assigned a name for identification. Moreover, we used this form [number/type/offender/stage] to distinguish them in the case descriptions, as presented in the next section. For instance, Case 3 [theft/juvenile/prosecutors] refers to the Dormitory Cell Phone Stolen case.

The 32 cases achieved sufficient variation. We made the following distinctions:

1. *Typical cases*. The Case 3 *Dormitory Cell Phone Stolen*, committed by a dormitory mate, represented the juvenile offenses that were typically subject to mediation. The Case 8 *Assault against Taxi Driver*, involving physical harm, represented the typical cases that the court addressed using mediation.
2. *Critical cases*. The two involuntary manslaughter cases (Case 9 and Case 17) involving juveniles who accidentally killed a passersby while operating vehicles were somewhat unusual because of the severity of the harm.
3. *Deviant cases*. The Case 4 *Stealing at the Grocery*, which involved a juvenile, normally would have been resolved by a mediation agreement but was not, and it can be viewed as a deviant case. The Case 11 *Assault During the Poke Game*, in which mediation failed and the offender was sentenced to prison, is another deviant case.
4. *Sensitive cases*. The *Sexual Assault Two Female College Students*, in which a (male) college student watched pornography and engaged in sexual attacks on two female students several times outside the campus, is the one that is sufficiently sensitive.

Later, we provide a short summary of what we collected, which constitutes the basis for the analysis.

1.6 Note on the Extent of Information for Each Case

Although we tried to maximize the collection of information through the triangulation of methods, there was variance among the cases in terms of the extent and the kind of information that could be obtained. Five cases collected at the court had been closed before I arrived, and, therefore, the mediation could not be observed. With regard to cases that were collected during the police phase, only direct observation could be utilized.[2]

[2]As mentioned earlier, the mediator did not allow the researcher to contact parties outside the mediation session.

Table 5.2 Case list

Case 1	Interviews, observations, case file analysis
Case 2	Interviews, case file analysis
Case 3	Interviews, observations, case file analysis
Case 4	Interviews, case file analysis
Case 5	Interviews, observations, case file analysis
Case 6	Interviews, observations, case file analysis
Case 7	Interviews, observations, case file analysis
Case 8	Interviews, observations, case file analysis
Case 9–13	Interviews, case file analysis (finished cases)
Case 14	Interviews, case file analysis
Case 15	Interviews, case file analysis
Case 16	Interviews, observations, case file analysis
Case 17	Interviews, observations, case file analysis
Case 18–32	Observations

Below, we provide a short overview of the sources that were used to constitute the description of each case to make the case base underlying this study apparent to readers (Table 5.2).

2 Starting from a Local Project

The 5-month period of fieldwork was carried out at the level of the local state apparatuses – justice organizations including the police station, the prosecutor's office, and the court in a district of Nanjing between February and June 2014.

In China, in the criminal justice sphere, power resides in "the Communist Party, government and power organs" (Qu 2002, p. 4, as cited in Zhang 2004, p. 15). The power organs refer to the criminal justice institutions. As arms of the party-state power, the state justice apparatuses act as "the ultimate defence of social stability" (Ji 2013, p. 210).

As explained in Chap. 3, building a harmonious society was placed on the political agenda by the Chinese socialist state a decade ago, and this informs its criminal justice policy and practices (Trevaskes 2010, 2011). In 2010, the Several Opinions on Implementing "Combining Leniency and Harshness" Criminal Policy (hereafter the Opinions), issued by the Supreme People's Court of China, stated the tenets of this policy as such: "preventing and reducing crimes to the maximum, resolving social contradictions, maintaining social harmony and stability." The Opinions require that in handling criminal cases, attention should be given to whether support from the masses can be gained and whether a contribution is made to social stability; whether it resolves crime and conflict; whether it benefits the education, rehabilitation, and reintegration of criminals; and whether it reduces social friction.

Without doubt, the project with the local juvenile prosecutor's office (JPO), in collaboration with the local university, did not deviate from the goal of maintaining social harmony. To elaborate, the *xingshi hejie* center was established to better resolve conflicts that arise among college students on campus. The overall purpose was to maintain stable and harmonious campus surroundings, in line with the top-down harmony discourse. Highly informed by the idea of restorative justice, the guideline[3] clearly indicates that "the purpose of *xingshi hejie* was to restore the broken social relationships, to restore the harm to victims, and to rehabilitate and reintegrate offenders." *He* 和, in Chinese, means harmony, and *jie* 解 means understanding. Both words can be understood as reconciliation without any misunderstanding; hence, we simply translate them as the reconciliation center.

The establishment of an independent reconciliation center resulted from practical concerns and considerations. First, the prosecutors, in assessing the conditions for reconciliation, had to invest substantial energy and time performing investigations on their own, which created a considerable burden for the state staff. Secondly, given the role of the prosecutor as an investigator and decision-maker representing the state, neutrality and fairness are impaired if he also assumes the role of mediator. Hence, the reconciliation center, as a societal force and organization, would provide the best solution. This initiative was highly informed by the New Zealand conferencing model, in which the state authorities, such as the police, can be present but should respect the sequence and the script of the conference. As is indicated in the guideline for this project, the agreement made under the facilitation of the mediator/facilitator is subject to review by the state authority, and this right is legally enforceable.

What then was the structure and institution of the new societal organization? It was meant to be placed under the management committee of the local campus, but this option was not supported by its committee. Finally, the reconciliation center was installed in the local police station, where there was an office designated for it. There was no funding and no official approval from the local bureau of civil affairs, but the project did recruit mediators. One of the mediators was working on a daily basis at a mediation room, called *gong tiao dui jie shi* 公调对接室, a small product of the grand mediation, i.e., the top-down, government-initiated mediation process (Hu 2011; Zhang 2013).

[3] See the appendix.

The guideline of the project explicitly excluded the state apparatuses from performing mediation between citizens. Instead, the mediator pool among which the disputing citizens could select included college teachers, members of the mass committee for the well-being of youth, mediators from the local mediation committee, residence committee, villager's committee, or colleagues and friends.

Regarding the difference between the new initiative and the "old" practices, I learned about two strong tenets of the new project: First, a third party should be invited to be the mediator; second, the two disputing sides should be informed that they have the right to choose to reconcile with their offenders.

Although this project was initiated by the prosecutor's office, it also involved the police, the court, and the local bureau of civil affairs within the district. These three latter institutions all had to put an official stamp on the guideline, which outlined that each of them should employ this societal organization (the reconciliation center) exclusively in different stages to organize mediation to address youth offending.

Unfortunately, this guideline did not receive due attention but was apparently neglected. The project was then concluded by a nationwide conference that convened practitioners, experts, and scholars and was attended by the Supreme People's Procuratorate. The effects the new initiative had achieved, the social harmony embodied in the satisfaction expressed by all the participants, and the successful resolution of disputes was viewed as successes during the conference.

2.1 A Description of the Daily Work of the State Apparatuses and the Job of Mediation

Mediation, as a generic term, means bringing people into reconciliation with the help of a third party. It seems to be a powerful weapon that state apparatuses can use to successfully resolve conflicts of different types.

Based on the observations collected from the prosecutor's office, a local mediator was invited in only one case. The victims were not happy about being telephoned and asked to appear, but they cooperated nevertheless. The other five cases encountered setbacks with regard to having such a facilitator preside over the encounters between the victims and the young offenders. What kind of setbacks? As we learned from the prosecutors and the victims, (1) the victims lived in a distant city and could not afford to travel to Nanjing, but these victims had already expressed that they had chosen not to prosecute the young offenders at the police investigation level; (2) it had become routine for the prosecutor to perform the mediation himself for the purpose of educating the offenders and granting them leniency based on their remorseful attitudes; and (3) the victim saw that there was no opportunity to recover her property losses, and, personally, she did not want to meet because she was afraid of subsequent retaliation. In the first circumstance, to obtain the "agreement," the prosecutor asked the offender's father to make reparations to the victim; subsequently, the victim sent the signed agreement back to the prosecutor's office. For the same purpose, in another case, the prosecutor also learned of the victim' opinions face-to-face, and the latter explicitly expressed that she did not want to prosecute the offender; instead, she requested that the offender be expelled from the college they both attended.

At the court or the prosecutor's office, the mediation was often held around a big table in a meeting room, with the victims, the offenders and their supporters sitting on the two sides, and the mediator or judge sitting in the middle. This was not the norm, however. Mediation at the court could also be performed in the judge's office when both sides were called upon or in the courtroom when no other room was available. Finally, mediation was also performed during the court trial; at some point, the trial was suspended, and the judge shifted his role to a "mediator," although some readers might question the neutrality of the "mediator" under such circumstances. There was no exact sequence between the trial and the mediation (trial first vs. mediation first). As one judge explained, busy judges proceed straight to the trial and then ask both sides about their opinions on civil compensation if they agree to recess for mediation. Other judges try to organize mediation first out of court and then open the trial to sentence the offender. In the latter situation, it may be difficult to determine the harm in the legal sense because not all the evidential materials have been examined in court. Regardless of the situation, the judge must learn both sides' willingness and ideas, whether they agree to mediate, the minimum they will accept, etc. In some cases, it may take several meetings, i.e., between each side and the judge and between the two sides presided over by the judge.

At the local police station, there was a room specifically allotted for mediation (the aforementioned MR). The mediators were staffed at the bureau of justice within the same district and were responsible for mediating all the cases that the police diverted to them. The mediation room had a specific name, *gongtiao duijie shi* 公调对接室, which basically means that the mediation is combined with the normal criminal proceedings in order to reduce the caseload, as well as resolve the conflicts (*huajie maodun,* 化解矛盾). It was a manifestation of "grand mediation" (*da tiaojie*), which incorporates people's mediation, administrative mediation, and judicial mediation into maintaining social stability. The police office was just a few meters away. The policemen would sometimes call the mediators into the corridor to talk or come in during the mediation process to express their opinions. The mediators implicitly told the researcher that they did not like to be interrupted, but it seemed that there was nothing they could do.

2.2 A Presentation of the Cases

Between 18 February 2014 and 30 June 2014, seven cases were collected from the prosecutor's office (Cases 1 to 4, Cases 14 to 16) around the *xingshi hejie* project. A study of these seven cases was presented in the form of a scientific paper.

By the end of March, four cases had been concluded with mediation. Starting from late March, I was introduced to a juvenile court as a researcher and then to an adult offenders' court. There, I collected Cases 5 to 13 and Case 17. The juvenile court received the guideline but did not implement it at all. They, as usual, employed mediation in order to achieve lenient treatment for the offenders, because the victims had to agree to "forgive" the offenders.

Finally, starting at the end of May, I had the opportunity to go to the local mediation room located within a police station. This was also where the reconciliation center had been installed with a plaque. I encountered and observed the mediation sessions (Cases 18 to 32). We did not encounter any mediation on juvenile offenses; but the mediator also told me that since the project had been launched, no one had come to inquire about it.

Most of the 32 cases were observed while they were in progress. With regard to Cases 9 to 13, the finished cases, we received some input from the lawyers or judges, who described the scene. Ten of the cases fell into the category of juvenile offending and were prosecuted and tried, respectively, by the juvenile prosecution office (JPO) and the juvenile court (JC). Prosecution was discontinued in only two cases, because the offenders were under 18; in the remaining eight cases, all were sentenced to suspended sentences (one received control).

Below, the case descriptions offer a base for the reader to understand what the cases involved, how they ended up in mediation, and what the actual practice was.

Case 1 Theft/Juvenile/Prosecutor

Multiple Thefts Against Strangers

Zhang and Zhao[4] had been involved in stealing multiple times before they were caught. Both families agreed almost immediately to attend mediation when they were informed that it would benefit them by reducing the punishment. They first assumed it was just to compensate the victims, but, later, they were told they would meet their victims face-to-face. A mediator from the bureau of civil affairs was invited to come. The victims were also notified by phone to attend; they were informed that the young offenders were identified and wanted to compensate them. Five victims agreed to participate. The sessions continued, one after another, with no breaks, in the meeting room situated within the prosecutor's building. The mediator briefly stated that the purpose was to reach reconciliation (*dacheng hejie*) and that the offenders were young, willing to cover their losses, and, hence, should be given a second chance. The mediators also briefly educated the young offenders. There was very limited exchange between the offenders and the victim. The sixth victim was scheduled to come the next morning, but there was no longer a mediator present. Then, one offender's father was asked to appear and to provide the reparations to the victims. When interviewed, the victims who had met the young offenders assumed that they had learned a lesson and should be given another chance, but they did not know exactly what the exact judicial decision awaiting them would be. The victim who did not meet with the offender wanted to know whether the offender had truly repented.

[4] All the participants in this study have been anonymized.

Case 2 Theft/Juvenile/Prosecutor

Teenage Boy Cell Phone Theft

Huang was a teenage boy when he was apprehended for stealing a mobile phone. The police later returned the phone to the victim, and she told them she forgave the offender and did not want to see him prosecuted. Nevertheless, the case was sent to the prosecutor's office. The prosecutor contacted the victim and informed her of the offender's situation. Although the victim could not come to meet the offender, she was willing to put her signature on the agreement drafted and printed by the prosecutor. The offender's father was asked to reimburse the victim's travel expenses to retrieve the stolen phone, despite the fact that it was beyond the victim's expectations. Prosecution against the offender was then discontinued. Not only was it not convenient for the victim to come, but the offender had already been sent by his father to an enclosed work-study school. A face-to-face meeting between the victim and the offender was not possible. The father, when contacted by the researcher, disclosed that he had not seen any change in his son during his time at the school.

Case 3 Theft/Juvenile/Prosecutor

Dormitory Cell Phone Stolen

The victim, Lu, and the offender, Jiang, were college students and dormitory mates. The victim and the grade teacher were asked to accompany the offender to the prosecutor's office to attend the mediation. The teacher had no idea what he would be asked to do that day, and according to the prosecutor, they should have let the teacher be the mediator. However, it was presided over by the prosecutor who was in charge of this case. Both the victim and the teacher were asked their opinions about the offender's behavior, in addition to the formal education by the prosecutor. Both the victim and the offender considered this "mediation" procedure to be redundant and overdue. Six months earlier, the offender had apologized to the victim face-to-face after he had been released by the police. The victim said he had forgiven him at that time and did not expect the offender to be prosecuted for something trivial that had occurred between them.

Case 4 Theft/Juvenile/Prosecutor

Stealing at the Grocery

Qian assisted his friends in stealing from a shop. He was caught at the scene by the victim, who was the manager of the store, and, then, the police were called. Qian was held in custody for several days. Qian felt sorry about what he had done to the victim, whom he believed made a living with difficulty, similar to his own mother. Feeling regretful, he was too poor to offer any monetary compensation. The victim was not interested in meeting him, because she had learned from the prosecutor that the offender could not compensate her at all. She said that given the disorderly society, she feared the offender might seek revenge afterwards. She gained the impression at the scene that the offender was unintelligent and might have a lack of legal awareness. Therefore, the victim believed that the offender should be taught a lesson, but in the meantime, she felt pity for him if, according to the law, he must eventually be sent to prison. No mediation was arranged between them, as the prosecutor saw no possibility for the victim to obtain financial reparations.

Case 5 Assault/Adult/Court

Assault Against Apartment Roommates

The offender, Ma, and the victim, Liu, shared the same apartment with their respective partners. Outraged by a message from the victim's wife saying that his girlfriend had had an affair with the victim, he assaulted Liu, causing him minor injury. The victim did not call the police until he felt very helpless while he was hospitalized. He then helped the police to apprehend the offender by inviting the latter to meet for a conversation. All the mediation during the first criminal stages failed, which eventually led the case to be brought to court. The court trial ended up in mediation, with the judge as the mediator. The victim had no other choice but to accept the mediation agreement. Although he remained angry at the offender, he also felt a deep sense of unfairness about the law and society at large. The offender, who was given a suspended sentence, refused to be interviewed.

Case 6 Assault/Adult/Court

Business Rivalry Assault Case

This case was unusual in that the victim was, in the meantime, the offender in another assault. The two assaults happened on the same day but were prosecuted at two different local courts. The victim in this case suffered in a fight with the offender, but in the related case, the victim's son assaulted the offender's son. Prior to this offense, both sides had had infractions arising from their competing businesses. The victim was accompanied by his lawyer to the judge's office (his son was held in custody by another court) where the case was mediated, and the offender was accompanied by his son. The victim felt that there was "no alternative" choice but to accept this situation. The victim's son had been sentenced to prison in another case, and the offender in this case was given a suspended sentence. The hostility between the two sides remained significant.

Case 7 Assault/Adult/Court

Assault Against Upstairs Neighbor

Wang, outraged by the noise caused by the neighbors who lived upstairs, had a verbal dispute with them, which then escalated into an assault resulting in a minor injury. The offender intended to settle the issue in private; the victim originally agreed but later reported the assault to the police because the offender did not compensate him as promised. Later, the offender agreed to compensate the victim on the condition that the prosecution against him would be discontinued. When this attempt failed, the case was sent to court. The mediation occurred quickly under the judge's direction and was attended by the victim's father and uncle (the victim was absent, as he worked in a distant city) and the offender and her mother. Based on several concerns, the victim had to accept the mediation agreement. The offender was given a suspended sentence.

Casc 8 Assault/Adult/Court

Assault Against Taxi Driver

The offender, Ren, who was slightly drunk, had a quarrel with a taxi driver, Qin, who refused to drive him. The quarrel escalated into a fight, which was joined by

Qin's friends. In the middle of the fight, Ren used his fruit knife to stab Hu, whom he believed was coming to Qin's rescue. Ren's claim of self-defense was not accepted; instead, his act constituted an assault with a minor injury. Prior to the court procedure, mediation had been arranged twice between Ren and Hu, but both attempts had failed. At court, an agreement was finally reached despite an intense atmosphere, and Ren was given a suspended sentence. The victim, Hu, refused to be interviewed, as he said he no longer wanted to have any contact with the officials (*gong jia ren*). The victim, Qin, who was initially ignored, but later added as a victim, was asked to accept the agreement with the offender. Both the offender Ren and the victim Qin were later interviewed by the researcher by phone.

Case 9 Involuntary Manslaughter/Adult/Court

Involuntary Manslaughter A

The offender, in operating an excavator under a bridge cave early in the morning, killed a passerby. The offender was taken into custody immediately. His father, the employer, and the company were all involved in compensating the victim's family. The minutes of the mediation did not contain any details about the negotiation process. Five months after the case was concluded, the offender's two lawyers refused to be interviewed for the following reasons: One lawyer believed that the way the case was handled was illegal, so he did not want to talk about it. The other lawyer stated that he needed to protect his client, who was still very young. The victim, who lost his wife in this case, refused to be interviewed: "I don't want to speak of it again." Only one interview with the victim's lawyer could be conducted, which was facilitated by the judge.

Case 10 Assault/Juvenile/Court

Joint Assault Against a Young Girl

The offenders (several juveniles) assaulted the victim, severely damaging her left eye. The evidence was not clear about whose blow directly damaged the victim's eye, but all the juveniles were held liable for committing the assault (with serious injury). The case file noted that the judge had organized the mediation. All the parents of the offenders were present, and the result was a one-off payment to the victim. On the same day, the same judge opened the trial for the offenders, convicting them and issuing non-custody sentences. However, the case did not conclude. The victim and her parents contacted or visited the court several times, filing a complaint that one offender had been left out of the criminal procedures and had evaded responsibility. It was also found that, 1 month before the court mediation, the victim had issued a statement of "no forgiveness" stating that "the offenders did not repent, and they even threatened the victim."

Case 11 Assault/Adult/Court

Assault During a Poker Game

The offender, while playing cards with the victim, had a quarrel with him. He battered the victim, resulting in a minor injury. The offender paid part of the medical fees (10,000 RMB, 1250 euro) to the victim after the event and prior to court. As recorded in the case file, the offender turned himself in to the police and confessed what he had done. Two attempts at mediation were set up by the police to address the compensation, but both failed. The judge sentenced the offender to prison on the grounds that he had not fully covered the victim's losses. The case was not concluded until after I left the field. Before I left, I was not permitted to contact the parties because the court procedure was ongoing.

Case 12 Assault/Juvenile/Court
Assault Between Dormitory Mates
Li, in a trifling dispute that escalated to an assault, caused his roommate, Hou, to permanently lose sight in his right eye. This event had a traumatic impact on the families of both sides. Li's family, poor and disadvantaged, collected as much as they could to pay the victim's side. Li was finally given a non-custody sentence. The mediation agreement did not bring an end to the dispute. The lawyer disclosed that the victim was planning to sue the college for non-action in this event; the victim remained traumatized from the event and became angry upon hearing the offender's name.

Case 13 Assault/juvenile/court
Assault Causing Several Injured
Qing caused actual physical harm (to the level of minor injury) to the victims with a knife but claimed he had acted in self-defense against the victims' assault. Subsequently, the offender's family made an out-of-court payment to the less severely hurt victims in this case. Nevertheless, he was prosecuted in court. The offender's family made considerable financial reparations to the victim who was the most severely hurt, and in return, the offender received a letter of forgiveness from the victim. In the end, the offender received a suspended sentence.

Case 14 Theft/Juvenile/Prosecutor
High School Classmate Theft
The victim, Li, and the offender, Wang, were former classmates in high school and were on good terms during that time. When Li insisted on reporting a lost phone to the police, he did not expect the perpetrator to be Wang. While Wang was being held in custody by the police, Li's mother realized that Wang's parents must be extremely sad about Wang's behavior; therefore, she chose to forgive him during the investigation stage to save him from further judicial dispositions. Nevertheless, Wang was sent to the prosecutor's office for further judicial action. Li's mother, however, did not have time to travel to Nanjing at that time, because her son Li had too much school work and various exams. Although she then spoke to Wang briefly on the phone, as arranged by the prosecutor, she had a few questions that still needed be addressed. The prosecution against Wang was discontinued. He was looking for another school that would admit him but was concerned that his criminal record would have a negative impact.

Case 15 Theft/Juvenile/Prosecutor
Two Female Students Theft
Yu and Tang, college students, entered their neighboring dormitory at midnight and stole a handbag, a cell phone, and a purse. Yu tried to conceal it when the police intervened because she was afraid of losing face in front of all her classmates. During the police investigation, both students were expelled from the college.

Learning from the prosecutor of the possible benefits associated with meeting the victims and seeking to apologize, Tang agreed to be taken to the college. Yu also agreed because she felt she needed to take responsibility for what she had done. The victims were unaware they were going to meet with the offenders. The prosecutor convened the meeting, which was attended by teachers (*fudaoyuan*) from each side, the security guard of the college, as well as two police officers. Pressure and tension was felt throughout the room.

Case 16 Sexual Assault/Juvenile/Prosecutor
Sexual Assault Two Female College Students

The sexual assault against two female students was considered serious and sensitive. The young offender was arrested, which was usually a sign that there would be a custodial sentence. The offender remained in custody while the meeting was held. It started with a discussion between the prosecutor, the police officers, and the college cadres. The principal of the college expressed his shame about the occurrence of this criminal event, as well as his hope that the offender would be granted leniency. Other college cadres reported to the prosecutor about the follow-up work they had done and what they had learned from both the offender and the victims. The message was conveyed that the victim was indeed traumatized, but she did not want to continue this experience, and ultimately felt that the harm was not substantial. Subsequently, the victim was called, and she told the prosecutor that she did not want to see the offender prosecuted due to the nature of the offense and the fact that the offender's parents had apologized to her. The victim signed the agreement but insisted that the offender should be expelled from the college. Eventually, the prosecutor gave a non-arrest decision. The case had not yet been prosecuted when I left the field.

Case 17 Involuntary Manslaughter/Adult/Court
Involuntary Manslaughter B

The offender, when moving an excavator from one site to another, accidently killed a passerby. He was still being held in custody when the court organized the mediation between the victim and the perpetrator's sides. The offender's father and employer were listed as responsible for compensating the victim. But there seemed to be an issue about how to divide the responsibility between the offender and his employer. The judge organized mediation twice: out of court and during the trial. The perpetrator's side had tried to approach the victim's family to seek reconciliation after this tragedy happened. Mediation was also organized at an earlier criminal justice stage but had failed due to the gap in the amount of compensation both sides would accept.

Case 18 Assault/Adult/Mediation Room
Assault in a Local Residence

An assault happened in a local residence unit, where the residence manager (a female) was battered by a man. The community police brought the sides together to engage in mediation. The victim was accompanied by her husband, and the perpetrator was accompanied by his wife. The two sides sat across from each other, with the mediator sitting at the short edge of the table, between each side. Later, the perpetrator's employer hurried in to attend. The atmosphere was tense and confrontational but informal. The mediation lasted almost 50 min but failed to reach any agreement. The "failure" case would not be kept in the file. Moreover, I was not allowed to approach the participants afterward.

Case 19 Assault/Adult/Mediation room

Assault in Teacher's Residence

The fight happened in a teachers' residence unit at a local university between two females. One was the residence gatekeeper (the victim), and the other (the perpetrator) was a woman who came to look for her mother. The perpetrator had waited in the mediation room since noon, after being interrogated by the police. She was accompanied by a security guard, who prevented her from escaping. She appeared very anxious and kept making calls to people seeking help (seeking "connections"). She said she was afraid of being extorted by the other side and was anxious about being in the police station. She did not want to bring this issue to court, which would involve a lengthy procedure. Once the mediator (G) entered the office, the police asked him to come out and told him that because the woman had left a scar on the victim's face, the mediator should ask her to provide more compensation. Then, the police entered the room with the mediator and announced to the perpetrator that "if the mediation fails, it's possible that you will be kept in custody (*xingzheng juliu*, 行政拘留, administrative punishment). There are two counts, one for disturbing the social order and the other for assault. Luckily no injury has been caused to his ear, otherwise you would be sentenced and sent to prison (*zuolao panxing*, 坐牢判刑). If it is successful, then we settle this; if not, then we go about legal proceedings." The mediation lasted one and a half hours, and an agreement was finally reached through bargaining, confrontation, persuasion, and compromise.

Case 20 Assault/Adult/Mediation Room

Assault Causing Mediation Three Times

This dispute arose from two quarreling mothers over a petty fight between their children. One mother slapped the other on the face, causing the latter to claim that there was a problem with her hearing. Mediation was set up between the two parties three different times. Because the first mediation took place before I arrived, I only observed two of the mediation sessions. The victim's side requested the mediation, so the mediator was asked by the police to do it. The first mediation session failed due to a power imbalance because of the economic statuses of the two sides. The victim's side proposed one intimidating request. The second mediation faced difficulties, with several dramatic ups and downs, but it finally concluded with an agreement. During the second mediation, the victim's husband came alone on behalf of his wife, and the other side was attended by the perpetrator (who had come alone the first time) and her parents (the grandparents of the child).

Case 21 Assault/Adult/Mediation Room

Assault Claimed in a Traffic Dispute

A girl (who was accompanied by her boyfriend) claimed that she had been assaulted by a man, and her phone had broken when it fell on the ground. Both sides entered the room shortly after they came out of the police office, agreeing to the mediation. The girl showed anger and contempt while seated face-to-face with the man but did not speak. Instead, her boyfriend spoke and insisted that the other side should apologize and should provide compensation for the medical fees and replace the broken phone. Surprised by the claim that the phone was broken and informed about its astronomical price, the man refused to give it back but insisted that the phone should first be repaired. Disagreeing on the terms, the mediation failed to reach an agreement. The girl and her boyfriend claimed that they would bring this issue to court. The process was saturated with direct confrontation and distrust. At some point, the girl's side even made a call to someone occupying an important office post. They threatened the man by showing that they had relationships with officials who might aid them. The power imbalance was quite obvious during this mediation session.

Case 22 Assault/Adult/Mediation Room

Business Infraction Leading to Assault

There was a fight between two sides arising out of a business infraction, which resulted in the victim being injured and her door being broken. The police intervened and presided over the mediation with the assistance of another mediator because the principle mediator was not present. The perpetrator was accompanied by his mother and their neighbor, while the victim was accompanied by her relative. The mediation process was very confrontational and quarrels continuously erupted. The perpetrator made a payment but refused to apologize. The assisting mediator tried to persuade both sides and to lessen the confrontation and ensured that an agreement was eventually reached.

Case 23 Debt Dispute/Adult/Mediation Room

Paying Back the Debt

There was little work left to do in this case, because the two sides had already reached an agreement at the police office. This short mediation (around 25 min) was simply to witness the signing and performance of the agreement. The mediator, however, still explained the procedures of the mediation to each side. He also suggested, in a persuasive tone, that the most important thing for one side was to get their money back. The facts were not as important as each side's willingness to end the dispute. According to the mediator, each side was clear about what had happened and what they had done. A solution package was preferred over endless discussion of the matter.

Case 24 Accident and Injury/Adult/Mediation Room

Accident and Injury

The dispute arose from a child falling down and suffering a bone fracture at a playground owned by a company. The mediation lasted 2 h and 20 min. The injured side included the mother, the father, and the child's uncle, while the company was represented by the vice manager of customer service and an employee. At the beginning, the atmosphere was relaxed and friendly, and both sides seemed to have agreed on some terms. However, the mediator started by proposing his own solution package. His authoritarian and directive style made both sides reluctant, but they had to consider what he had proposed. This caused a direct confrontation between the two sides. The company's side was urged with great pressure to make a one-off payment, which they found difficult to accept. This unwillingness upset the injured side. Open expression on both sides was cut off, and the supposed dialogue was guided into a discussion over monetary compensation. Moreover, the mediator did not allow a more detailed and deep discussion of how this matter had arisen, because he was afraid that further confrontation between two sides would emerge.

Case 25 Assault/Adult/Mediation Room
Criminal Settlement Organized by the Police

The police performed a criminal mediation, which was as short as 30 min. The perpetrator was a young adult who was represented by his father and his uncle. The victim was an old man who was represented by his son and a lawyer. There seemed to be no dispute about the major facts – the young adult had hurt the old man during a quarrel – and the disagreement lay in the reparations. This case occurred between a criminal punishment and an administrative punishment, depending on whether and how the perpetrator would make reparations to the victim. Pressured and persuaded by the police, as well as the victim's side, the perpetrator's side finally agreed on the amount. As assumed, many minor offenses eluded intervention by the criminal justice system (prosecution or sentencing) in this way.

Case 26 Assault/Adult/Mediation Room
Assault Between Two Female Friends

This assault happened between two friends. Because both sides had fought against each other, there was no clear distinction between who was the perpetrator and who was the victim. Both women were accompanied by their husbands, and the quarrel was ongoing when the mediation began. The mediator had to ask one to remain silent while the other was speaking. This turned out to be difficult. The facts remained unclear, as each side presented different arguments. As a matter of fact, both sides were ordered several times to stop expressing their opinions and emotions. In the end, although the two sides, at the request of the mediator, offered apologies to each other, they seemed unwilling to agree on what the mediator had proposed. Their need to have the truth established was not met, and one side's claim of damage to her reputation in her company was not addressed.

Case 27 Debt Dispute/Adult/Mediation Room
Dispute over Business Debt

This dispute arose from business conduct, when one side claimed that the other side owed them payment for goods. The mediation lasted around 40 minutes. The mediator, in particular, used "admiration" skills (with relation to people's notion of saving face) to urge the debtor to perform her duty to repay. Both sides were confrontational throughout the mediation. The mediator also educated the debtor without causing her to lose face.

Case 28 Assault/Adult/Mediation Room
Assault Between Two Security Guards

The assault happened between two security guards who had committed small infractions prior to the fight. Two managers from their company came to attend the mediation. The atmosphere appeared serious. Silence emerged occasionally, and the managers, as well as the mediator, dominated the mediation session. The manager criticized the behavior of the perpetrator but also voiced his concern for the perpetrator's family, i.e., that it would be a disaster for the perpetrator's family if he was thrown into prison. The police also intervened and lectured the perpetrator. There was little exchange between the victim and the perpetrator. In the end, all agreed that such a thing should never happen again. Upon leaving, the manager thanked the mediator, and the perpetrator shook hands with the police.

Case 29 Dispute Over Housing Contract/Mediation Room

Dispute over Housing Contract

This was a dispute over a housing contract between a buyer and a housing service agency. The buyer had fully paid the price, which was a huge sum, but he had not been allowed to move in. Prior to the mediation, he went to court, filing a lawsuit, and, then, he applied for execution of the judgment. Even then, he still could not obtain the ownership certificate from the seller. He claimed that this was because the agency did not perform their duty properly, and he asked for a return of the service fees and proper compensation for his losses in this deal. Out of anger, he locked the gate of the agency, and the latter had to call the police. Two mediation sessions had been organized but had failed to reach an agreement. It was noted that both the mediators and the police felt angry for the buyer and criticized the agency for failing to take responsibility and insisting on going to court, which the buyer did not wish to do.

Case 30 Assault/Adult/Mediation Room

Assault Between Migrant Workers at a Construction Site

The perpetrator and the victim were workers on the same construction site. Outraged by the victim's suspicion that the perpetrator's brother had stolen his phone, the perpetrator slapped the victim on his face. Both issues were still in dispute during the mediation, because the victim claimed that he did not doubt the behavior of the perpetrator's brother, but the perpetrator insisted that he did doubt it. In front of the police, they shook hands and grinned. Later, the victim went to see the doctor and was diagnosed with a nose fracture. Immediately, the perpetrator was taken into custody. The police then called on the managers of the construction site to resolve this matter within their company. Upon the warrant letter from the manager, the police released the perpetrator, lectured him, and agreed to "reduce major issues to minor ones and minor ones to nothing."

Case 31 Dispute on the Use of Garage/Mediation Room

Dispute on the Use of Garage

This was a dispute on the use of a garage between the residence management company and the proprietor. The company locked the garage, and, as a result, the proprietor called the police. The mediation at the police office failed, but they were asked to return and participate again. The mediation lasted around half an hour, and the mediator suggested that they should check a few more details of the contract. In the meantime, the mediator educated one side that he should have been more careful in making the contract to avoid such a dispute.

Case 32 Assault/Adult/Mediation Room

Assault between Business Partners

Former business partners who had separated had a fight arising from a verbal altercation. After they were lectured in the police office, the two parties were brought to the mediation room. Both sides were still angry, and the perpetrator was unwilling to make any reparations, although the other side claimed there was a medical fee involved. The mediator tried to persuade the perpetrator to accept it but failed. The perpetrator claimed that the person who had been assaulted had engaged in stealing. Seeing that there was a standoff and the police disposition lying ahead, the mediator had a chat with the perpetrator. Then, the mediator referred to a third person that both the perpetrator and the mediator knew well. The perpetrator relented and agreed to pay for the medical fees. The person who had been assaulted said he would receive the money at the mediation room instead of having any direct contact with the perpetrator again. It could be concluded that there was deep mistrust between the disputing parties, as later, the perpetrator returned and asked for a copy of the medical bill, as he intended to check the authenticity of the bill.

References

Hu, J. (2011). Grand mediation in China. *Asian Survey, 51*(6), 1065–1089.

Ji, W. (2013). The judicial reform in China: The status quo and future directions. *Indiana Journal of Global Legal Studies, 20*(1), 185–220.

Liao, M., & Shi, L. (2014). The specialization of justice organs and professionalization of justice personnel in Chinese juvenile criminal cases. *Frontiers of Law in China, 9*(3), 403.

Tanenhaus, D. S. (2012). The elusive juvenile court: Its origins, practices, and reinventions. In B. C. Feld & D. M. Bishop (Eds.), *The Oxford handbook of juvenile crime and juvenile justice* (pp. 419–441). New York: Oxford University Press.

Trevaskes, S. (2010). The Shifting Sands of punishment in China in the era of 'Harmonious Society'. [article]. *Law & Policy, 32*, 332–361.

Trevaskes, S. (2011). Political ideology, the party, and politicking: Justice system reform in China. *Modern China, 37*(3), 315–344. doi:10.1177/0097700410394776.

Yao, J. (2004). A reflection on the necessity of creating juvenile courts [*chuangshe shaonian fayuan biyaoxing yanjiu de fansi*]. *Issues on Juvenile Crimes and Delinquency, 2004*(3), 55–59.

Zhang, H. (2013). Revisiting people's mediation in China: Practice, performance and challenges. *Restorative Justice: An International Journal, 1*(2), 244–267.

Zhang, X. (2004). *A restorative justice audit of the Chinese criminal justice system*. London: The London School of Economic and Political Science.

Zhao, G., & Chang, L. (2010). The development of juvenile system in China [*zhongguo weicheng-nian ren shenpan zhidu de fazhan*]. *Academic Forum of Nandu (Journal of the Humanities and Social Sciences), 30*(1), 97–102.

Chapter 6
Thematic Analysis

1 Introduction

In this chapter, we utilize the line of process to outcome in mediation to present the findings. The previous literature review suggested that substantial attention has been attached to the outcome, but the understanding of the communication process between the victim and the offender is underdeveloped. Thus, this chapter draws on the field data, which were mainly collected by observations and interviews, to reveal the processes and the outcomes of mediation practices. Here, the process is defined as the sequence of the initiation of the mediation, the preparation for it, and the direct and indirect encounters between the victim and the offender; the outcome is defined as the results based on the agreement made between the two sides.

2 Initiating the Mediation

In compliance with the suggestions from previous studies, in this study, the state authority must initiate criminal reconciliation. "Streamlining" is found when a case had been unsuccessfully mediated prior to the court stage, and mediation occurs again in court. The judicial assessment takes the following into account: the type of conflict, the wrongdoer's remorse, the willingness of the wrongdoer to make reparations, and the opinion of the victim. This complies with the practices reported by the judicial practitioners in Chap. 3 (Song and Yuan 2009).

The justice authority's assessment consumes substantial time. Juvenile cases can be considered as an example. While the social investigation of the offender's circumstances and family background should be performed by the local justice bureau, which must assist the justice authority, the reality is that the justice authority also must perform substantial work to provide a sounder and more reliable investigation.

X. Yuan, *Restorative Justice in China*, Springer Series on Asian Criminology and Criminal Justice Research, DOI 10.1007/978-3-319-63922-2_6

There are possible benefits for offenders who are offered the option of reconciliation, such as a reduction of the sentence or an exemption from prosecution. Cooperation from the offender is expected, and coercion cannot be utterly avoided. One offender told us he was "encouraged" by the authority to make reparations to the victims in exchange for penal reduction: *If I were not making reparations, then I could only go to prison.*

When they informed the victim's side, the state actors would also determine whether the victims agreed to be compensated, giving the offenders a second chance. With respect to youth offending, there appears to be an expectation that the victims will agree to what has been proposed by the authority.

> I don't know who contacted me. I guess it was the judicial staff from here. She said on the phone that the offenders' families agreed to make compensation, and asked me if I could give them this opportunity… I was angry because my motorcycle was stolen. But giving it a second thought, we were all adolescents, so it's OK to give them a second chance (interview with the victim, Case 1 Multiple Thefts against Strangers).

The initiation of mediation does not solely serve the purpose of reconciling the opposing sides. It appears that the restoration of personal relationships does not seem to be the authority's first priority. Instead, maintaining social stability is the paramount concern. The political pressure imposed by the Chinese government on its criminal justice system can easily be felt.

The overall impression of the situation facing the local courts is that they are busy and shorthanded. Because of their overloads, the state authority is left with very little time to perform its duties. It is not uncommon for them to work very late and during the weekend. Judges, who are not guaranteed independence from the government, are burdened with tasks such as attending various training sessions and party ideology education. An informal conversation with a judge during a work lunch revealed her complaints: *The people at the upper level court have enough free time, and they convene us to attend the training on our working days. Burdened with so many cases, we local court judges do not have so much time…We have to work extra hours to settle the cases before us… The [current criminal justice] system is too bureaucratic*. By "bureaucratic," she meant that many formalities, such as various training and political studies, occupied the judges' time, which should have been used to handle cases (researcher's diary, April 3, 2014).

In addition to these routines, the court must perform political, administrative, and practical tasks, such as a big cleanup to prepare for the arrival of the Youth Olympics, which involved physical labor. Young judges were also assembled for extreme body training sessions to prepare for the fight against terrorism and any possible social events (*shehui shijian*, 社会事件).

This shortage of time meant that the judges had no time to listen to the opposing sides in a given case. They clearly knew the essential information about the cases that came into their hands, and they were also experienced in handling them. Nevertheless, the work pressure each day caused them to lose patience. In one mediation session, the judge asked the researcher to mediate because he had a meeting to attend. In another session, the judge was asked to attend a political study organized for new party members, leaving the victim to wait in his office for one hour. On another occasion, both the offenders and the victims were present, waiting for mediation, but the judge had to attend a meeting elsewhere; she had to call another judge, who had no knowledge of the case, to perform the mediation on her behalf.

3 Observation of the Encounter

3.1 Education

In the mediation sessions, the mediators usually provided aspects of "education" to the perpetrator.

Education of the Perpetrators by the Mediator Although the context seemed rather formal, the mediator in the mediation room appeared much more relaxed than the one who was invited to the prosecutor's office. They both provided education during the mediation, albeit to different degrees.

In Case 1, Multiple Thefts against Strangers, the mediator asked the offenders to learn a lesson from the situation; at some point, he acknowledged that young people could not always avoid making mistakes. However, the extent to which these statements had an educative impact on the offender was questionable. It seemed as if the mediator said those words because he had to say them under the circumstances. Faced with great pressure as a result of being situated there, he proceeded with the mediation in a very superficial manner. For instance, the mediator simply talked of the purpose of reaching an agreement, knowing that both sides would agree. One session in Case 1, which lasted longer (almost one hour), was an exception to this because of the victim's incongruent opinion about his losses. The other sessions lasted 20 minutes or less. The mediator also left the room to take the printed agreement from the prosecutor, leaving both sides sitting there in silence. At one point, it was observed that both the mediator and the victims began to look at their mobile phones or chat in order to kill time. The offenders and their fathers barely spoke. Nevertheless, the offenders' side had already shown their sincerity by agreeing to compensate the victims' losses; face-to-face encounters involving more shaming can risk stigmatizing young offenders.

In addition to the education by the mediator, we also noticed efforts by the prosecutors to educate the offenders. However, young offenders felt that they had already learned a lesson, so these words seemed redundant and annoying.

In the local mediation room, the mediators also sometimes educated the perpetrator, usually in an indirect way. "It doesn't matter when one did something wrong; anyone can make mistakes, but he should learn this lesson" (Case 18). "Since it happened, he should reflect upon where he was wrong" (Case 19). "If he did receive the eggs and refused to pay you, he should be tortured by his conscience" (Case 32). Instead of accusing the perpetrator directly of the wrongfulness of his behavior, the mediator usually used an indirect pronoun "he," showing that he was standing on the side of the victim, acknowledging his status, without causing the perpetrator to lose face. In other words, the education must not be "harsh," because the perpetrator is considered to have a sense of shame.

However, in the high shame and power context in which the mediation is situated, the impact of education on the perpetrator may be minimal. Being detained at the police station was already perceived as the price; the fear of being a loser in the power game compelled both sides to seek connections. Under these circumstances, the mediators' educative words did not seem sincere.

Educating the Offender by the Victim's Side We rarely saw victims speak directly to the perpetrators in an educative tone, except in the juvenile cases. In the mediation sessions in Case 1, we observed the victim saying: *Since you want to turn good, I will give you an opportunity for sure. How to correct your behavior is your business. Do not go astray anymore.* The victim also asked the father not to blame the youths, because this had occurred previously (observation notes, Feb 18, 2014).

During the direct confrontation with the offender, the education may be too punitive and stigmatizing, as the offenders already bore a stigma based on the exposure of the crime when they had been brought into contact with the criminal justice authority. The offenders felt ashamed to meet their victims face-to-face; when the encounter was inevitable, further harm to both sides was also possible. An example is provided below.

In Case 15, Two Female Students Theft, the offenders, who were alone, were confronted by their peer victims, the class teachers, a campus security guard, two police officers, and the prosecutor. Reconciliation was set as the aim of the face-to-face meeting. When the victims were reluctant at first to speak up at the request of the judicial authority, their class teacher[1] (*fudaoyuan*, 辅导员) felt he should break the silence: "OK. As a matter of fact, I knew you before this (the crime) happened. To resolve this matter, you should apologize to our classmates sincerely. With regard to the nature of this matter, it is a business left to the court." He continued, "At that moment you two appeared very calm. But our classmates were very disturbed, and they were afraid of going to sleep at night. You, as a female student, should reflect and realize your mistakes" (observation notes, May 22, 2014).

The two female students, pressured by all sides, had to repent in front of the victims, who did not consider their apology to be sincere. Between the interference from the police officers and prosecutors at the scene, the peer victims offered words that sounded educational:

> You returned the goods, just because of the pressure or whatever. You have to realize your mistake. You said you had three siblings in your family. I also have, but did I go to take other's stuff? You should be thankful for us reporting to the police, to help you avoid bigger mistakes in the future. You should reflect deeply on your deeds and their impact on others. I hope you reflect upon where you were wrong.

Another victim also spoke to the offenders in this way:

[1] *Fudaoyuan*, 辅导员, in China, they are faculty assigned to monitor and counsel students in personal and political matters and are different from academic advisors and psychological counselors.

> You are not a kid anymore. You should stand up to take your responsibility. We are not asking for compensation. We just could not understand why you, after having made a mistake (or commit a wrong?), could still live happily, but we had to live in fear every day. We asked the police, and the police told us not to tell others in case you would do something. I just felt that you could still have fun. It's not that we couldn't forgive you, but rather, it's your attitude that did not make us feel you are remorseful (observation notes, May 22, 2014).

It was observed that the offenders were not given a chance to respond to these questions; rather, the prosecutor spoke to the offenders in a threatening and appealing tone:

> This opportunity is precious for you. Even when you go to court, you still have to speak up. You should take advantage of the time because we have no more time for you. If you miss this opportunity, the rest of your life will be influenced by this....You will surely go to court. But if you obtain the other side's forgiveness, you will have your sentence fifty percent off. You are not bad at speech. If you realize your mistake, you will say it (observation notes, May 22, 2014).

Between these two scenes, the victims believed that the offenders were genuinely remorseful in the first case when the state authority was not present; in the latter case, in which the state authority was present, the victims believed the apology was merely in exchange for a reduced sanction.

3.2 *Communication*

Here, we define communication as a dialogue between the two sides about the impact of the crime and how to resolve the issue. The victim and the offender did show emotion when they encountered each other, which was indicated in nonverbal gestures, such as remaining silent, having a long face, etc.; however, the communication was quite difficult. The victims did have the opportunity to convey the impact the crime had had on them; but very often, they were interrupted because the state authority considered that mentioning it again was unnecessary; the key issue now was how to resolve the situation. As one victim recounted, the state authority was concerned that further confrontation would be caused by bringing people into a physical encounter; continued listening may also be a burden on the state authority.

As indicated above, in Case 15, Two Female Students Theft, the offenders were not allowed to say anything aside from showing remorse. As she was not accompanied by any supporting persons, one of the offenders was afraid to say anything the victims knew was not true, as she later said: *I was afraid of causing awkwardness, so I did not speak, but I felt hurt... I felt they misunderstood me... I felt very low that day* (interview with one of the offenders, Case 15 Two Female Students Theft).

In Case 8, Assault against Taxi Driver, the judge asked me to mediate (as he had a meeting to attend) between the two sides. He instructed me that I should attempt to learn each side's bottom line. I noted in my diary:

> I did not want to impose pressure on them, but tried to give them time and space to talk about their feelings and opinions. Persuasion was needed, as I found that both sides were not voluntarily taking the opportunity to speak up, but rather relied on me to negotiate. When it seemed that the talk would not go beyond the issue of monetary compensation, I reported to the judge what had occurred and waited for the order (field diary, April 16, 2014).

It was very difficult for communication to occur within that sober or suffocating context. The case file indicated that both parties had participated in mediation at a previous stage but that it had failed; the police recorded the following statement: *I (the offender) have no other thoughts. The victim asked too much. At this moment, I only expect that the final decision will be delivered as soon as possible so that I can put an end to this matter.*

One may wonder whether direct communication is really needed when the state authority dominates the process. An authoritarian style of concluding the matter renders direct communication less important. It follows that, in most cases, there was a limit to the expression of emotion, and the victim was persuaded to compromise.

3.3 Victims' Voice

In the mediation sessions performed by the mediators, the victims were given an opportunity to talk about their experience and their suffering in general. A few examples are: *Since I was battered on May 9th, every afternoon I have a headache* (Case 18). *I suffered a loss of dignity, and I don't want to talk about it anymore* (Case 19). *I'm feeling better now, but not fully recovered* (Case 20). In some cases, the victims became very angry, especially when they saw that the perpetrators had a negative attitude, not admitting to their mistakes and making apologies that were insincere.

Such angry victims could certainly gain sympathy and support from the mediators and the policemen. In Case 29, although it was a civil case, the complainant party was angered that the court did not help him resolve the problem. He claimed the company should take responsibility and partially cover the losses, but the company maintained that the court had concluded the case and that they had no longer had any legal responsibility. All of the mediators and the policemen stood on the side of the victim and persuaded the company to take responsibility.

There seems to be a limit to the expression of emotions by the victims. On many occasions, the mediator stopped them immediately, even at the beginning of the mediation session, which started with the victims talking about their experiences. The mediator considered that "more talk is useless, since you guys know what happened with the most clarity." He always tried to prevent the two sides from engaging in further argument about the matter. However, both sides had something to say and continued to have different opinions, and they did not really believe in the positions the mediator asked them to accept.

In Case 18, we observed that the victim's supporter wanted to discuss how the event had happened and its impact, but, clearly, the mediator attempted to control the process and bring the matter to a close. Although the perpetrator's side (the manager on behalf of the perpetrator) apologized, they could not agree on the issue of the work subsidy, which had been raised by the mediator; the victim considered that this was a signal of distrust from the perpetrator toward him, and the mediation failed. The perpetrator considered that the victim's side had a negative attitude, had made unreasonable requests, and were unwilling to compromise. From the mediator's perspective, asserting one's claim and expressing strong emotions were a sign that too much was being demanded, and it certainly would not lead to a successful resolution of the matter. In this case, the perpetrator was only willing to agree when he thought the victim's requests were reasonable.

The mediator disclosed that the victims had the upper hand (占上风) because they had suffered as a result of someone else's wrongfulness. If the case is to be resolved successfully, one should prevent the victim from taking advantage of the fact that they are a victim to demand more. In such cases, the victims' desires or needs should be played down.

In various mediation sessions, the dialogue was not oriented by what the victims wanted to say but was directed toward the final conclusion of the matter. Below are some examples.

Case 1 Multiple Thefts Against Strangers

During one mediation session, we observed that the victim wanted to know how to avoid being stolen from again; obviously, the impact of the crime on him was not addressed during the mediation.

Case 14 High School Student Theft

The prosecutor's office asked the offender to make a call to the victim. However, the interviews with the victim's side (the victim's mother) suggested that they had several concerns that needed to be addressed. They included the following: would Wang's (the offender) father feel that it was unfair for the school to expel his child and as a result take revenge on Li (the victim); why had Wang stolen from Li, i.e., was it because of any previous misbehavior on Li's side; was Wang remorseful; and was Wang's behavior habitual or reckless (*hutu*, 糊涂)? The mother was also worried that Wang's family might be brutal to their son because of the crime; the offender needed to be corrected (*ganhua*, 感化), not severely punished.

Case 7 Assault Against Upstairs Neighbor

The victim's side (the father and the uncle represented the victim) wanted the offender to compensate for part of their losses. What mattered more to the victim was the attitude of the offender, who until then had only considered his behavior "bad luck"; the offender was also not actively making reparations (researcher's note). As stressed by the victim, *the central point is you need to give me psychological balance. What matters most is the attitude from the old lady (the offender's mother). You pay if you have money, pay less if you don't. If you are truly penniless, I can even cross it out. But you cannot just turn away from it* (= not take responsibility) (interview with the victim's side, Case 7 Assault against Upstairs Neighbor).

However, there was another story when it came to the mediation. The judge had no interest in what the victim expected out of the mediation. Instead, he told the offender's side about the possible punishment the offender may receive. *If the issue is resolved, it does good to your life; and they (the victim side) will obtain the compensation. Today, we won't discuss the legal issue or the facts, but only the compensation. If we mediate today, tomorrow you send in money, and the day after tomorrow we could issue a judgment.* Then, the victim side was called in, followed by a discussion on the monetary matter, which, to the victim, felt like "bargaining on the market." The judge stressed that "this is mediation" (observation notes, April 14, 2014).

Case 26 Assault Between Two Female Friends

Because both parties had fought with each other, there was no clear distinction between who was the perpetrator and who was the victim. When G was the mediator, D1, D2 the disputants with S1, S2 their respective supporters, we observed the following dialogue, during which the mediator wanted to control the process and prevented the disputing side, who had claimed to be assaulted, from arguing about the matter any further.

D2: She refused to drop the trash.

G: This is not the point.

D2: When she did the cleaning, she began scolding me. When she saw me put the dishes in the kitchen, she called me "stupid." And she said I took the company's stuff home. The manager asked her why she didn't work and told her that her wage would be reduced if she continued this way. Then she began her work but didn't stop cursing. The manager asked her who she was scolding and asked her to stop working the next day. Another time, she began scolding from 2:30 pm on and ordered me to work.

G: Stop please! It's pointless that you continue.

D2: Please listen to me.

G (interrupting her): What's your idea now?

D2: The next day, I rested at home…

G: What is the relationship between you, D1 and S1?

D1, S1: We are a couple.

G (speaking to D2): I don't think your words have any point.

D2: I want to speak.

G: Again, what's your idea now?

D2: I still want to talk.

G: You listen to me.

D2: D1 hit me at night.

G: Again, what is your opinion now?

D2: She hit me during the work time.

…….

G: We do not need to talk about the process and details. Then, what's your general idea?

D2: D1 should allow me to see the doctor because I'm feeling uncomfortable.

G: What time did she hit you?

D2: 4 pm, yesterday.

G: You meant you want to take a CT scan test?

D2: Yes.

G (speaking to D1 and S1): What is your idea? Only answer this question.

D1: She sent a message to my husband's cell phone.

D2: Master (G), please let me finish my talk.

G: Don't talk about it now! I don't think you can get to the point in one hour.

Clearly, the mediator did not want to hear the victim speak continuously about her experience and the stories behind the fight but tried to find a quick solution that both sides could agree on in order to put an end to the dispute. Nevertheless, the victim did not agree to that. As the supporter from one side said: *Now, it has not yet been made clear who beat whom, and you talk about how to resolve it*?! Moreover, one side's concern over the damage to their reputation and their request that the other side make an apology at the workplace were not addressed by the mediator. The mediator simply stated: *That's none of my business* (observation notes, June 13, 2014).

In Case 20, Assault Causing Mediation Three Times, we noticed the following. In the second mediation session, the mediator sought to compel both sides to reach an agreement based on an apology and economic compensation (the medical expenditure was 440 RMB or 55€). When the calculation turned out to be a substantial sum (10,054 RMB or 1257€), the perpetrator's side became angrier. The tension rose to a level that led the victim to ask the perpetrator to remove her child from the same kindergarten.

During the third mediation session, the victim did not appear but was represented by her husband A1, and the perpetrator B1 was accompanied by her parents S1, S2. Again, the mediator did not want one side to talk continuously about the matter but moved directly to the compensation issue. This type of mediation was questioned by the perpetrator's side, but finally, based on persuasion from the police, they agreed to pay even though A1 refused to give ground.

The mediation began with greetings between both sides. S2 explained that there was no verbal assault the last time, but due to the different meanings of the term, A1's wife considered that there had been. At the beginning, the atmosphere was friendly.

A1 started: "I have persuaded her (A1's wife) several times since it happened that 'we shouldn't make this issue more complicated'. Now that we are advocating the harmonious society, we should settle it peacefully. She is recovering physically. If she goes to Shanghai to have a medical check-up, it will add more time and be a greater financial burden. I persuaded her to stay and get treated in Nanjing."

B1 wondered what they were asking for now.

A1: We want to settle it peacefully. We don't have time to waste on this issue. In fact, it arose from a trivial thing. My wife was reckless as well and may have said something disrespectful.

S1 wanted to say more about this verbal abuse, but G asked her not to discuss it further. "There is no need to talk about the process. Since you quarreled and fought, we should put an end to this now."

A1 asked B1 about her opinion now.

B1: No matter what the result will be, it all depends on us. First, it was a quarrel, and then, it was a fight. If someone had come to stop us when we were quarreling, the fight would not have happened. We are now trying to find a fair, just way that both sides can accept. Up until now, that scene has always been on my mind, like a movie. It stirs my emotions every time I think about it. We all hope to get it resolved. Back to the issue, the police kept a video.

G: There is no need to talk about this.

……

A quarrel began.

The police entered and asked them to stop. However, the argument continued between the mediator and one disputant. B1 insisted on sticking with the last mediation; however, she did question the amount set by the mediator. S1 and S2 also began to question the mediator about the way he was conducting the mediation.

Overall, in the cases at the prosecutor's office and at the court, the victims usually refrained from expressing their opinions or their feelings when the judicial authority was present. In the cases that were diverted to the mediation room at the police stage, the victims appeared to be more active in expressing their opinions, but they were very frequently interrupted or asked to stop. When the victims began to talk about their suffering, complaints, dissatisfaction, etc., they were rarely able to continue, as the authority who was guiding the encounter would stop them.

3.4 *Compromise Expected from the Victim*

The observation of the mediation sessions suggested that it was not at all exceptional for the victims to compromise as a result of persuasion. Compromise was expected of the victims under certain circumstances.

In cases involving young offenders, the victims were expected to extend forgiveness and to give young offenders a second chance, rather than to put them in a riskier situation. From the standpoint of the mediator, we found that he felt that it was necessary for the victims to compromise or, in Chinese terms, to bear some of the losses (chi kui, 吃亏) in order to achieve the settlement. As he said:

> During our last mediation, we put the victim's side in the place of suffering losses (chi dian kui, 吃点亏). We found that he lost his vehicle, which perhaps did not cost that much, but had tremendous use value for him, e.g., in commuting to his workplace every day. Although the Price Evaluation Department assessed that it was only valued at 1,000 RMB, he probably could not accept the assessed value at the bottom of his heart, so we expected him to be a humanitarian. Because, after all, those who commit this crime usually have a poor economic background, low education level, or are young and easily misled; hence, they more or less belong to a socially disadvantaged group. We expect the victim to be tolerant, which means to give up some of his interests, which could even be larger than those in civil cases.

Interestingly, the victim who was mentioned by the mediator recognized the fact that he was being persuaded, but he agreed to the settlement in spite of his dissatisfaction with the reparation plan, which had been predetermined. He explained that he appreciated that the mediator had stood in his shoes and had tried his best, on the one hand, but that on the other hand, he should nevertheless give the young offenders an opportunity to renew themselves.

In some cases, the victims were also considered to have contributed to the event. In other words, they were not completely innocent, which may contradict the legal classification that the person who was beaten is the victim. For instance, in Case 30, the wrongdoer believed that the victim had initially been at fault. Based on this circumstance, both were asked by the mediator or the police to apologize to each other. In another case, the victim went to the police again because he was dissatisfied with the previous settlement, as the wrongdoer had failed to compensate him for his losses. The mediator responded that *you are not irresponsible, although you suffered the pain*. He then listed two issues for which the victim was at fault in a persuasive tone. In Case 26, the mediator tried to educate the disputants in a persuasive tone, as he spoke to the side who had claimed to be battered: *What's the point of staying angry? You stood there and gossiped about another family's affairs? If your husbands joined in the fight, would you two women be happy then? To be a good woman, you should only take good care of the children and the family, shouldn't you?* Her husband seemed to support her in an indirect way: *Time will tell who is good and who is bad. Once you have done it, there is no need to regret it.*

Even in critical cases such as involuntary manslaughter, we also observed that compromise from the victim was necessary in order to put an end to the conflict. In Case 17, Involuntary Manslaughter, the court trial was suspended for mediation based on the agreement of both sides. The judge was proactive in negotiating between the two sides. She convinced the victim's side (the wife of the deceased victim, her relatives, and the lawyer) by citing the benefits of mediation and the disadvantages of a judgment. *Mediation is based upon consensus. If he is willing to give more, I would not disapprove it. Moreover, they send the money to the court, so you will have it in cash. You calculate it yourself; there is a huge difference between what you will get from mediation and that from executing the judgment.* Upon hearing this, the wife of the deceased victim could not control her emotions and burst out crying, begging the judge to speak for her. The supporters of the victim, at this point, persuaded her not to insist. The judge, after learning that the offender's side was making efforts outside the door, continued to try to persuade the victim: *If they can borrow it, they will give it to you...Good people are rewarded by good things. You have a long road ahead of you. If you can put an end to this matter, you will start a new life. We are trying our best to work for you. If their capability is to take out 800,000 RMB (100,000€), I would not allow them to only take out 600,000RMB (75,000€). Stay strong.* Again, her relatives reminded her that her emotions would affect others. The judge continued: '*Take it as if you have spent the money on traveling abroad, as if you have pardoned him, as if you have bought a happy future*'. Then, the relatives and the lawyer joined in the persuasion: '*If the court issued the judgment, there would only be a little you can get. Which one of these options helps your child more?' (the lawyer). 'What's your purpose? You cannot bring his life back (the deceased victim). What's the sense if you have earned yourself more money today?!' (the relative)*. In the end, under all the pressure, the crying wife "agreed" to sign on the letter of forgiveness (observation notes, May 27, 2014).

One of the mediators expressed that the parties' disputes could be resolved only when they were brought face-to-face but that mediation should focus on both sides' weaknesses. He explained that one could not place the victim's status above the offender's because under those circumstances, the victim's expectations would be raised.

3.5 *The Importance of* Shouren

As explained above, the implementation of the fieldwork was facilitated by a person who had connections with the judicial institutions. The connections were at a personal level, but they worked smoothly, as favors and mutual obligations are essential to Chinese life. One Chinese term for "connections" is *shouren* (熟人), i.e., someone you know. Likewise, the existence of such an acquaintance greatly facilitates the mediation process. The mediator used it to achieve settlements between two disputing sides.

In Case 32, when the disputing sides reached an impasse, *shouren* played a crucial role in facilitating a smoother dialogue. For example, the mediator persuaded the wrongdoer by saying "everyone takes a step back. There is an acquaintance. Just take it as bad luck"; this was accepted by the wrongdoer, who said he had a good relationship with the man mentioned. He had to give in to the mediator on the basis of the face given to the *shouren*. But does this mean that the wrongdoer really believed he had any responsibility? The wrongdoer later returned to the mediation room to request that the authenticity of the documents presented by the other side be verified.

In Case 19, although the victim was not happy that the amount the perpetrator agreed to pay did not meet her expectations, she also said she knew the perpetrator's mother, as they worked in the same building, citing her words in Chinese, *taitou bujian ditou jian* (抬头不见低头见), which refers to people who meet frequently.[2] She was unwilling for the perpetrator to leave with a criminal record, because they still might meet in the future; striving to meet her own desires would break their interdependency.

The mediator said he was unwilling to act as the third party when one or both sides belonged to his *shouren*, as he could not afford to offend one side, which would put their relationship at risk.

3.6 Persuasion Leading to Harmony

The mediator would sometimes try to make peace between two angry disputing sides. Some of the persuasion techniques he used were very much like "harmony education." This is portrayed by the following quotes: "Mutual understanding is needed, no discord, no concord", "since you know each other now, it's possible that you will become friends in the future; he was drunk, had no malice" (Case 21), "At least, you are from the same hometown. There is no winner in this dispute", "don't intensify the disagreement, which will result in both sides being hurt and suffering (liangbai jushang, 两败俱伤)" (Case 29), "Now, you all are in psychological imbalance, right? We should resolve it soon if you are sincere, because you will still work together" (Case 26).

A phrase frequently cited by participants who had a voice in the mediation was the following: "reducing major things to minor ones and minor ones to nothing (大事化小,小事化了)." Driven by this ideology, the police asked the work unit to address the matter. If it were handled properly, no further judicial action would be taken, as occurred in Cases 28 and 30. In the mediation performed by the police, the

[2] Literally translated: People do not see each other when they lift their heads, and people see each other when they lower their heads.

"harmonious society" was also on tip of their tongues; for example, in Case 25, the police would not make a criminal case as long as an agreement was reached between the two sides.

Harmony, as a guiding principle we observed during the mediation sessions and our interviews, does not refer to an agreement reached between two conflicting parties, but rather to maintaining harmony as a broader common perspective among all members of society.

4 Outcome

Mediation produces an agreement signed by both sides or consent from the victim's side to show leniency to the offender's side. The agreement does not address how to rehabilitate the offenders but is more like a restitution agreement. Nevertheless, the outcome is significant for the victim, the offender and the state authority. We shall now look at what occurs following the agreement.

As one mediator stated, it is difficult to achieve a result that is completely satisfactory to both sides. We rarely saw two disputing sides shake hands with each other, but they did shake hands with the mediator, because they appreciated his efforts to resolve the matter. Hostility did exist between the two sides in many of the cases we collected. We will consider the outcomes of mediation in relation to the three sides: the perpetrator, the victim, and the state actors and the system.

4.1 Reintegration of the Offender

Mediation gives the offender an opportunity to stay out of prison. Having a family member in prison stigmatizes the whole family. One offender's family told us:

> We are living in sorrow as our child was in prison. If it were not for their small child, my son's wife would have sought a divorce from him. My son has an illness, and the medical expense is a big sum. When he is released from prison in the future, he will not be able to find a job. Who would dare to have an employee who has two criminal records. Once they go to police, they will find the record out (interview with the victim, Case 6 Business Rivalry Assault Case).

Leniency granted to the offender is also an opportunity for the family. In juvenile offending, the family clearly has the role of shaming and reintegrating the young offender. Shaming takes place when young offenders are placed under the supervision of their family, for example, the young offenders perceive the emotional distress experienced by their parents or their parents verbally criticize their behaviors. Crime is not only deemed to be a disgrace to the family but also to be an indication of the failure of the parental efforts to steer the child in the right direction.

> They (his parents) did not tell this to others (relatives and friends). I felt very ashamed (ting kechi, 挺可耻), because now all the students have learned of it (interview with offender 1, Case 15 Two Female Students Theft).

> In the meantime, they faced great pressure and feelings of losing 'face' living in the village. His mother felt unhappy now and suffered physical illness due to her bad mood. His father was looking forward to Jiang's graduation in the near future and sharing the burden of earning a livelihood. His family is shielding this 'bad reputation' from their relatives (case description, researcher's notes).

The offenders' families felt an obligation to reintegrate him/her and to restore society. In most of the cases in our study, the offenders (not held in custody) were accompanied by their families, close relatives, employers, and neighbors. Almost every family, irrespective of their economic background, modest or poor, took great pains to make reparations to the victims to save the offenders from harsh criminal sanctions. The interviews with offenders suggested that their families, while criticizing their behaviors, accepted them as good people instead of seeing them as bad elements.

> My dad said to me that he believed that I wasn't a bad child. I feel the same about myself. Because, he said, I wasn't like the guys on the street who keep doing bad things, I wasn't wicked to the extreme (interview with one offender, Case 15 Two Female Students Theft).

> My dad and mom know that I'm feeling sad right now. They want to talk to me until my mood turns better. They ask me to stay at home and correct my thinking. They need to see first that my thinking has changed and then they will help me to find a new school (interview with one offender, Case 14 High School Student Theft).

> A fault confessed is half redressed (or translated as: a prodigal who returns is more precious than gold; lang zi huitou jin bu huan, 浪子回头金不换). As long as he can repent, I would be willing to spend whatever I have. He confessed to me yesterday that he would never do such illegal things again. He plans to find a job, and I want him to learn how to drive (interview with offender's father, Case 1 Multiple Theft Against Strangers).

The societal efforts to reintegrate young offenders were reflected in the sensitive case, Case 16 Sexual Assault Two Female College Students. During the meeting between the prosecutor, the police, and the school leaders, the leader of the college tried to save the young offender from being arrested.

> I felt very ashamed. For 16 years, a criminal offense had never occurred on our campus. We should learn a lesson and engage in self-criticism. Second, we hope that the prosecutor and the police could grant care and understanding. To be honest, the parents of this youth came to my office twice. It was not easy for a family from the countryside to send him to college. We hope the youth can be given a restrained penal disposition. Lastly, the college will handle the follow-up properly.

On the victim's side, reintegration required them to accept a less punitive sanction for the offender based on the offender's apology and reparations to them. In Cases 1, 2, 3, 14, and 16, the apology made from the offender's side to the victim was accepted, meaning that the victims in these cases did not wish to prosecute the young offenders. Nevertheless, in Cases 2, 3, and 14, although the victims had expressed earlier that they did not desire a prosecution, the system still pursued the process, resulting in the victims being consulted again at the prosecution phase. The job left for the prosecutors and judges was to grant leniency for these young offenders under the shadow of the punitive system. Further stigmatization can be prevented if the offender can reach an agreement with their victims at a very early phase. The police imposed pressure on them to reconcile with the victims in some way so that a case would not be opened. Thus, strain on the criminal justice system as a whole was avoided.

When we examined the face-to-face encounters closely, we found that reintegration in a verbal form from the victim's side was very rare during these encounters. Moreover, the encounter did not counteract the labeling effect from the criminal justice process. According to the CPL 2012, the police do not have the power to dismiss the criminal case but can only refer it to the prosecutor's office for a further decision. The options for leniency are circumscribed, as the authority is only able to decide between proceeding with prosecution with the suggestion to the court of a lenient sentence and discontinuing the prosecution. Among the seven cases collected at the prosecution phase, two were dismissed on the grounds of the age of the young persons; the rest were prosecuted to court and eventually resulted in suspended sentences. One offender, who reconciled with his victims, told us after his case was concluded: *I feel there is a different eye watching me* (interview with the offender, Case 1 Multiple Thefts against Strangers). The label would follow the young offenders throughout their search for new schools or new employment. However, in this case, the offender felt that he had been forgiven by the victims because the agreement was signed.

The offenders' contact with the criminal justice system was stigmatizing for them, both adults and juveniles. Deeply embedded in the justice system, mediation was felt as a formality that was imposed. They wanted to get away with it and to "put an end to this matter."

> Nobody wants to commit mistakes. When he does, please do not continue repressing (打压) him. Because the law should be fair, and everyone is equal before the law, no matter whether he commits mistakes or not. After he does, please do not give him a psychological blow. The way you (the judge) speak, the tone, should be gentle and mild. Please do not say 'Now you have committed a wrong, we will sentence you; if you don't compensate the victim, you wait to be sentenced'. I felt sad. I committed a wrong, and I admitted it, but you should not rub the salt into one's wound (雪上加霜). This tone shouldn't be used towards criminals (interview with one offender, Case 8 Assault against Taxi Driver).

> If I did not explain the misunderstanding between us (to the victims), they would never know. I felt no need to explain, however. Even if I enabled others to trust me, there is no need to do it; why should I? To put it honestly, everyone's life is so different. I will never come across them again in the future, so there is no need. I don't want to mention it anymore (interview with one offender, Case 15 Two Female Students Theft).

Bangjiao, helping and educating the convicts, which has been regarded as a reintegration effort (Braithwaite 1999), seemed to focus on preventing more crimes and ensuring societal stability as opposed to anything else. The young offenders informed us about what they were asked to do, including reporting once a month to the local justice bureau. They did not receive any assistance with regard to looking for jobs or other related help. Case 4 can probably convey some meaning about *bangjiao*. The young offender in Case 4 was prosecuted in court. The prosecutor's office intended for the judge to announce a judgment as soon as possible so that the offender could be sent back to his hometown; the social aid station could not accommodate him very long due to his criminal status. The judge imposed a "control" measure instead, placing him under a *bangjiao* contract, and then released him after the specified days were completed. What does *bangjiao* mean? The judge said that it was to control him and prevent him from creating trouble while he was serving a suspended sentence. In other words, the judge had to ensure that his sentence was safe, i.e., that no trouble would arise. The court, as the last defense of social stability (Hu 2011), carries the political task and pressure of ensuring the correctness of its judgment. This "correctness" includes no appeals, no visits and letters, and no deviant behavior following the judgment. This brings us to the implications of mediation for the criminal justice system.

4.2 Benefits for the Justice System

The conventional procedure focuses on punishing offenders and excludes the participation of victims, which results in some negative consequences: The victims do not receive reparations, and the offenders are sent to prison. As one lawyer stated, the current penal stipulation on assault is too punitive, as in reality, perpetrators may act out of recklessness, with no malice; nevertheless, because of the legal rule, the offender must go to prison, paying a heavy price. Thus, the hope is that mediation will provide an opportunity to offenders who have learned a lesson. Meanwhile, the criminal procedure law does not fully restore the victims' losses, and it disregards their emotional losses (精神抚慰金). Thus, mediation provides better options to both sides, not least that the weaknesses of the conventional procedures are thus addressed.

However, the system restrains the judicial authority from conducting mediation properly. To control judicial discretion and possible judicial corruption, the prosecutor's dismissal decision must be approved by the prosecution committee (检察委员会); in reality, this adds more hurdles to a lenient judicial decision. The internal non-prosecution indicator not only impedes the interests of other departments but also the police organizations, because the evaluation of their job performance is based on the prosecution rate.

In spite of the internal tension and constraints, the promotion of reconciliation between offenders and victims is also meant to avoid greater damage to social stability. The imprisoned offenders and trouble-seeking victims can cause further harm to societal stability. Thus, the resolution of the dispute, which is secured with the victims' consent, reduces the likelihood that they will seek justice by visiting and sending letters (信访) to the higher authority.

4.3 Restoring Victims

Compared with the conventional procedure, criminal mediation gives a place to victims, in theory, allowing their voices to be heard. However, in practice, more emphasis is placed on the financial compensation. This finding is congruent with observations made by other scholars. If the offender is ordered or coerced to make reparations to the victim, are the victims then satisfied with the reparations, and why did they accept the agreements, given the relatively high success rate in terms of reaching agreements? A high success rate was also reported in Song (2009).

For the victims, crime causes harm to their property and their psychological wellbeing, and it affects the stability of society. *This matter is a problem for our society and has a psychological impact on us* (interview with the victim, Case 4 Stealing at the Grocery). *He is clear about what he has done. He should realize that his behavior was wrong. You say, your behavior has caused losses to others, to society, and to our families* (interview with the victim, Case 8 Assault against Taxi Driver).

The offenders, lawyers, mediators, and criminal justice actors in our sample believed that the victims had suffered losses, either materially or spiritually. The offenders also recognized that they should be responsible for their behaviors and sought reconciliation outside court, e.g., they apologized to the victims face-to-face or through a phone call, or they visited the victims. One offender said that he had done this based on his conscience and that he guessed that the victim had been hurt by his behavior, which had broken their relationship as classmates. We also found that the victims in Cases 5 and 7 did not report the event to the police when the offenders tried to reach reconciliation by offering an apology and reparations; they chose to bring it to court only when the reparations were not sufficient. Likewise, the victim's side in Case 6 wondered why the other side did not seek reconciliation with them after the offense occurred; according to them, this failure was unreasonable (*bu heli*).

The harm to the victim's side was usually not perceived as affecting only one person but, instead, the whole family. The victim in Case 8 expressed that because he had been assaulted; his family also felt anxious and fearful. The victim in Case 7 also spoke of his relatives' response in his case, which had persuaded him to settle it and move on. The victim in Case 18 did not tell her family members about her experience, because she was afraid they would be angry, which would have made resolving the conflict more complicated. The disputants in Case 20 confessed to each other during the mediation session that their families had been troubled and affected by the matter. They all wanted to put an end to it and, consequently, had organized mediation sessions three times. In fact, it was observed that during the mediation sessions at the local mediation room, the family members were very often present.

One lawyer, citing the involuntary manslaughter case, in which he had represented the victim's side, described how the victims perceived the harm: *The Chinese have family-oriented minds. They usually start from whether and how the death or the injury of the family member can have an impact on the whole family. If they conceive that the reparations they have received from the offender can offset their family's livelihood for the 10 or 20 years, they are more likely to accept it, thus achieving a psychological balance.*

It is true that the crime breaks downs the victims' psychological balance. Some felt angry about what they had experienced, some felt insecure and fearful, and some felt helpless after being left in the hospital, facing the financial burden of their medical treatment. The victims had varying degrees of victimization experiences depending on the losses and harm they had suffered, as well as their expectations about whether any reparations should made to them. For instance, we found that some of the victims in Case 1 did not expect their lost property to be found nor did they expect their perpetrator to be located and their losses recovered. Although this happened more often with offenses against property, offenses against the person, such as assault, were experienced more intensely. Notwithstanding the type of harm, their psychological imbalance did not appear to end with the intervention by the criminal justice system. Rather, the contact with the criminal justice system appeared to make the victims more anxious and worried, or to result in a "secondary victimization," to use a more general term. Some victims could not understand why they were approached by the criminal justice authority after they had chosen to pardon the offenders.

> He was locked in the police station for one night. The next day, he came back, made an apology to me and explained why he had committed the theft…This should be arranged earlier, because it has been a long time since it happened. I think he should not be prosecuted. After all, he is a first-time offender, and this decision is overly punitive (太过了) toward him (interview with the victim, Case 3 Dormitory Cell phone Stolen Case).

The criminal justice actors, i.e., the prosecutors and the judges, tried to achieve satisfaction for the victims in their judicial decisions. There was a concern for the victim, as one prosecutor opined: "If we don't provide an opportunity for reconciliation to the victims, their lives would become a mess, and their families would be destroyed."

If the victim's individual interests must be compromised during the process leading to an agreement, to what extent and in what terms do they feel restored? Based on our empirical research, we found five determining factors.

4.3.1 Countering the Weaknesses of the Normal Procedure

Various victims in Cases 1, 5, 6, 7, and 8 expressed their views of the weakness in the law: On the one hand, the law fails to provide sufficient protection for the victims' rights; on the other hand, the law is ineffective at guiding the offender and making him admit his mistake and repent, and giving him short-term custody will not change his behavior at all.

> I would rather say that this mediation is coercive. If I do not agree, the case just gets stuck here. What if I insist? The court will never decide as I want; plus, there is the problem of executing the judgment (if the normal procedure is taken). Currently, the law lacks measures to protect the victims' interests (interview with the victim, Case 5 Assault against Apartment Roommates).

As the victim in Case 6 Business Rivalry Assault case said: *Their (the offender's side) purpose was to shut down our business. Now, my son is in prison. What could I do if I didn't accept reconciliation with them?* This was confirmed by the interview with his lawyer: *The other case (in which the victim's son was the offender) was sentenced. The victim has changed his mind, since that case was closed. His economic status was not good, and he retired long ago, so he wanted to benefit more (than in the normal court procedure) in financial terms.*

4.3.2 Hate the Act But Give the Sinner a Second Chance

Seldom did any victim express that they wanted to see the offender sent to prison. Instead, the victims believed that prison is a dark place where even a good person could turn bad, and, hence, imprisonment should not be pursued. In juvenile offending cases, the victims generally held the opinion that because the wrongdoers were still young and were remorseful, they deserved a second chance.

The victim in Case 5 Assault against Apartment Roommates talked of sending the offender to prison in this way:

> I can say I want to see it happen, because I'm still very angry; I can also say I don't want to see it; that's because of my soft heart, and he will waste his youth there. Detention centers and prisons are the darkest places.

4.3.3 Time-Consuming and Moving Past the Matter

The quick pace of their lives also prompted the victims to attempt to move past the matter as rapidly as possible, and mediation provided a quicker solution than a lengthy court trial.

> I go on business very often and my hands are full. I cannot afford to spend lots of time and energy on this matter. Although it's not too much going to court to submit materials, my mind is focused on that, right? (interview with the victim, Case 7 Assault against Downstairs Neighbor).

4.3.4 Leaving the Psychological Disturbance Behind

> I'm not satisfied at the bottom of my heart, but a little is better than none. When I think this way, my psychological imbalance is remedied (interview with the victim, Case 1 Multiple Thefts against Strangers).

> Whatever, since things have happened, I should face reality. How should I put it, I will just take it. After all, they are still very young; nothing would change even if you took them out and beat them (interview with the victim, Case 1 Multiple Thefts against Strangers).

> This (being victimized) is not a good thing for us. In other words, it's OK if we can put an end to this matter. We ordinary people live a life; we don't wish to have so many disturbances and troubles. It's not good for our family, is it? (interview with the victim, Case 8 Assault against Taxi Drivers).

> Why? Harmonious society…We do not have a conflict involving class struggle. We do not want to get trampled here. Who would want to go to court every day? (interview with the victim, Case 6 Business Rivalry Assault Case).

4.3.5 Avoiding Anything Too Confrontational with Offenders

The victims tried to avoid anything that was too confrontational, which would have caused further harm to the relationship; they accepted the agreement despite having to compromise.

> He has an elderly mother. If he goes to prison and something bad happens to his family, he will not think this is his own fault, but instead he will blame us for that. We have that concern. Chinese people want to settle matters peacefully; they hope the matters will be resolved and the people can return to peace (息事宁人). Big things dissolve into small ones, and small things dissolve into none (大事化小, 小事化了). Judge Li also said that the other side would write a guarantee that they wouldn't hurt us anymore (interview with the victim, Case 7 Assault against Downstairs Neighbor).

Instead of insisting on imprisoning the offender, the victim did not want to see the matter become worse. When it is possible to let people off, they should be spared (得饶人处且饶人). The relatives of the victims tried to persuade them as well, as the same victim told us:

> Our relatives also persuaded us that we should make peace with others (结善缘). We prefer losses (吃亏) and render good for evil (以德报怨).

Some of the victims did not desire a face-to-face encounter with the offenders. They were concerned that the other party would take revenge because the interpersonal harmony had been broken following the crime.

> I don't want to have any contact with them. I do not want to see them. Now, our society is insecure, and some might seek revenge later. It's better to give me back my losses. There is no need to meet face-to-face (interview with the victim, Case 4 Stealing at the Grocery).

> If his parents are evil people, it's possible that they will take revenge. I now remain a bit conservative, and I will allow my son to avoid this matter (interview with the victim's mother, Case 14 School Classmate Theft).

In Case 14 High School Classmate Theft, the victim's mother, as a way of protecting her son, transferred him away from his original school following the discovery of the perpetrator. She feared not only that the perpetrator's side would take revenge on the victim for reporting the event to the police but also that the school authority would be unfavorable in decisions related to the victim.

References

Hu, J. (2011). Grand mediation in China. *Asian Survey, 51*(6), 1065–1089.

Song, Y. (2009). Empirical analysis of the status quo of criminal mediation in China *[woguo xingshi hejie xianzhuang shizheng fenxi]*. Paper presented at the Criminal Mediation and Improvement of the Criminal Procedural Law, Beijing.

Song, Y., & Yuan, J. (Eds.). (2009). *Theory and practice of criminal reconciliation in China*. Peking: Peking University Press.

Chapter 7
What Is the Harmony Approach?

1 Introduction

Chinese people, like their Western counterparts, are unfamiliar with terms such as "restorative justice" or "repairing the harm." Nevertheless, they are probably one of the most largely populated nations in the world that has embraced both the ideas and practices of mediation. Resolving conflict through mediation is currently a practice across the criminal justice spectrum. Although it might be overshadowed by this study's singular focus on mediation practices in the field, the fact is that various mediation practices are taking place throughout the punishment-based justice system. The story is fundamentally about repairing harm in the Chinese societal and legal landscape. This chapter explains why it is "about repairing the harm" and why I view it in this way.

1.1 Harm Reduction

Being caught in the legal system or captured by the police is considered a harm caused to an individual and his interpersonal relationships. To an individual (including his family or close networks), being caught by the police is deemed shameful because it reveals that the person has committed a wrong. While a Westerner may harbor the idea that there should be "no crime without a judgment from the court," Chinese people may wonder how a person could be caught by the police if he had not engaged in wrongdoing. An upright person would keep away from justice organs such as the police, the prosecutor's office, and the court. Our findings provide evidence that ordinary people feel ashamed about involvement with these institutions.

X. Yuan, *Restorative Justice in China*, Springer Series on Asian Criminology and Criminal Justice Research, DOI 10.1007/978-3-319-63922-2_7

A dispute or a crime, depending on the level of seriousness of the behavior, damages interpersonal relationships. In Chinese history, "making peace" was always preferred over "going to court"; punishment was only used when mediation attempts had failed at the community level. Going to court risks escalating the confrontation between the two sides. Invariably, the findings show that reconciliation/mediation is sought immediately after the dispute/crime has happened. It is only when reconciliation/mediation has failed that the cases are brought further toward the "deep end" of the criminal justice system. Albeit not always very satisfied with what they receive from the mediation, the disputants eventually compromise because confrontation will only result in more harm if one side persists in seeking it.

At the "deeper end" of the criminal justice system, i.e., the prosecutor's office and the court, the state authority continues to assume the role of a mediator. The findings show that the prosecutor believed that for some of the poorer victims, not offering a reconciliation option would only have caused further harm to them and their families; in addition, as long as the offenders have repented and the motivations behind the crime were not egregious, they should be spared, and their families should be given a second chance. Based on the aforementioned accounts by the father whose son had been imprisoned, sending a person to prison would certainly cause a destructive blow to the entire family. In many cases, the victims sacrifice their own interests, because they do not want the offender to be imprisoned, which would cause further hatred and deepen the conflict.

Harm reduction also implies minimizing the intervention from the criminal justice system. In local community-based policing, after both sides agree to mediation or their work units take responsibility for resolving a conflict, the police normally will not open a case. Some "threatening" words and tones were used, but we never saw any side stand up against such "coercion." For them, it is perhaps not even perceived as being "coerced." Compromise from the victim often occurs; the victims refused to agree to a compromise in only a few cases. People appeared to have little faith in the legal system's ability to provide a quick solution to their disputes, nor did they believe they should proceed to the court of appeals to continue arguing over their interests.

Thus, the idea of "harm reduction" is shared by all parties involved in dealing with the crime, including the judicial authorities.

1.2 Repairing Social Relationships

Justice does not mean one side wins and the other side fails. Justice must be balanced and should take both sides into account. In the case studies, we did not encounter one case in which the victim insisted on sending the offenders to prison. Their judgments seemed to be based on whether the other side had repented and taken (sufficient) responsibility. However, this does not mean that their emotions were suddenly or fully recovered. For example, on a few occasions, both sides shook hands when they were leaving; when the victim was interviewed, he said he was still angry but that he believed that the young person had apologized and taken responsibility. Based on this, many other victims would concur that a second chance should be given to young persons. In other cases, although an idealized scene such as "shaking hands" did not occur, the judge assured the victims, in the presence of the offender, that the offender would never commit such an act again.

China is a "relationship-based" society, according to Liang (1949, as cited in Stacey 1983; Yang 1994). The relationships are variously based on hometowns, workplaces, a person commonly known, schools, etc. In the accounts from the field, we invariably captured a sense of connectedness, e.g., the victims asked the offenders where they were from – because they were from the same city, they would meet regularly and often (抬头不见低头见); the victim who had been sexually assaulted said she came from the same hometown as her perpetrator; hence, she chose not to prosecute the latter as long as he was expelled from the college and had no opportunity to cause her further harm. The victim said she worked in the same place as the perpetrator's mother, and, thus, she should not pursue her own request, which risked the perpetrator being left with a criminal record. Victims who went to the same schools as their perpetrators never wanted to escalate the conflict by bringing the latter into the justice system. In all these accounts, the victim chose to make peace; the parties did not necessarily leave as friends, but at least there were no further risks to their ability to remain in the shared connected groups.

The social relationships not only existed between the victim and the offender but also expanded into the relationships with the justice staff (or the state authority). In the local mediation room, the disputing sides sometimes gave ground in order to grant "face" to the mediator in an effort to maintain their harmonious relationship with the mediator. The police also had connections with the workplaces, the schools, the residences, etc. within their policing area; consideration was also given to these sorts of relationships when the police made penal decisions. Relationships also existed among the state authorities; they frequently communicated with each other, regardless of their ranks in the various horizontal and hierarchical levels. State authorities also have collaborative relationships with the defense counsels, the victim's lawyers, and even the disputing sides. As stated above, my contact with the lawyers was facilitated by the state authority.

The social webs into which people are woven clearly point toward one aim: harmony in their social relationships. Below, we interpret the harmony approach, that is, doing justice to achieve harmony is not based on individual rights or personal needs but on relationship-oriented harmony.

2 A Harmony Approach

To elaborate on the harmony approach, the discussion will proceed in several steps.

2.1 Not About Rights

We did not encounter a person who claimed that his rights had been violated; instead, people expressed and implied that they wanted the other side to learn a lesson from the event and not commit such actions again. Very often, people doubted that the legal system could fully protect their interests. The victims complained that their interests were not recognized by the law; moreover, if the court sentenced a person to prison, this would only lead to a failure to guide and educate him. Based on our observations, the victims sought to bring the issue to court only when they failed to achieve an apologetic attitude from the perpetrator. Additionally, it is widely agreed that the court procedure takes a tremendous amount of time and energy and operates based on strict evidentiary requirements, which is definitely not beneficial to the victims. Hence, when negotiations occurred between the victim and the perpetrator (or the disputing parties), the legal stipulation regarding the status of each side became an Achilles' heel – it failed to supply strong and balanced protection.

Instead of safeguarding human rights, Chinese law provides legal benefits for those who repent through by making a confession (*tanbai*, 坦白) or "turning oneself into" the authority (*zishou*, 自首). The cultural underpinning is that a wrongdoer can become good through self-renewal, with the help of his family and local community. This certainly differs from the Western approach, which situates the state as the offender's opponent. Rather, it strongly advocates for the protection of the offender against any possible abuse of the state power. Griffiths (1970) consistently compared the typical American battle model with the family model he constructed based on the Japanese experience; in the former, there is "the inevitability of a state of irreconcilable hostility between the individual and the state" (p. 413), but in the latter, the state places the offender's interests at the heart, and there is useful communication between them. Foote (1992) further developed this idea, proposing the "benevolent paternalism model," which places great emphasis on the reintegration and rehabilitation of suspects in accordance with their individualized circumstances. Indeed, this model may intrude on personal autonomy, but it greatly encourages moral responsibility and reparations to the victims and to society.

Now, our attention will shift to Chinese mediation practices. Across various stages of the criminal process, we saw that the offender was encouraged to confess and take responsibility. In cases involving juvenile offenses, the victims concurred with the authority that young persons should be given a second chance if they repent. In the court, we once observed a young person come to see the judge, who asked him whether he admitted his guilt. When the offender hesitated, stating he would consult his lawyer, the judge appeared dissatisfied and let the young person leave. In juvenile court, the case files always included repentance letters from the young suspects describing how they had reflected on their behavior; the judge received letters from those who were far away about how they had corrected their behavior and had engaged in self-renewal. A juvenile judge, if she is female, is usually called "mother judge" (*faguan mama*) in Chinese.

Such a relationship exists not only between the state and young persons but also adult offenders. For example, the state authority has clear knowledge of the family background and the individual circumstances of the suspects. In one court trial, shortly after it recessed for mediation, the prosecutor asked the offender in a surprised but persuasive tone: "You haven't made reparations to the victim yet? If you had done it earlier, the case would have already concluded." On another occasion, while making the agreement, the judge, in a casual tone, asked the offender: "You are going to marry? Is that true?" The police also sometimes patted a perpetrator's shoulder, telling him not to maintain his psychological burden and to not be afraid to take responsibility.

Thus, it is not an exaggeration to say that the Chinese mediation practices under study are not based on the abstract concept of individual freedom or rights. Are they instead based on personal needs?

2.2 Not Just About Needs

We cannot conclude that personal needs are completely ignored in practice; rather, the extent to which these needs are met should be considered. In cases in which the victims are engaged in the discussion, their opinions are consulted and heard, but in some circumstances, they must compromise. The victims inform the authority about their needs, but they are not satisfied if the authority or the other side considers their needs to be unreasonable. We found that the unmet needs that caused the mediation to fail usually included "making a public apology" or "covering the losses raised." The authority may fail to address these needs because they are beyond the scope of his mediation capacity or the perpetrator does not perceive them as reasonable (*heli*).

More importantly, justice is relational (Burnside and Baker 2003; Llewellyn and Howse 1999; Llewellyn 2008). The victim, who occupies the moral high ground, should not merely pursue his own emotions or needs; he should also take the other side's "face" into account if the resolution engages both sides. Hu (1944) has been attributed with discovering the importance of *lian* (脸) and *mian zi* (面子) for the Chinese. *Lian* is a social sanction for enforcing both moral standards and internalized sanctions. People who have failed to live up to moral standards by committing a crime suffer a loss of *lian*, which is felt by him toward his family and the people who have trust in him. *Mian zi* extends the concern to others; thus, the person who has been harmed should avoid deprecating the perpetrator if the latter is expected to renew himself (Zhai 2011). Even victims who appeared angry or revengeful during the mediation restrained themselves from directly labeling the perpetrator as "a villain," a term they only used when speaking to the researcher. The term "villain" was only used in situations in which the victims did not see any remorse in their perpetrators. In other words, society expects an unhardened offender to repent, and as a member of the collective, the victim is supposed to give "face" (留有余地) to a repentant delinquent, to defer his own needs and interests in favor of the needs of the collective. Moreover, when the emotions were very intense, we usually observed that no agreement was reached. Pye (1996) commented that, for the Chinese, acting properly is not to follow one's feelings but to conform to standards.

2.3 *Compromise and Harmony*

Instead of insisting on one's own rights and interests, compromise was a typical characteristic of the resolutions of all these conflicts. In the process of conflict resolution, the Chinese are more likely to be non-confronting, avoiding, obliging, and integrating and to adopt an authoritarian approach (Chen 2002).

Strong expressions of personal feelings are discouraged. An emotional victim was always accompanied by his/her family, relatives, or colleagues, who kindly appeased him/her when his/her emotions were too strong. Indeed, when emotions do surface, they tend to be destructive and not constructive and only indicate dissatisfaction or deep animosity toward the other side, therefore hindering closure in their social relationships. In our case studies, when intense emotion was involved, no harmony or agreement emerged.

The reliance on intermediaries in conflict situations reduces the need for direct and emotional involvement (Hsü 1970). Direct confrontation with the perpetrator is a source of anxiety and anger; very often, the fight and disagreement continued when the disputants were briefly brought together. From the local mediation room to the court, the persuasion to compromise stemmed not only from the authority but also from the disputants' own family members and relatives. Even though they may not be completely happy with the agreement, the trouble was finally removed. Closing the matter gives the disputants peace of mind. Citing one victim, despite disagreeing with the way his case was handled, he said "we ordinary people make a living, and don't like to have troubles as such." He believed that being a victim was not a glorious thing, and he and his family all wanted to put it behind them.

To an equal extent, for the perpetrators who were involved with the criminal justice system, internal and external sanctions were induced, such as feeling ashamed, being subject to negative social judgments, expulsion from school or work, etc. A direct encounter with the victim was another source of shame; thus, if justice is meant to be balanced, should it not involve some compromise by the victim?

3 An Authoritarian Approach

A related issue, which is one of the salient themes in this study, is the authoritarian approach adopted. In the historical sense, mediation is normally performed by individuals who enjoy prestige, have moral power, etc. Until recently, mediation has been institutionalized in people's mediation committees in Communist China; the legislation has further formalized the practice and has made it an integral part of the legal procedures, e.g., mediation is a required procedure in court divorce cases. With the deepening modernization China is currently undertaking, more conflicts of both a civil and criminal nature are inevitably ending up in court, causing further strain on the system.

China's mediation model has been described as coercive or arbitrative (Yeo 1993, as cited in Johnstone and Van Ness 2007). In our study, the mediators were indeed active and directive in giving advice; however, it may also be true that people rely heavily on the opinions of the authority. My own experience as a potential mediator was a failure: I wanted to remain neutral and allow the parties to communicate, but instead, they relied on me to give verbal directions.

The victims very often refrained from speaking up but relied on the authoritative mediator to educate the perpetrator and to require him to take responsibility for his actions. Did the disputants feel coerced by the authority? The findings show that although the victims cooperated with the authority, they did not necessarily feel pressured by the latter, e.g., by being asked to come over. Instead, the authority felt a bit worried if the victims were not cooperative. In this study, the cases that reached the court level did so because the victim did not agree on the matter of compensation. Pressure was felt, but not to the extent of "coercion"; however, in some circumstances, the authority used a threatening tone. This is probably a bold claim, but not if we consider that people in different cultures may experience voluntariness differently.[1] A "left-over" woman can still get married voluntarily based on social pressure, although this voluntariness may be rejected by people in a freer Western society.

I will use two reversed examples to illustrate this.

In a situation in which we observed substantial pressure, which was admitted by both the victim's side and the offender's side, we found that the victims were not opposed to pressure but wished that they had been given more time to think. While the pressure from the authority was for them to reach an agreement, the victims said they did not disagree about forgiving the offenders, but it would take time.

In another interview, the victim explicitly expressed that the mediation agreement was coerced. We found that this was because he believed there was no use/necessity to bring the dispute to an upper court. In his opinion, the road to legal justice was blocked. He also witnessed how busy the judge was and did not want to make things difficult for him.

The role of the mediator is widely recognized and trusted. The following are among the comments we heard: the authority is experienced in handling disputes, in being persuasive, in being patient, or in balancing two sides, etc. The "experience" mentioned by the disputing sides is not just legal knowledge but refers more to insights into life and the dispute, which is accumulated based on their personal life experiences and their understanding of people's real lives. By contrast, a young judge who offered mediation on a totally voluntary basis was criticized by the victim as "too young to understand the implications (利害关系) of this case." Not only "experience" but also

[1] For instance, a study comparing the freedom of contract in China and Europe found that for China, the voluntariness of contracts, although recognized, was subjected to the public interest and the collective interest (Fu 2013).

"patience" is important for the disputing sides. Patience requires full negotiations between the authority and the disputants. When the authority is perceived as patient, the disputants tend to appreciate this, but when the judge does not have enough time, the disputants feel neglected.

The authoritarian approach may downplay the need for expression by the disputing sides, which indeed caused some bitterness. However, we only saw two cases in which the disputing sides shifted the blame to the mediator, who was too assertive in his own proposal. Apart from that, even when the authoritarian style contradicted what was expected by the disputants, they recognized the authority's conduct as legitimate. Thus, the victims stated: "The judge has so many cases to handle, and I don't want to make this case difficult for him," or "I know, the prosecutor does not let me meet the young person, because she is afraid of any conflicts arising from the meeting. As a matter of fact, she should let us meet." Even in the case involving involuntary manslaughter, all the victim's relatives joined in the persuasion, telling the victim not to be too emotional or to make things difficult for the judge at the scene.

Patriarchy, a term that defines the nature of authority in China (Hamilton 1990), has lived through the exclusionary history of socialist China (Stacey 1983) and remains a factor that shapes China today (Hamilton 1990; Fukuyama 2011). Hamilton (1990, p. 96) found that:

> [i]n Chinese thinking, power (that is, the act of command) is an aspect of a role, and a person in such a role has the obligation to command others in conformity with his role. Hence, in theory, power is impersonal, non-intentional, and directed toward maintaining the harmony of the whole. In developmental terms, this line of reasoning led to the specification of roles and of role-defined actions and emotions, a trend that in turn reduced the legitimate discretionary spheres of individual action.

Along the same line of thinking, Pye and Pye (1985, pp. 27–28) asserted that "in most Asian cultures leaders are expected to be nurturing, benevolent, kind, sympathetic figures who inspire commitment and dedication." Rule by man is not stigmatized as it is in the West, as long as the ruler is benevolent and cares about the citizens' interests.

By contrast, authority is conceived as closely related to power in the Western political sphere. Power must be contained. While the government is simply an institutionalized apparatus of concentrated power, the rule of law needs to be in place in order to protect the individual from government oppression (Tamanaha 2004). Bills of human rights, which are widespread throughout democratic societies, stand against the abuse of power by the authority. Rather than deference to authority, Western democracies assert individual decision-making and equal participation.

4 Harmony: Reconciliation in a Broad Sense

Nader's (1990) "harmony ideology" described how the Zapotec mountain villagers tried to preserve local autonomy using local legal practices, keeping a system of courts that was based on a law foreign to the social conditions of rural Mexico at bay. As an important international player, China has been advancing in the construction of a legal system for almost four decades. However, Chen (2011), a professor in criminal procedure law, found that some legal procedures had actually been bypassed; one reason for this is that they were not in accordance with the social conditions. The current study also partly reveals how the legal structure is not attuned to people's conceptions and their lives. In the following discussion, I will expose some of these incongruences.

First, among the social conceptions of justice and legal justice, there are conflicts between the traditional conceptions of right and wrong and the legal definitions of crime. As voiced by a disputant, "why does a physical assault violate the law, but verbal abuse does not?" Perhaps the harm caused by the verbal abuse was greater than being beaten; the verbal abuse was from a young woman toward an elder. Similarly, why does the law differentiate between the perpetrator and the victim based only on who first reported the incident to the police or who suffered more physical harm if the fight involved both sides? This implies that when the law defines the incident in "black and white" terms, the complexity of the dispute itself dwarfs the legal definition and approach.

The victims stated that they wanted an apology, but an apology may not always come; they wanted the offenders to truly learn a lesson, but the court and the law fail to guide them and send them to prison. Both the victims and the offenders questioned why a state punishment was imposed on the offenders, because they have already suffered a loss, e.g., through a sense of shame or being expelled from their schools. Once the two sides have reconciled, why should there be any further decisions by the government (公家)?

These questions reflect the worries and confusion echoed by Qiuju, who wondered why the offender was taken away by the police when she only wanted an apology from the wrongdoer.[2] The current study, which is based on a local level in a moderately prosperous city in the Eastern part of China, is very different from the village setting in the movie. In spite of economic progress and deepening modernization, traditional conceptions of justice persist.

Essentially, Chinese society is not grounded in individual rights or freedom but is highly interdependent and obligation based, which, to the greatest extent, amplifies human feelings (人情). The *shouren* society is embedded in all types of social relationships; people get along by means of mutual favors and obligations that reinforce social and interpersonal harmony. The resolution of a dispute is endowed with the expectation that interpersonal harmony will be restored, especially when a relationship existed prior to the dispute. Many of the disputes in this study occurred among classmates, roommates, colleagues, neighbors, etc., and indeed, such people have a high likelihood of meeting again regularly. A harmonious approach to resolving the matter sustains this interdependency, while considering only one's own interests allows disharmony in the community to continue.

---

[2] As mentioned at the beginning of this book, this movie was released in 1992. For a legal review of this movie, please refer to Su (1996), The Puzzle of Qiuju, and the Tragedy of Shang Gang Ye (秋菊的困惑和山杠爷的悲剧), in his book *Rule of Law and Local Resources* (法治及其本土资源), Beijing: Press of China University of Political Science and Law.

In this study, the police, although they wielded power, tried to leave a certain amount of autonomy to the disputants. If the offender successfully reached an agreement with the victim, no penal decision was taken. Many criminal conflicts are diverted away from the justice system at the police level (Liu et al. 2012; Chen 2011), thus avoiding a "degradation ceremony" (Garfinkel 1956).

However, there is, again, a conflict between the formalized system, which incorporates every legal dispute into its purview and the reintegration efforts aimed at avoiding further stigmatization of the offenders.

As found in the field study, once the conflict is categorized as criminal, then the police have no authority to dismiss it but must bring it to the prosecutor's office. The victims' opinions are consulted; even if they do not want prosecution, their will is not decisive. The prosecutor's dismissal decision is then subject to review by the prosecution committee (*jiancha weiyuanhui*), not to that of the prosecutor who is in charge. At the prosecutor stage, only two observed cases were dismissed based on the age of the offender. The rest of the cases were prosecuted in court and resulted in suspended sentences. The prosecution authority believed they were trying to provide leniency to repentant offenders by giving them an opportunity to reconcile with their victims.

Thus, it can be said that not only the disputants but also the state authorities are engaged in a type of collaboration. It is not just a "victim-offender collaboration model" (私力合作模式) (Chen 2006); rather, the state authority is a central actor in guiding both sides toward reaching reconciliation. The reconciliation achieved through confession and forgiveness avoids intervention by the penal state (Garland 2013), ensuring the autonomy of social institutions, such as schools, families, work units, etc.

Minjian (民间), the private sphere in China, is perhaps devoid of a national civil society (Pye 1996). In China, no legal, public, or institutionalized structures or associations exist that are not part of or subordinate to the state (Yang 1994). This is a reminder of the destiny of the reconciliation center, mentioned above in this study, which was an epitome of the status of third-party organizations in China. Its establishment required approval from the Bureau of Civil Affairs, which is a lengthy procedure; also, it lacked funding and staff. For unknown reasons, the local campus management committee refused to have such an organization installed under its purview. Nevertheless, the project, which catered to the state's harmony discourse, was able to elicit other state organizations to work together to accomplish the enterprise. While everyone knew that the reconciliation center was simply a plaque hanging on the wall, people tried to cooperate with and help each other, so to speak. For instance, one mediator, although very dissatisfied with the "empty box," told me to praise it when the media, another institution controlled by the state, came to do an interview. People who are embedded in all sorts of social networks work based on mutual obligations and indebtedness. While the legal system is not presently enforced in a way that protects individual rights, no one can doubt that reparative efforts to redress harm are made throughout the criminal process. Social relationships, which also made the current study possible, constitute the civil sphere under the banner of the formal legal system that brings people together to reduce harm and restore broken social relationships. Social harmony is restored, a goal pursued by the Chinese people for centuries.

5 A "Harsh" Harmony

Nevertheless, if the goal is for the broken relationship to be restored, is this goal always achieved? Why is the communication so difficult despite the genuine need to sit down and talk? I describe this as a harsh harmony, because the process and the outcomes appear to be harsh.

First, there is the power setting in which the mediation is situated. Tremendous pressure is placed upon each of the participants to resolve the conflict in a "harmonious" way. The victims can present their arguments or opinions but are limited to discussing the financial terms. The offenders rely on the "agreement" to determine their destiny. Formalizing the mediation and endowing it with the coercion of the state leaves real needs and opinions unaddressed. One may question whether the practice is more about achieving a settlement than engaging in actual mediation. The authority must bring the conflict under control and move it toward the outcome of social stability, as opposed to being genuinely concerned about the individuals' well-being. The impetus of maintaining societal stability has tightened the grip of the justice system, placing stability as a priority over other concerns. It does not exclude the possibility for political will to infringe upon the citizens' reasonable and legitimate request for justice. A virtuous harmony may thus be yet to come.

This study suggests that the absence of an effective forum for communication is crucial in explaining this rigid harmony. In this study, mediation must put an end to the dispute, but the real causes of the dispute, the details of the dispute, and what the disputants actually want or need are not considered before the matter is closed. Without doubt, such an approach would require much more time and effort from a third party. If a genuine apology is a requirement for reconciliation, how can such an apologetic attitude can be conveyed by the perpetrator to the victim in a settlement that is superficial and rushed? Because it is likely that the disputants will reach reconciliation to restore the balance of the collective, individual satisfaction may not always occur or be an important factor in the dispute resolution.

Closing a matter means that society as a whole has been ridded of a dispute, but no one can be certain that the "settled" dispute will not reemerge to strike the system again.

6 Conclusion

In this chapter, I have explained what the harmony approach involves. There are at least two layers of social harmony: the top-down approach of maintaining social stability and the pursuit of interpersonal harmony at the expense of individual sacrifice in daily life. This study reveals that mediation is more about restoring harmony to society than healing interpersonal relationships. Social order is thus achieved on the basis of everyone's obligation to community harmony, rather than by addressing the needs and rights of those directly harmed. The risk, however, lies in an overemphasis on social stability, which can lead to an increasing tension between the societal needs represented by the authority and individual demands for justice.

References

Burnside, J., & Baker, N. (2003). *Relational justice: Repairing the breach*. Winchester: Waterside Press.

Chen, G. M. (2002). The impact of harmony on Chinese conflict management. In G. Chen & R. Ma (Eds.), *Chinese conflict management and resolution* (pp. 3–17). Westport, CT/London: Ablex Publishing.

Chen, R. (2006). The victim-offender collaboration model in criminal proceedings: The emergence of criminal mediation in China [*xingshi susong de sili hezuo moshi: xingshi hejie zai zhongguo de xingqi*]. *Chinese Legal Science, 2006*(5), 15–30.

Chen, R. (2011). Initial research on the malfunctions of the criminal process. *Pacific Rim Law & Policy Journal, 20*, 359.

Foote, D. H. (1992). The benevolent paternalism of Japanese criminal justice. *California Law Review, 80*(2), 317–390. doi:10.2307/3480769.

Fu, J. (2013). Freedom of contract in the EU and China. *Journal of International Commercial Law and Technology, 8*, 274.

Fukuyama, F. (2011). *The origins of political order: From prehuman times to the French Revolution*. London: Profile Books.

Garfinkel, H. (1956). Conditions of successful degradation ceremonies. *American Journal of Sociology, 61*(5), 420–424. doi:10.2307/2773484.

Garland, D. (2013). Penality and the penal state. *Criminology, 51*(3), 475–517.

Griffiths, J. (1970). Ideology in criminal procedure or a third "model" of the criminal process. *The Yale Law Journal, 79*(3), 359–417. doi:10.2307/795141.

Hamilton, G. G. (1990). Patriarchy, patrimonialism, and filial piety: A comparison of China and Western Europe. *The British Journal of Sociology, 41*(1), 77–104. doi:10.2307/591019.

Hsü, F. L. (1970). *Americans and Chinese: Purpose and fulfillment in great civilizations*. Garden City, NY: American Museum of Natural History.

Hu, H. C. (1944). The Chinese concepts of "face". *American Anthropologist, 46*(1), 45–64.

Johnstone, G., & Van Ness, D. (Eds.). (2007). *Handbook of restorative justice*. Cullompton: Willan Publishing.

Liu, J., Zhao, R., Xiong, H., & Gong, J. (2012). Chinese legal traditions: Punitiveness versus mercy. *Asia Pacific Journal of Police and Criminal Justice, 9*(1), 17–33.

Llewellyn, J. (2008). Bridging the gap between truth and reconciliation: Restorative justice and the Indian Residential School Truth and Reconciliation Commission. In M. B. Castellano, L. Archibald, & M. DeGagne (Eds.), *From truth to reconciliation: Transforming the legacy of residential schools* (p. 183). Ottawa: Aboriginal Healing Foundation.

Llewellyn, J., & Howse, R. L. (1999). Restorative justice: A conceptual framework. Prepared for the Law Commission of Canada.

Nader, L. (1990). *Harmony ideology: Justice and control in a Zapotec mountain village*. Stanford, CA, Stanford University Press.

Pye, L. W. (1996). The state and the individual: An overview interpretation. In B. Hook (Ed.), *The individual and the state in China* (pp. 16–42). Oxford: Clarendon Press.

Pye, M. W., & Pye, L. W. (1985). *Asian power and politics: The cultural dimensions of authority*. Cambridge, MA: Harvard University Press.

Stacey, J. (1983). *Patriarchy and socialist revolution in China*. Berkeley, CA/Los Angeles, CA/ London: University of California Press.

Tamanaha, B. Z. (2004). *On the rule of law: History, politics, theory*. New York: Cambridge University Press.

Yang, M. M.-h. (1994). Gifts, favors, and banquets: The art of social relationships in China. Ithaca, NY: Cornell University Press.

Zhai, X. (2011). *Perspectives on Chinese "face": Psychological motives and social representations [zhongguoren de lianmian guan: xingshi zhuyi de xinli dongyin yu shehui biaozheng]*. Beijing: Peking University Press.

Part IV
Doing "Restorative" Justice: China and the West

Chapter 8
Restorative Justice

1 Introduction: Restorative Justice – A Movement Within the Criminal Justice System

Today, although the extent to which restorative justice has moved from the margins to the mainstream in state crime policies is subject to debate, it remains undisputed that restorative justice has prospered as a new paradigm, in contrast to the traditional punitive one. Restorative justice, which is aimed at transforming penal justice or even completely replacing it, is now widely used to address less serious offenses and forms of deviance. In countries such as New Zealand and Northern Ireland, restorative justice has acquired a central place in handling juvenile offending (Zinsstag and Vanfraechem 2012). Moreover, the impact of restorative justice is also evident in numerous legislative amendments, governmental reports, judicial policies, etc. (Gavrielides 2007; Dünkel et al. 2015; Miers and Aertsen 2012).

Restorative justice is also widely practiced in other domestic settings, such as schools, communities, and workplaces.[1] From the international perspective, its application has moved beyond traditional offenses within a specific society in accordance with its own jurisdiction to reach mass atrocities, which have usually been dealt with based on international legal frameworks (Bueno 2013; Aertsen et al. 2008). Nevertheless, to stay within the scope of this study, we will examine restorative justice in domestic judicial contexts.

[1] Some scholars, e.g., Green et al. (2013), have restricted the application of restorative justice to criminal matters, whereas similar practices in schools, neighborhoods, and other settings are called restorative approaches or practices.

X. Yuan, *Restorative Justice in China*, Springer Series on Asian Criminology and Criminal Justice Research, DOI 10.1007/978-3-319-63922-2_8

2 Two Origins of the Western Restorative Justice Movement

Restorative justice is a convenient umbrella term for a variety of related theories and practices concerned with the restoration of the offender, the victim, and the community. According to John Braithwaite (2002a), the term "restorative justice" incorporates various traditions of justice, such as "making amends," reconciliation, redress, relational justice, transformative justice, community justice, etc. There are many strands of ideas that may intersect with RJ to varying degrees. However, the restorative justice advocacy literature has identified two main lines regarding its origins. The first line starts by addressing a series of social movements that swept the Western world in the second half of the last century that should be understood within the societal context following World War II. The second root can be identified in historical accounts of justice models, specifically the model of informal justice, which the literature has claimed can be found in the customary practices of indigenous communities.

The social movements during the 1960s and 1970s across Western societies provide the flavor of the societal background to the understanding of the growth of restorative justice, i.e., the feminist campaigns against male violence, the civil rights demands, and the victim movement (Cunneen and Hoyle 2010). The most salient among these is the demand for reforms of the criminal justice system by groups representing support for both prisoners and victims. The rising crime rates prompted people to reflect on rehabilitative models and to search for "what works" because "nothing seemed to work" (Martinson 1978). Moreover, for victims, the era of disenchantment had lasted too long. Proposals for restitution to victims can be traced back to scholarly work at the start of the twentieth century, e.g., by Enrico Ferri (1968), but they did not lead to a social movement until the 1950s, when intensive claims for victims' rights were part of publications by criminologists and legal experts. Their call finally led to the birth of victim support schemes in the UK, the USA, and Canada, which were later studied and borrowed by other Western countries, including continental Europe, Australia, and New Zealand. Remarkably, this victimological surge inspired the early authors of articles regarding restorative justice, such as Eglash (1977), who is widely recognized as having coined the term "restorative justice" (Maruna 2014); Barnett (1977), who argued for a new paradigm, restitution; and Christie, whose article "Conflicts as Property" (1977) carries tremendous weight in the restorative justice field. However, restorative justice was not fully embraced by victims' advocates, as concerns existed among them regarding the possible re-victimization of the victims, the exacerbation of power imbalances and restorative justice being an excessively soft option for victims (Curtis-Fawley and Daly 2005).

Restorative justice advocates have also tried to ensure the legitimacy of their claims by asserting the dichotomy of state justice and non-state (community) justice. The yearning for community involvement is commonly held by the Western world with regard to handling crime (Cunneen and Hoyle 2010). Restorative justice advocates have claimed that restitution to the victim and the community has long existed in the legal history of European and other civilizations. From the sixth to the tenth century, the basic law of the peoples of Europe, as in many non-Western cultures, was founded on the customs and common consciousness of the community, and vengeance, upon the violation of those bonds, usually gave way to negotiations for pecuniary sanctions and restitution (Berman 1983). Restitution was probably the most common form of resolving a conflict in non-state societies (Weitekamp 2000).

This tradition in Europe lasted until approximately the twelfth century, when central authorities assumed control over the criminal law and formalized a body of legal rules. A crime was no longer considered a violation of human bonds but rather an offense against the state; hence, criminal conflict resolution fell within the monopoly of the state. As a result, punishing the offender became the paramount task facing the justice apparatuses and professionals. In the meantime, the rights of the victim were gradually overshadowed and supplanted. The core of the justice process is that the offender should suffer pain that is equal to the harm his/her acts have caused. Although the concept of retribution was later slightly adjusted to a rehabilitative model at the turn of the twentieth century, on the whole, it was offender oriented and punitive by nature. The way that restorative justice differentiates itself from both retributive justice and rehabilitative justice lies in its claim that it aims at restoration, not punishment or unilateral rehabilitation.

Many restorative justice theorists position restorative justice as opposed to retributive justice, which the latter view as harsh and punitive. Whether in medieval times or in the far distant history of human existence, retributive punishment has always existed, e.g., in the form of individual revenge within the community. Even in today's indigenous communities, to which restorative justice theorists frequently refer in their literature, cruel punishments, such as exile, still exist. John Braithwaite (2002a) also noted that in premodern societies, restorative traditions existed side by side with retributive traditions, which, in many ways, were much more punitive than modern retributivism. It is understandable that restorative justice needs to position itself as something different, but placing itself against retribution, without clearly defining the concept of retribution, can be problematic. Some authors, such as Daly (2000), have stated that it invites confusion to call the old system "retributive" and the new justice system "restorative"; she argued that restorative justice must also have elements of retribution in it.

While some restorative justice theorists may wishfully assert that the state is evil and does no good for the restorative justice movement, the fact remains that the initial impetus of what was later termed as restorative justice eventually received support from the state. The first victim-offender mediation program in the world was operated and guided by probation officers. The Canadian First Nations' notions of healing circles, the Navajo justice and healing ceremony, the Maori in New Zealand and the South African indigenous restorative notion of Ubuntu did not exclude the involvement or support of the state. Moreover, currently, in most jurisdictions, restorative justice is developing under the auspices of traditional criminal justice (Dünkel et al. 2015). Although many argue for its potential to replace retribution, its further development requires support from the conventional justice system (Walgrave 2002).

As a movement that was initiated in the Western world and that assimilated the traditional practices of indigenous communities, restorative justice cannot be naively seen as a concession to premodern society or as extolling the advancement of tradition over modernity. Rather, it is a reflection of the problems that have emerged in postmodern societies (Blad et al. 2013). This may sound alien to many societies, such as those along the Asian-Pacific region, which are still on the road of advancement to "modernity." According to authors such as Steels and Goulding (2013), restorative justice theorists and researchers should search for more localized practices around the world. These authors noted that some localized practices may not use the term "restorative justice" but display many of the desired components in terms of processes and outcomes. They argued that during this journey, indigenous people and societies should avoid being hijacked by white examiners who arrive with a Western standard of what is understood to be "restorative justice." In other words, Said's (1978) notion of Orientalism should be considered as an admonition.

3 Defining Restorative Justice: Various Attempts

This section will provide a brief examination of various attempts to define RJ made by academics, NGOs, and international governmental institutions. The purpose of this section is to expose the core elements shared by different actors at different levels, which will lay a foundation for the subsequent analysis. All the reviewed literature is Anglophone.

3.1 Scholarly Attempts

Although the international movement is widely termed as "restorative justice," so far, there has been no consensus on its definition. Arguably, the most frequently cited and probably the most widely accepted definition was given by Marshall (1999) in his project for the UK Home Office: "Restorative Justice is a process whereby all the parties with a stake in a particular offence come together to resolve collectively how to deal with the aftermath of the offence and its implications for the future" (p. 5). The central concern of RJ, according to Marshall (1999), is the restoration of (a) the victim, (b) the offender to a law-abiding life, and (c) the damage caused by the crime to the community.

However, Marshall's definition has been criticized by several theoreticians in the field. Zehr and Mika (2002), while acknowledging that the Marshall definition captures the core idea of RJ practice as a collaborative process to resolve harm, pointed out that "despite the seductiveness of his succinct definition, however, we feel it is important to be more explicit about the elemental features of a restorative approach"

(p. 62). From an RJ perspective, things are viewed differently. They listed three major headings that they considered to be the essential elements originally associated with RJ: (a) crime is fundamentally a violation of people and interpersonal relationships; (b) violations create obligations and liabilities; and (c) RJ seeks to heal and put right the wrongs (pp. 64–69).

John Braithwaite (2002b) noted that the definition given by Marshall does not tell us who or what is to be restored or what the core values of restorative justice are. Dignan (2005), in his book, *Understanding Victims and Restorative Justice*, addressed the weaknesses associated with this definition, including the lack of reference to outcomes, as well as the aim of the process. Moreover, there are questions about the identity of the parties who have a stake in a specific offense.

Walgrave (2002) considered restorative justice as "an option on doing justice which is primarily oriented towards restoring the harm that has been caused by a crime" (cited in Bazemore and Walgrave 1999, p. 48). His later book, however, provides an adaptation of this definition, in which restorative justice is proposed as "an option for doing justice after the occurrence of an offense that is primarily oriented towards repairing the individual, relational and social harm caused by that offense" (Walgrave 2008, p. 21). As a maximalist advocate, he contended that restorative justice is categorized by its aim of restoration, not by a process that typically favors restorative outcomes. The harm considered by restorative justice should be public and caused by crime (Walgrave 2008). The focus of restorative justice on the reparation of harm establishes it as a new paradigm, different from both the punishment and treatment approaches to crime.

3.2 *Definitions in NGO Working Documents*

Various NGOs are also important players in promoting and advancing the restorative justice movement in the Western world. In reality, the close exchange between scholars and practitioners who are active in NGOs has constructed an important landscape in the development of RJ in Western countries. Below, we display some of the definitions of RJ that have been supplied by the NGO sector.

3.2.1 Ron Claassen's RJ Principles

The "Working Party on Restorative Justice," which was an international alliance of NGOs on Crime Prevention and Criminal Justice, aimed to give RJ a profile that was sufficiently high that it would be placed on the agenda of the tenth United Nations Crime Congress in 2000. However, their project failed to reach a common definition. Eventually, they accepted Tony Marshall's definition but suggested adding Ron Claassen's RJ principles; they believed that in this way, a more complete picture of RJ was painted. Ron Claassen (1995, as cited in Gavrielides 2007, p. 47), from the "Center for Peacemaking and Conflict Studies" (Fresno, USA), proposed the following "Fundamental Principles of Restorative Justice"[2]:

(a) Crime is primarily an offense against human relationships.
(b) RJ is a process to make things as right as possible.
(c) As soon as the immediate victim's, the community's, and the offender's safety concerns are satisfied, RJ views the situation as a 'teachable moment' for the offender.
(d) RJ prefers responding to the crime at the earliest point possible and with the maximum amount of voluntary cooperation and minimum coercion, because healing in relationships and new learning are voluntary and cooperative.
(e) RJ recognizes that not all offenders will choose to be cooperative and that those who are significant safety risks should be placed in settings where the emphasis is on safety, values, ethics, responsibility, accountability, and civility.
(f) RJ recognizes and encourages the role of community institutions and requires follow-up and accountability structures (Claassen 1995, as cited in Gavrielides 2007, p. 47).

3.2.2 The Victim-Offender Mediation Association (VOMA) Guidelines

The "Recommended Ethical Guidelines" adopted by the American Victim-Offender Mediation Association (VOMA) in 2001 were targeted at practitioners and cover the process and procedures used in handling cases involving victim-offender mediation. Some of these principles are[3]:

(a) Victim-offender mediation is a restorative conflict resolution process that actively involves the victim and the offender in an effort to repair the emotional and material harm caused by a crime.
(b) Presenting choices to the parties whenever possible maximizes their opportunity to feel empowered by the process.
(c) Training in victim-offender sensitivity issues is provided for the mediators.
(d) The mediator shall reach an understanding with the participants regarding the procedures to be followed in the mediation.
(e) The primary responsibility for the outcome and restitution agreement rests with the participants. The mediator's obligation is to assist the disputants in reaching an informed and voluntary settlement and/or to have an informed and voluntary dialogue.
(f) Contact with the media for purposes of education and information regarding the underlying philosophies of restorative justice, and victim-offender mediation is generally supported. However, programs are encouraged to use great caution

[2] This set of principles can also be found at http://peace.fresno.edu/docs/rjprinc2.html. October 10, 2013.

[3] For the complete contents of the "Recommended Ethical Guidelines," please refer to http://www.voma.org/docs/ethics.pdf. Retrieved on October 15, 2013.

and care in responding to media requests for direct involvement in cases, particularly live settings or the taping of cases for later viewing (Victim Offender Mediation Association 1998, as cited in Gavrielides 2007, p. 50).

3.2.3 Statement of Restorative Justice Principles by the Restorative Justice Consortium of the UK

The 2002 Statement of Restorative Justice Principles (Restorative Justice Consortium 2002) replaced the 1999 Standards for Restorative Justice (Restorative Justice Consortium 1999). The principles provide a basis for a series of standards in particular settings of practice, namely, adult criminal justice, youth criminal justice, schools, workplaces, prisons, and neighborhoods. The Restorative Justice Consortium, which has been known as the Restorative Justice Council since 2016, is a British group of organizations and individuals with an interest in RJ. They defined restorative processes in both criminal justice settings and non-justice settings, with the former named "restorative justice" and the latter "restorative approaches (or practices)". One of their recent endeavors was the proposal of principles for restorative practice. In simplest terms, these six principles are restoration, voluntarism, neutrality, safety, accessibility, and respect.[4]

3.3 Definitions in International and Regional Instruments

Not all attempts to define restorative justice have been made by academics and practitioners; policy-makers at the international level have also been enticed to engage in this endeavor.

In the 1990s in Europe, various local and national mediation programs and experts argued in favor of a uniform document to guide and promote its further implementation. The Council of Europe's Recommendation N° R(99)19 on mediation in penal matters defined mediation as a "process whereby the victim and the offender are enabled, if they freely consent, to participate actively in the resolution of matters arising from the crime through the help of an impartial third party (mediator)". This definition is limited to mediation, which is the dominant model of restorative justice in Europe. In 2007, the European Commission for the Efficiency of Justice (CEPEJ), in an attempt to improve the implementation of the mediation principles contained in the 1999 Recommendation, issued the guidelines for a better implementation of the existing recommendation concerning mediation in penal matters, which specifically addresses the issues of availability, accessibility, and awareness.

The European Union is another player. In early March 2001, the Council of the European Union passed the Framework Decision on the Standing of Victims in

[4] https://www.restorativejustice.org.uk/sites/default/files/resources/files/Principles%20of%20restorative%20practice%20-%20FINAL%2012.11.15.pdf. Retrieved on February 20, 2016.

Criminal Proceedings (2001/220/JHA), in which mediation was also addressed. However, this framework decision was replaced by the Directive of the European Parliament and of the Council establishing minimum standards on the rights, support, and protection of victims of crime (2012/29/EU), which ensures that victims of crime receive appropriate information, support, and protection and are able to participate in the criminal proceedings. Article 2 specifically addresses the definition of restorative justice, namely, "any process whereby the victim and the offender are enabled, if they freely consent, to participate actively in the resolution of matters arising from the criminal offence through the help of an impartial third party." It seems that the European Parliament and the Council adopted the definition of the Council of Europe. Restorative justice is considered a service that is to be provided to victims when they choose to participate. Moreover, in the context of restorative justice services, a series of procedural safeguards, such as free consent, access to full and unbiased information, voluntariness, and confidentiality, are clearly laid out in Article 12.

The United Nations is another prominent player that has guided and promoted RJ programs, as indicated in the 2002 United Nations Basic Principles on the Use of Restorative Justice Programmes in Criminal Matters (ECOSOC Resolution 2002/12). The purpose of the principles was to assist the member states in adopting and standardizing RJ in their own justice systems; however, the principles should not be taken as prescriptive or mandatory. The use of terms with relation to restorative justice has been specified as follows. "Restorative justice programme" means any program that uses restorative processes and seeks to achieve restorative outcomes; "restorative process" means any process in which the victim and the offender, and, where appropriate, any other individuals or community members affected by a crime, actively participate together in the resolution of matters arising from the crime, generally with the help of a facilitator; "restorative outcome" means an agreement reached as a result of a restorative process, which includes responses and programs such as reparation, restitution, and community service, which are aimed at meeting the individual and collective needs and responsibilities of the parties involved, while achieving the reintegration of the victim and the offender. The UN instrument expanded the scope of restorative justice to include community service, at least when it is the result of a restorative process.

However, these instruments, except the Directive from the European Parliament and the Council, do not extend beyond the role of guidelines for national governments to provide a clearer vision about what restorative justice is and how it should be implemented.

3.4 Discussion

In sum, restorative justice is a contested concept that is beset by confusion (Dignan 2007; Strang 2013). At its core, restorative justice defines crime as "a violation of people and relationships… It creates obligations to make things right. Justice involves the victim, the offender and the community in a search for solutions which promote repair, reconciliation, and reassurance" (Zehr 1990, p. 181). In other words, crime is, in essence, harm to individuals, their communities, and society in general.

Restorative justice identifies three sides that have a stake in the process and outcome in the resolution of the conflict: the victim, the offender, and the community. Restorative conflict resolution should include reparations to the victim and the community, as well as the reintegration of the victim and the offender into society.

Notwithstanding the disparities in the various endeavors made to establish a definition, the three traditional stakeholders of restorative justice constitute a pillar of RJ theory. However, two additional concepts, the society and the state, also merit further discussion.

3.4.1 Victim

As Strang (2002) asserted, RJ is not value-free: It begins with a presumption that the victims have been harmed and that their restoration is a priority. Dissatisfied with the fact that the conflict between the victim and the offender had been usurped by the state, in the second half of the last century, the precursors of RJ advocacy called for a return of conflicts to their real owners.

The "discovery" of victims in Europe and beyond went further than simply recognizing victims' rights in the criminal justice system. A series of international and supranational instruments have made victims' rights explicit and concrete. As a step further, the needs and feelings of victims have been incessantly explored in many countries. For instance, victims have been found to be less likely to desire their perpetrators to be convicted and sentenced. Instead, they want restoration, an explanation and the possibility of continuing their lives in peace (Strang 2002; Aertsen et al. 2004). Moreover, the victims seek answers to questions, such as why they were victimized, what made the perpetrators go in the wrong direction in their lives, what the offenders think about their acts after considering the harm that has been done, etc. The concept of a "healing process" in the RJ literature has been largely described as a mechanism through which these needs and opinions can be addressed and can help the victim to feel better. Thus, the victim is said to be treated with respect and dignity.

Although it has been pointed out that the concept of restoration has not been insufficiently investigated (Bolívar Fernández 2012), there is no doubt that the victim should be the first to be restored. A large proportion of victim-focused research has indeed attempted to understand and evaluate whether and how the victim benefits from the restorative mechanism. For example, Bolívar Fernández's (2012) thesis identified the meanings associated with restoration by the victims, and she argued that mediation could contribute to closure for victims in terms of either communication with their perpetrators or distance from them.

The ideal image of the victim has been depicted in RJ as vulnerable and respectable and not contributing to their own victimization (Daly 2000). In contrast to the "ideal victim" (Christie 1986), some scholars have proposed adopting multi-victim perspectives (Young 2000; Dignan 2005), because in real life, practical situations are more complicated than the fabricated single perspective. For instance, some crimes are victimless, and in some cases, the victims share the blame with the offender. There also are cases in which there is no clear distinction between the "offender" and the "victim." Overall, the victim in RJ practices is usually represented by a natural adult individual who should have the capability to comprehend or understand the significance and meaning of the restorative process and outcome. In cases in which the victims are juveniles, the parents or guardians are usually invited to participate. Still, there are differing opinions about whether a victim that is an institution or a corporation should be allowed to attend the RJ process. Some authors have argued that a corporation can also be a victim that can participate in the RJ process, and in this case, the legal representatives could represent the interests of the company. Others have rejected the idea that a legal person should be given the opportunity to participate on the grounds that there could hardly be any meaningful communication or dialogue (Zehr and Toews 2004).

3.4.2 Offender

Although, in theory, the victim remains central, research has found that many RJ programs are mainly offender oriented, such as those in Austria, France, Germany, and Spain (Dünkel et al. 2015; Muncie 2001). The theories underlying restorative justice have mainly focused on offenders. Braithwaite's (1989) reintegrative shaming theory suggested that when shaming is directed toward the offender's "deed" rather than the "self" by those who are significant to him, it could achieve constructive effects on the offender's behavior in terms of rehabilitation and the prevention of reoffending. The procedural justice theory proposed by Tyler (1990, 2006) – although also relevant to the victim's experience – suggested that people abide by rules and laws when they are perceived as legitimate and valid. In particular, offenders who have gone through a restorative process experience procedural justice and are more likely to perform the reparation agreement.

While the restorative process does not necessarily encourage an admission of guilt (Cunneen and Hoyle 2010), it is expected that the offender will take responsibility and accountability for his/her acts and will undertake reparative actions toward the victims and the community. "Responsibility" seems to be a very central concept, as it provides a rationale for engaging the offender (Braithwaite and Roche 2001). The traditional penal system imposes responsibility on the offender in a very passive way. It delivers punishment to the offender in the form of forcefully taking something away from him. By contrast, restorative justice theorists have argued that the main objective of judicial intervention against an offender should not be to punish or even to (re)educate but to repair or to compensate for the harm caused by the offense (Walgrave and Aertsen 1996).

One major problem is the degree to which the offenders freely participate in restorative justice programs. Voluntariness is a principle that underlies restorative justice programs. Some authors have argued that coercion should be excluded from the process, as it disrespects the willingness and concern of the parties, making the RJ process no different from a court procedure. However, others have supported the existence of coercion to a certain degree. Hence, this creates doubt about whether confessions in such a process would arise out of true repentance or only as a means to avoid court procedures.

3.4.3 Community

Christie (1977) proposed community committees to replace state professionals to deal with conflicts at the local level. Community is an icon in restorative justice (Walgrave 2008), but it has been defined in a loose way.

McCold (2004) noted the difference between restorative justice and community justice in their definitions of community. Restorative justice defines community as the "natural networks of personal relationships, community is perceived in a very positive light" (p. 20). Among this natural network, the family is recognized as the primary support system. For restorative justice to be "restorative," it must involve those most directly affected (McCold 2004, p. 15). "Community" means everyone who is affected by the crime, i.e., persons who have some relationship with the victim or offender or who have been affected in other ways by the incident (Fellegi and Szegö 2013). Based on the idea of community healing, the engagement of the group of people who were affected has been considered essential. In victim-offender mediation, the community is perceived as those who have a relationship with the offender or the victim. In family group conferences or sentencing circles, the participation of members from the micro-neighborhood through community representatives or police officers is seen as the "involvement of the community." In sum, in RJ, "a community" can be considered either as a close-knit group of family members and supporters or as a geographic entity or an interest group (Shapland et al. 2006).

A consideration of the extent to which "community" can be found in today's European society, which is organized around the nuclear family, is inevitable. What is the role of the community in restorative conflict solving? Braithwaite (1993), in *Shame and Modernity*, argued that the fluidity in Western societies does not necessarily weaken the communitarianism that is conducive to reintegrative shaming. Rather, in late modern societies, communities are formed around new forms of associations and types of activities. For instance, city dwellers may have stronger communities than people living in villages. Yet a recent study by Fonseca Rosenblatt (2015) on the functioning of youth offender panels in the UK suggested that the role of community is very limited and narrow in these restorative processes. The following are some striking illustrations: the so-called community panel members do not necessarily carry a mandate from the community but simply voice their own opinions and ideas; young people in general are quite indifferent to the involvement of community members; the decision-making lies in the hands of youth offender panel workers instead of community members; etc. Hence, such empirical findings have posed serious challenges to the important notion of community involvement as proposed by RJ advocates and practitioners.

To sum up, in restorative justice, the "community" is generally seen as subject to restoration, just like the victim. The offender is supposed to restore the harm caused to the community in the form of community service or work, for example. Moreover, the community bears the responsibility of supervising and rehabilitating offenders. It is the place to which the offender must eventually return.

3.4.4 Society and State

Society and state are not mentioned as often as community in the RJ literature. Van Ness and Strong (1997) seemed to view society as a larger community, which also suffers injuries from crime. Yet the injuries to society differ in both form and degree from the injuries to the local community and the community of interest. Moreover, injuries to the latter two appear to be more direct than the general injuries to society as a whole. Walgrave (2000) conceded that the role of society in the settlement of a crime is not often discussed because of the fear that the recognition of society as a victim will result in a shift back to penal retributivism. Moreover, the ways in which society can be represented in restorative practices remain unclear (Vanfraechem 2007).

Because harm has been defined broadly enough to include a societal dimension, Walgrave (2008), for example, argued that harm should be understood at the individual, relational, and societal levels. Moreover, RJ theories have continued to maintain ambiguous attitudes about the role of society. Vanfraechem (2007) asserted that following the community as a third party, society is a fourth party whose primary role is confirming the norm (McCold and Wachtel 2002). Overall, the harm to society (the societal aspect) does not seem to move beyond the need for safety, which is felt by the whole community.

The role of the state is another area in which there is a gap in RJ theory. The precursors of RJ called for conflicts to be returned from the state to the community based on the fear that if the state is involved, the parties would lose their central role (Christie 1977). More recently, however, the view of RJ scholars has changed, as they have gradually realized the broad support the state can provide (Cunneen and Hoyle 2010). The state can have an important role as "power-container and norm-enforcer" (Crawford and Clear 2001, p. 141), or the government needs to play their (its) parts in upholding order and establishing peace (Van Ness and Strong 1997). In addition, faced with criticism from retributivists in terms of protection of the human rights of the offender and due process (Ashworth 2002; Ward and Langlands 2008), RJ theorists have come to recognize that the state should also have a role in ensuring that the practices take place in a fair way. The state should protect its "dominion," a concept that was first proposed by Braithwaite and Pettit (1990) and further elaborated by other RJ scholars.

4 Restorative Justice Values

"Values are the foundation of restorative justice, the touchstone to which we return when in doubt about what to do or how to do it, the yardstick for accessing action" (Pranis 2007, p. 72). The uniqueness of the modern restorative justice movement lies in the values it advocates, which have been said to have existed in earlier human history but has been absent in Western countries' mainstream systems of justice for the last 200 years. Strang (2010, p. 538) also argued that "it is the values attached to restorative justice that make the process unique and distinguish it from conventional court-based justice." Addressing values can be very tricky, however, because each society, or even a specific region within the borders of a modern country, carries its own values. Further, the personal beliefs of the practitioners themselves, as human beings, could influence their restorative justice programs; moreover, the values advocated may be closely related to their own experiences. Pranis (2007) noted that "just as there is no single agreed definition of restorative justice, so there is not a single definitive list of values; rather, people have articulated those essential aspects of restorative justice in a variety of ways" (p. 61).

In addition to the indefiniteness and immaturity of restorative justice, if we consider Braithwaite's view that its development is too recent for there to be any settled views on the conception of restorative values (Braithwaite 2002a), a third difficulty emerges. The problem is that in the RJ literature, values are sometimes intermingled with other concepts, such as principles, assumptions, objectives, and so on. An attempt to provide greater clarity follows below. The assumptions of restorative justice usually refer to normative statements of "what ought to be" in a restorative justice program; for example, the *UN Handbook on Restorative Justice Programmes* delineates the assumptions of restorative justice by specifying what the roles of the victim, the offender, and the community should be. The objectives and aims offer a very broad picture, and people may define them in relation to their own perspectives, which may be very different. For example, although the *UN Handbook* specifies that "the goal is to create a non-adversarial, non-threatening environment in which the interests and needs of the victim, the offender, the community and society can be addressed" (p. 8), scholars have defined different aims; for example, some have argued that the aim is to activate urban citizenship in contemporary Western society.

Nevertheless, the trickiest question may relate to the principles of restorative justice. Zehr and Mika (2002, pp. 64–69) elaborated on the principles of RJ in the landmark book *The Little Book of Restorative Justice* as follows: (1) crime is fundamentally a violation of people and interpersonal relationships; (2) violations create obligations and liabilities; and (3) justice should seek to heal and make wrongs right. Braithwaite (2003) proposed three groups of values: constraining values, maximizing values, and emergent values. "Constraining" values are those values that must be present, as they reflect fundamental procedural safeguards, such as non-domination, empowerment, respectful listening, etc. "Maximizing" values are those values around which the success of restorative processes can be evaluated, covering different forms of restoration. "Emergent" values are no less important than the previous two sets of values and include remorse, apology, and censure of the act, forgiveness, and mercy. Emergent values cannot be imposed or expected. Braithwaite seemed to consider that the principles of restorative justice fall within the maximizing values, i.e., the "different forms of healing/restoration," which include the "restoration of property loss and emotional restoration, and more abstract ones like restoration of dignity, compassion and social support" (p. 11).

There is a need to distinguish RJ's principles from its values. While Braithwaite (2003) considered the principles of RJ as enablers of restorative justice values, we also agree with Zehr (2002) that the principles of RJ are useful only if the underlying values are respected. For RJ scholars, values are the core and the ultimate end of RJ. For instance, Tschudi (2008) believed that dignity is one of the most important values, while Zehr (2002) viewed the value of respect as being the most fundamental. Walgrave (2008) advanced the quality of social life as a justification (common self-interest as the socio-ethical ground) for restorative justice interventions. In his viewpoint, both the harm done to the victim and the damage to social life must be repaired.

Here, we recognize our own limitations, as well as the limitations of the discussion of restorative justice values; it is almost impossible to identify all the values. We must adopt a much simpler and more pragmatic strategy by listing several values about which restorative justice scholars seem to agree. Therefore, we will address respect, inclusion, and healing.

4.1 Respect

Respect for human beings derives from recognizing and esteeming their intrinsic value (Walgrave 2008). First, respect for offenders in RJ is very different from the understanding of it in punitive criminal justice. Although the offender in the classic criminal justice sphere is seen as a moral agent who is able to make rational choices and to foresee the outcomes of his act, this responsibility is forced upon him in a negative way. The traditional proceeding treats the offender not as a whole person with dignity but as an abnormal "other" who has deviated from mainstream society. He deserves to be punished and to suffer pain. By contrast, restorative justice acknowledges the harm that was caused by the offender's acts but engages the offender in the active repair of the harm in a constructive way. A restorative justice process channels the offender toward true repentance and remorse through a meaningful dialogue with the person who suffered from the offender's criminal behavior. The traditional punitive paradigm obstructs this process by simply passing down a sentence and executing the punishment. In addition, the offenders' other needs, beyond their responsibilities to the victims and communities, must be recognized (Zehr 2002).

Second, equal respect is also granted to the victim. Restorative justice gives tremendous attention to the victim and regards the victim as the first bearer of the harm. The victim is no longer an abstract person but an individual with flesh and blood who is visible to society. In contrast to treating the victim merely as a witness, secondary to the public interests shared by the community, restorative justice first asks "what is the harm caused to the victim" and "what does the victim need." The victim's willingness and voluntariness are fully respected during this process, e.g., if he feels uncomfortable, he can withdraw from the process at any time. Instead of considering material reparations as the only remedy to which the victim is entitled, an idea deeply embedded in the traditional paradigm, restorative justice addresses the material, psychological, and spiritual needs of the victim. The victim is empowered as the real owner of his case, and he should be able to move on after the mediation session.

The value of respect is also acknowledged in *The Vienna Declaration on Crime and Justice: Meeting the Challenges of the Twenty-first Century* (2000) as the "development of restorative justice policies, procedures and programmes that are respectful of the rights, needs and interests of victims, offenders, communities and all other parties" (as cited in United Nations Office on Drugs and Crime 2006, pp. 1–2).

4.2 Inclusion

One of the fundamental principles of restorative justice programs is that criminal behavior not only violates the law but also injures the victims and the community. Any efforts to address the consequences of criminal behavior should, where possible, involve the offender, as well as these injured parties (United Nations Office on Drugs and Crime 2006). Braithwaite (2002b) has consistently defined the scope of the stakeholders of restorative justice as primarily "the victim(s), the offender (s), and the affected communities (which includes the families of victims and offenders)" (p. 11).

The ideal situation is for the offender, the victim, and the affected communities to jointly participate in the dialogue and negotiations and to reach decisions within their "dominion." Should the victim or his supporters be present in these conferences or meetings? What if they are absent or choose not to attend, which seems to occur in most of the cases? Restorative justice, in this context, may lose its credibility as a participatory process. Some researchers have denied the "restorativeness" of conferences when there is a lack of participation by the victim's side (Zinsstag and Vanfraechem 2012). However, others (Walgrave 2008) have argued in favor of its "restorativeness" in terms of the restorative outcomes, even when the process is not satisfactory.

Nevertheless, inclusion has been widely accepted as a fundamental value of restorative justice. The participatory value for the stakeholders may be what sets mediation in restorative justice apart from adjudications in traditional proceedings.

4.3 Healing

Within the ambit of criminal law, justice has traditionally been considered complete when the offender receives a punishment. Punishment may satisfy the inclination for revenge and placate feelings of indignation, but what happens after the punishment? The offender serves his sentence, the victim remains on the sidelines, and the community remains disrupted and broken. The call of RJ advocates is to make things right in a positive way.

There lies a rift between "wrong" and "harm." The traditional punitive paradigm is built on the notion of a "wrong" – an offense is a violation of the law and the public interest – but restorative justice is concerned about "harm," which, according to Walgrave (2008), applies to the individual, relational, and community levels. Duff (2002) contended that an offense not only affects the relationships of citizens in particular or in general but also creates a public concern; it should go beyond the scope of "harm" and should be treated as a "wrong." In his eyes, the restoration could and should embrace punishment. However, the civilizing thesis (Dignan 2005, 2007) considers that punishment only produces more harm, and therefore, should be repressed or even abolished. Despite the arguments between RJ advocates and "just desert" adherents, and within the RJ group, it seems that many agree that the aim of RJ is healing.[5]

Healing, in its concrete form, would be the result of a successful meeting or conference. The apology and forgiveness induced through these encounters signify a restoration of the harmed relationships, although neither of the foregoing should be imposed. The level of satisfaction achieved for both sides shows that, to a certain degree, their feelings and needs have been restored; healing has a heavy therapeutic bearing.

The values discussed above are in no way definite or all-inclusive. Restorative justice is an evolving practice which has, or will have, its own ebbs and flows. Thriving in Western societies and borrowing experiences from indigenous communities, restorative justice provides an extremely important framework for understanding crime and responding to it in modern industrialized democracies (Umbreit et al. 1994). Given that focusing only on its theoretical perspectives seems to cause more confusion than clarification, we will now shed light on its most widely recognized modalities.

5 Restorative Justice Modalities

Three distinct forms of restorative justice have traditionally been acknowledged: victim-offender mediation (reconciliation), family group conferences, and peacemaking circles. However, there are other programs, such as community restorative boards and local mediation schemes, which, to varying degrees, are considered to be restorative justice practices. Schemes for victim support have worked toward repairing the harm to the victim; however, the repair does not come directly from the offender but mainly from the state or the community. Whether or not community service should be seen as restorative remains debatable (Walgrave 2008). McCold

[5] European scholars have been opposed to the goal of healing, as they consider it too unrealistic and too idealistic.

and Wachtel (2002) proposed a range of restorative practices, from "fully restorative" to "mostly restorative" to "partially restorative." Yet it is not our intention here to argue about whether or not certain schemes are within the realm of restorative justice. Rather, we are focused on these diversified programs in relation to different stages of criminal justice. The realization of restorative justice can thus be divided into several levels: the pre-prosecution level, the presentencing level, and the post-sentencing (prison or community service) level. Here, we will discuss several established models of RJ; an analysis of the restoration based on each model will be provided in the next chapter. Notwithstanding the considerable variation across programs, a common element is a direct voluntary encounter between the perpetrator and the offended.

5.1 Victim-Offender Mediation (VOM) Programs

Victim-offender mediation was born in Canada in the 1970s, but by the mid-1990s, there were over 300 such programs in North America and over 500 in Europe (Umbreit 1998). Mediation programs have occupied a central place in RJ modalities in continental Europe (Aertsen et al. 2006, 2010). Depending on the stage of the criminal justice proceeding in which it is situated, victim-offender mediation may have different relationships with criminal justice, namely, independent, relatively dependent, and dependent.

In the *independent* type, the community intervenes immediately once a conflict has occurred. Its settlement is completely outside of the criminal justice system. Usually, a mediator (a community worker or volunteer) is designated for the specific case. The disputes may have a criminal nature but may be among the low-level offenses within a specific jurisdiction. Through direct or shuttle mediation, the party who has caused the harm is committed to making reparations to the offended side and to the community of care. Thus, both the perpetrator and the offended party are able to avoid the criminal justice system. The offender, to the maximum extent, avoids any possible punitive sanctions, and the victim avoids the "secondary victimization" associated with contacts with the criminal justice system. This alternative way to settle criminal disputes falls on the right end of the continuum of restorativeness (fully restorative). Restoration not only means that the victim and the offender have reached reconciliation through actions of restitution, apology, etc., but also relates to the peace and healing of the community through its own resolution of the disputes.

Mediation, at the level of prosecution, *depends entirely* on the justice system for case referrals and reports back to the justice staff about the mediation process and outcome. In most European countries, victim-offender mediation at this stage usually takes the form of "penal mediation." The agreement reached by the offender and the victim can influence the decision made by the criminal justice professionals about whether to proceed with the prosecution or not. For example, according to the Belgian Criminal Code, the justice officers can take the agreement into account

(Van Camp and Souter 2012), and in most cases, they do so. It is likely that both the offender and the victim face great pressure, as they are told that any action involved in the mediation could influence their fate in the justice system. Moreover, although mediation has been provided to the victim and the offender as a service of the welfare state in the European context on the basis of voluntariness, coercion unavoidably remains. The mediators, usually NGO workers, volunteers, and prosecutors working in the field, have indicated that the offender and the victim typically choose not to meet each other directly (Dünkel et al. 2015). Low victim involvement has also been reported in many programs. Mediation is supposed to respect both the offenders' and victims' willingness, and, therefore, it must be discontinued if either side does not agree to continue with it. Based on this fact, the extent to which the restoration of the harm and relationships can be achieved is a concern.

At the post-sentence level, mediation is usually arranged, while the offender is serving his sentence, and it can be initiated either by an offender who wants to meet the victim or by the victim through the victim's services. This is *relatively dependent* on the criminal justice system. The process and outcome of this type of mediation do not influence the sentence delivered, but an offender's repentance may be evident in his offer to meet the victim and to make penitent reparations, such as an apology, in order to redeem himself. These actions could be taken into account by the prison authority concerning the prerelease decision. As a result of the intense emotions involved in the encounter, this does not necessarily lead to forgiveness from the victim, but in some cases, the victims have voiced that the offenders were not very hateful. Through mediation, a deeper understanding of the causes of the crime and what both sides have suffered in its aftermath can be gained. Compared to mediation occurring at earlier stages, mediation at the prison level usually deals with more serious crimes, such as homicide or violent offenses. Scholars have suggested that RJ may work better for victims of more severe crimes (Sherman and Strang 2007).

5.2 Family Group Conferencing (FGC)

Family group conferencing (FGC) is built upon the traditional way the Maori, an aboriginal group in New Zealand, have handled community conflicts. In response to the overrepresentation of Maori youth and the missing voices from Maori communities in the justice system (Strang 2002), in 1989, legislation – the Children, Young Persons, and Their Families Act – established family group conferences as the primary mechanism for addressing almost all youth crimes. The New Zealand model quickly spread to Australia with a few adaptations, in particular, the ability of the police to act as conferencing facilitators. The differences between the two models have been described (Vanfraechem 2009). FGC, which is at the heart of the procedure in New Zealand, deals with serious crimes within the judicial proceeding, with the police present as a representative of the society. The lawyer is present, and there is no script throughout the conferences. However, in police conferencing, the police works as the facilitators to address less serious crimes, the conference diverts the offense from the criminal justice system, no lawyer is present, and a script must be followed. It is noted that there are now several different models of conferencing in different jurisdictions (Zinsstag and Vanfraechem 2012).

Conferencing has also been incorporated into the legislation dealing with juvenile offending in Northern Ireland and Belgium. The link to restorative justice was made because there was a shift "from deciding on penalties to deciding on outcomes that repair harm and reintegrate offenders" (Maxwell et al. 2004, p. 8). The main difference between mediation and FGC is probably that the latter involves the local community in the discussion of the offense and its aftermath (Strang 2002). A conference usually involves the victim, the offender, the families and friends of both, and, sometimes, other members of the community in a discussion of the aftermath of the crime, a workable reparative plan, and how to prevent the offending behavior from reoccurring.

5.3 *Peacemaking Circles (PMC)*

Circles, or peacemaking circles (PMC), initially emerged during the 1980s as a way for people in the First Nations in Canada to deal with the offenses occurring within the community. It includes a wider range of participants: the victim, the offender, their respective families, the judge, the lawyers, the prosecutor, the police officers, and the community residents. Usually, it centers around a "peace stone" or a "touching peace" and ensures that the voice of everyone sitting in the circle is heard. The discussions are tailored to topics such as how each one has been impacted by the crime, how they feel about it, and what they consider to be the best way to deal with it, with an eye to balancing the needs of the victim, the offender, and the community. Despite the fact the model was originally developed in North America, such circles have also been growing in importance in Europe, e.g., the research project involving Germany, Belgium, and Hungary (Aertsen et al. 2013; Fellegi and Szegö 2013). Some scholars have held that its rise in Europe possibly has nothing to do with the indigenous practices.

Conferencing and circles have some similarities, as well as differences, from victim-offender mediation. While mediation may only involve the victim, the offender, and their "communities of care," conferencing and circles expand into the wider community, possibly with the presence of authorities, such as the police, the prosecutor, and the judge. There is no clear line that can be drawn regarding the number of participants (Zinsstag and Vanfraechem 2012), although conferencing and circles are usually larger. To differentiate between conferencing and circles, the features of circles have recently been summed up as: (1) ceremonies and rituals are used as a framework; (2) the circle format creates a special dynamic in the dialogue; (3) the wider community and the judicial representatives (if possible) are included; (4) circle participants have the potential to define the values and rules of the discussion; (5) the keeper's role is different from a mediator's or a conference facilitator's role; and (6) the consensus-based decision-making covers all the participants (Fellegi and Szegö 2013).

References

Aertsen, I., Arsovska, J., Rohne, H.-C., Valinas, M., & Vanspauwen, K. (Eds.). (2008). *Restoring justice after large-scale violent conflicts: Kosovo, DR Congo and the Israeli-Palestinian case*. Cullompton: Willan Publishing.

Aertsen, I., Daems, T., & Robert, L. (Eds.). (2006). *Institutionalizing restorative justice*. Cullompton: Willan Publishing.

Aertsen, I., Dhondt, D., & Parmentier, S. (2013). *Implementing peacemaking circles in a European context.* Paper presented at the Beyond punitiveness: Crime and crime control in Europe in a comparative perspective, Budapest, September 5, 2013.

Aertsen, I., Mackay, R., Pelikan, C., Willemsens, J., & Wright, M. (2004). *Rebuilding community connections—Mediation and restorative justice in Europe*. Strasbourg: Council of Europe.

Aertsen, I., Vanfraechem, I., & Willemsens, J. (2010). Restorative justice in Europe: Introducing a research endeavor. In I. Vanfraechem, I. Aertsen, & J. Willemsens (Eds.), *Restorative justice realities: Empirical research in a European context* (pp. 1–9). The Hague: Eleven International Publishing.

Ashworth, A. (2002). Responsibilities, rights and restorative justice. *British Journal of Criminology, 42*(3), 578–595. doi:10.1093/bjc/42.3.578.

Barnett, R. E. (1977). Restitution: A new paradigm of criminal justice. *Ethics, 87*(4), 279–301. doi:10.2307/2379899.

Bazemore, G., & Walgrave, L. (1999). *Restorative juvenile justice: Repairing the harm of youth crime*. Monsey, NY: Criminal Justice Press.

Berman, H. J. (1983). *Law and revolution: The formation of the western legal tradition*. Cambridge, MA: Harvard University Press.

Blad, J., Wright, M., & Cornwell, D. J. (2013). *Civilising criminal justice: An international restorative agenda for penal reform*. Hook Hampshire: Waterside Press.

Bolívar Fernández, D. (2012). *Victim-offender mediation and victim's restoration: A victimological study in the context of restorative justice*. Leuven: KU Leuven.

Braithwaite, J. (1989). *Crime, shame and reintegration*. Cambridge, MA: Cambridge University Press.

Braithwaite, J. (1993). Shame and modernity. *British Journal of Criminology, 33*(1), 1–18.

Braithwaite, J. (2002a). *Restorative justice and responsive regulation*. Oxford: Oxford University Press.

Braithwaite, J. (2002b). Setting standards for restorative justice. *British Journal of Criminology, 42*(3), 563–577. doi:10.1093/bjc/42.3.563.

Braithwaite, J. (2003). Principles of restorative justice. In A. v. Hirsch, J. v. Roberts, & A. Bottoms (Eds.), *Restorative justice and criminal justice: Competing or reconcilable paradigms?* (pp. 1–20). Oxford: Hart Publishing.

Braithwaite, J., & Pettit, P. (1990). *Not just deserts*. Oxford: Oxford University Press.

Braithwaite, J., & Roche, D. (2001). Responsibility and restorative justice. In *Restorative community justice: Repairing harm and transforming communities* (pp. 63–84). Cincinnati, OH: Anderson.

Bueno, I. (2013). *Mass victimization and restorative justice in Colombia: Pathways towards peace and reconciliation?* Leuven: KU Leuven.

Christie, N. (1977). Conflicts as property. *British Journal of Criminology, 17*, 1–15.

Christie, N. (1986). The ideal victim. In E. Fattah (Ed.), *From crime policy to victim policy* (pp. 17–30). Basingstoke: MacMillan.

Crawford, A., & Clear, T. (2001). Community justice: Transforming communities through restorative justice. In G. Bazemore & M. Schiff (Eds.), *Restorative community justice. Repairing harm and transforming communities* (pp. 127–149). Cincinnati, OH: Anderson Publishing.

Cunneen, C., & Hoyle, C. (2010). *Debating restorative justice* (Vol. 1). Oxford: Hart Publishing.

Curtis-Fawley, S., & Daly, K. (2005). Gendered violence and restorative justice the views of victim advocates. *Violence Against Women, 11*(5), 603–638.

Daly, K. (2000). Revisiting the relationship between retributive and restorative justice. In H. Strang & J. Braithwaite (Eds.), *Restorative justice: From philosophy to practice* (pp. 33–54). Dartmouth: Ashgate.

Dignan, J. (2005). *Understanding victims and restorative justice*. Maidenhead: Open University Press.

Dignan, J. (2007). The victim in restorative justice. In S. Walklate (Ed.), *Handbook of victims and victimology* (pp. 309–332). Cullompton: Willan Publishing.

Duff, R. A. (2002). Restorative punishment and punitive restoration. In L. Walgrave (Ed.), *Restorative justice and the law* (pp. 82–100). Cullomption: Willan Publishing.

Dünkel, F., Grzywa-Holten, J., & Horsfield, P. (2015). *Restorative justice and mediation in penal matters in Europe: A stock-taking of legal issues, implementation strategies and outcomes in 36 European countries*. Monchengladbach: Form Verlag Godesberg GmbH.

Eglash, A. (1977). Beyond restitution: Creative restitution. In J. Hudson & B. Galaway (Eds.), *Restitution in criminal justice* (pp. 91–129). Toronto: Lexington Books.

Fellegi, B., & Szegö, D. (2013). *Handbook for facilitating peacemaking circles*. Budapest: PT Mũhely.

Ferri, E. (1968). *The positive school of criminology: Three lectures*. Pittsburgh. PA: University of Pittsburgh Press.

Fonseca Rosenblatt, F. (2015). *The role of community in restorative justice*. London and New York: Routledge.

Gavrielides, T. (2007). *Restorative justice theory and practice: Addressing the discrepancy*. Monsey, NY: Criminal Justice Press.

Green, S., Johnstone, G., & Lambert, C. (2013). What harm, whose justice?: Excavating the restorative movement. *Contemporary Justice Review*, 1–16. doi:10.1080/10282580.2013.857071.

Marshall, T. (1999). *Restorative justice: An overview*. London: Home Office.

Martinson, R. (1978). New findings, new views: A note of caution regarding sentencing reform. *Hofstra Law Review, 7*, 243.

Maruna, S. (2014). The role of wounded healing in restorative justice: an appreciation of Albert Eglash. *Restorative Justice, 2*(1), 9–23.

Maxwell, G., Kingi, V., Robertson, J., Morris, A., & Cunningham, C. (2004). Achieving Effective Outcomes in Youth Justice Final report. Wellington: Crime and Justice Research Centre, Victoria University of Wellington.

McCold, P. (2004). What is the role of community in restorative justice theory and practice? In H. Zehr & B. Toews (Eds.), *Critical issues in restorative justice* (pp. 155–172). Monsey, NY/ Cullompton: Criminal Justice Press/Willan Publishing.

McCold, P., & Wachtel, T. (2002). Restorative justice theory validation. In E. Weitekamp & H.-J. Kerner (Eds.), *Restorative justice: Theoretical foundations* (pp. 110–142). Cullompton: Willan Publishing.

Miers, D., & Aertsen, I. (Eds.). (2012). Regulating restorative justice: A comparative analysis of legislative provision in European countries (Vol. 2, Studies in Criminology and Forensic Sciences). Frankfurt am Main: Verlag für Polizeiwissenschaft.

Muncie, J. (2001). Policy transfers and 'what works': Some reflections on comparative youth justice. *Youth Justice, 1*(3), 27–35.

Pranis, K. (2007). Restorative values. In G. Johnstone & D. W. V. Ness (Eds.), *Handbook of restorative justice* (pp. 59–74). New York: Willan Publishing.

Restorative Justice Consortium. (1999). *Standards for restorative justice*. London: Standards in Restorative Justice Group.

Restorative Justice Consortium. (2002). *Statement of restorative justice principles*. London: Standards in Restorative Justice Group.

Said, E. (1978). *Orientalism*. New York: Random House.

Shapland, J., Atkinson, A., Atkinson, H., Colledge, E., Dignan, J., Howes, M., et al. (2006). Situating restorative justice within criminal justice. *Theoretical Criminology, 10*(4), 505–532.

Sherman, L. W., & Strang, H. (2007). *Restorative justice: The evidence*. London: The Smith Institute.

Steels, B., & Goulding, D. (2013). Restorative justice in the Asia Pacific region: Acting fairly, being just. In J. Liu, B. Hebenton, & S. Jou (Eds.), *Handbook of Asian criminology* (pp. 379–391). New York: Springer.

Strang, H. (2002). *Repair or revenge: Victims and restorative justice*. Oxford: Clarendon Press.
Strang, H. (2010). Exploring the effects of restorative justice on crime victims for victims of conflict in transitional societies. In S. G. Shoham, P. Knepper, & M. Kett (Eds.), *International handbook of victimology* (pp. 537–558). Boca Raton, FL: CRC Press/Taylor & Francis Group.
Strang, H. (2013). Conferencing and Victims. In E. Zinsstag & I. Vanfraechem (Eds.), *Conferencing and restorative justice: International practices and perspectives* (pp. 83–100). Oxford: Oxford University Press.
Tschudi, F. (2008). Dealing with violent conflicts and mass victimisation: A human dignity approach. In I. Aertsen, J. Arsovska, H.-C. Rohne, M. Valinas, & K. Vanspauwen (Eds.), *Restoring justice after large-scale violent conflicts: Kosovo, DR Congo and the Israeli-Palestinian case* (pp. 46–69). Cullompton: Willan Publishing.
Tyler, T. (1990). *Why people obey the law*. New Haven, CT: Yale University Press.
Tyler, T. (2006). Restorative justice and procedural justice: Dealing with rule breaking. *Journal of Social Issues, 62*(2), 307–326.
Umbreit, M. S., Coates, R. B., & Kalanj, B. (1994). *Victim meets offender: The impact of restorative justice and mediation*. Monsey, NY: Criminal Justice Press.
Umbreit, M. (1998). Restorative justice through victim-offender mediation: A multi-site assessment. *Western Criminology Review, 1*(1), 1–29.
United Nations Office on Drugs and Crime. (2006). *Handbook on restorative justice programmes*. (Criminal Justice Handbook Series). New York.
Van Camp, T., & Souter, V. D. (2012). Restorative justice in Belgium. In D. Miers & I. Aertsen (Eds.), *Regulating restorative justice: A comparative analysis of legislative provision in European countries* (Vol. 2, pp. 60–100., Studies in Criminology and Forensic Sciences). Frankfurt am Main: Verlag für Polizeiwissenschaft.
Van Ness, D., & Strong, K. H. (1997). *Restoring justice*. Cincinnati, OH: Anderson.
Vanfraechem, I. (2007). Community, society and state in restorative justice: An exploration. In R. Mackay, M. Bosnjak, J. Deklerck, C. Pelikan, B. v. Stokkom, & M. Wright (Eds.), *Images of restorative justice theory* (pp. 73–91). Frankfurt am Main: Verlag fur Polizeiwissenschaft.
Vanfraechem, I. (2009). *The relationship between restorative justice and restorative practices*. Paper presented at the Restorative justice and restorative practices: Are they the same?, Leuven, June 3, 2009.
Walgrave, L. (2000). Extending the victim perspective towards a systematic restorative justice alternative. In A. Crawford & J. Goodey (Eds.), *Integrating a victim perspective within criminal justice: International debates* (pp. 253–284). Aldershot: Ashgate Publishing.
Walgrave, L. (Ed.). (2002). *Restorative justice and the law*. Cullompton: Willan Publishing.
Walgrave, L. (2008). *Restorative justice, self-interest and responsible citizenship*. Cullompton: Willan Publishing.
Walgrave, L., & Aertsen, I. (1996). Reintegrative shaming and restorative justice. *European Journal on Criminal Policy and Research, 4*(4), 67–85.
Ward, T., & Langlands, R. L. (2008). Restorative justice and the human rights of offenders: Convergences and divergences. *Aggression and Violent Behavior, 13*(5), 355–372.
Weitekamp, E. G. M. (2000). Research on victim-offender mediation. Findings and needs for the future. In T. E. F. f. V.-O. Mediation (Ed.), *Victim-offender mediation in Europe* (pp. 99–121). Leuven: Leuven University Press.
Young, R. (2000). Integrating a multi-victim perspective into criminal justice through restoratie justice conferences. In A. Crawford & J. Goodey (Eds.), *Integrating a victim perspective within criminal justice: International debates* (pp. 227–252). Aldershot: Ashgate Publishing.
Zehr, H. (1990). *Changing lenses: A new focus for crime and justice*. Scottdale, PA: Herald Press.
Zehr, H. (2002). *The little book of restorative justice*. Intercourse, PA: Good Books.
Zehr, H., & Mika, H. (2002). Fundamental principles of restorative justice. In *The little book of restorative justice* (pp. 64–69). Intercourse, PA: Good Books.
Zehr, H., & Toews, B. (Eds.). (2004). *Critical issues in restorative justice*. Cullompton: Willan Publishing.
Zinsstag, E., & Vanfraechem, I. (2012). *Conferencing and restorative justice*. Oxford: Oxford University Press.

Chapter 9
Restorative Justice Practices: The Restoration Model

1 Introduction

Over the past 40 years, many restorative justice programs have been developed in Western societies. In the meantime, many studies on restorative justice practices have been produced, although they have been criticized as "a mile wide but only an inch deep" (McCold, 2003, as cited in Walgrave, 2011, p. 97). To move beyond what restorative justice claims to be as presented in the previous chapter, a focus on its practices may give us a better understanding of how restoration, as a central notion, is understood in these programs. In this chapter, we begin by presenting some case examples that demonstrate how RJ is actually practiced. Then, an overview of evaluation studies is presented, which should enable us to determine the terms under which the stakeholders claim to have been restored. Bearing in mind that RJ has developed different modes of practice in different countries, a restoration model is then delineated drawing on the body of literature on the reported practices.

2 Restorative Justice Practices

2.1 Case Examples

The RJ literature has provided case examples that show exactly how the restorative justice process has been conducted. Among such examples are Sherman and Strang's (2007) descriptions of three face-to-face conferences in London and Canberra, Fellegi and Szegö's (2013) introduction of peacemaking circles in countries such as Belgium and Germany, and Crosland and Liebmann's (2003) 40 accounts of what is being done in the name of restorative justice and victim-offender mediation. Although they are not intended to be representative, these cases may provide a direct glimpse of how restorative justice programs are run.

X. Yuan, *Restorative Justice in China*, Springer Series on Asian Criminology and Criminal Justice Research, DOI 10.1007/978-3-319-63922-2_9

Vanfraechem (2007, p. 83) described the steps of a conference meeting held in Belgium, according to a model borrowed from New Zealand:

> The police read out the charges so it is clear what the conference is about. When the offender does not deny the crime, the victim and his supporter can relate to how the crime has affected them. The offender can answer questions and explain what the criminal action meant to him. Members of his or her network have the opportunity to express their thoughts and feelings. When all stories have been told, the young offender and his network meet privately to develop a proposal about how to make amends for the harm. Problems in the youngster's life can be addressed. After these deliberations the proposal is discussed with the whole group and a well-balanced agreement is sought. The concerns of the victim, as well as amends to the community at large are considered. The meeting also identifies elements needed to ensure that the agreement will be implemented (e.g. addressing the young person's drugs problem or school attendance).

2.2 Evidence-Based Practices

According to Umbreit et al. (2005), RJ dialogue has been the most widely practiced and most thoroughly researched of the various practices in the context of criminal justice. Among these practices, VOM and conferencing have received far more coverage than other programs in evaluation studies (Kurki 2003). The 19 evaluation studies below were selected for review, and they differ from each other in the perspectives and methodologies adopted (Coates and Gehm 1989; Umbreit et al. 1994, 2001, 2005, 2006, 2007; Maxwell and Morris 1993, 1999, 2002; Morris and Maxwell 2000; Miers et al. 2001; Newburn and Britain 2002; Latimer et al. 2001; McCold and Wachtel 2002; Hayes and Daly 2003; Kurki 2003; Campbell et al. 2005; Bonta et al. 2006; Strang 2002; Sherman and Strang 2007; Shapland et al. 2008). These evaluation studies were retrieved from the Internet, printed books, and reports. In examining them, attention will be given to the effect or impact that these programs have had on the three stakeholders: the victim, the offender, and the community.

2.2.1 The Victim

Repairing the harm to the victim cannot merely remain as a protocol; it must be realized in concrete RJ programs. To date, in the evaluation literature, "restoring the victim" has mainly focused on the attendance rates, the reason for attending and not attending, the issue of satisfaction, and the perception of fairness and other psychological outcomes for the victims. The results seem encouraging and promising for victims, and the implications of these results will be analyzed below.

1. Attendance Rate

   Although they claim to enable victims and other stakeholders to participate in decision-making in their own cases, some restorative justice programs, mainly conferences, do not seem to meet this target very well in practice, given the very low attendance on the victim's side. For example, in Maxwell and Morris' (1993); Morris and Maxwell (2000) studies, only 41% of family group conferences were attended by victims. Campbell et al. (2005), in evaluating youth conference services in Northern Ireland, found that victims were present at 69% of the conferences. However, Crawford and Newburn (2003, 2013) reported that very few victims attended the conferences in their evaluations of the referral panels for young offenders in England and Wales.

2. Reasons for Attending and Not Attending

   Various evaluation studies have also uncovered the reasons that victims attend mediation or conferences. In a study of Victim-Offender Reconciliation Programs (VORPs) including both juveniles and adults in Indiana and Ohio, Coates and Gehm (1989) found the following reasons for victims to attend: to obtain restitution for loss, to help the offender, to participate usefully in the criminal justice process, to ask questions and express their feelings toward the offender, or to punish the offender more effectively than through the traditional criminal justice system. Doak and O'Mahony (2006) indicated that most victims who participated in conferences in Northern Ireland appeared to be rather altruistic: They sought to help the offender and to give young people a second chance. Umbreit et al. (2006) found that the victims chose to meet the offender for following reasons: to learn more about why the crime had happened, to share their pain with the offender, to help the offender change, to hold the offender accountable, to receive restitution, to avoid court processing, or to see that the offender is adequately punished.

   Of course, not all victims want to participate, nor do they all want to meet their offenders. The reasons for this vary across different types of crime victims and different restorative justice programs. A small survey done by Mercer (2006, cited in Liebmann 2007, p. 323) found the following reasons for not attending:

   > I felt too much time had passed since the offence; I just wanted to forget about the offence; I was too busy; My mother was too angry; I do not think it worthwhile; Nothing can be done about it as I have been burgled three times; There are issues around confidentiality; It wasn't a personal crime against myself; I have had excellent support within the organization; I have appreciated the contact but feel a counselling service meets my needs best; I don't want further information or involvement. I need to focus on looking after my son; I have other priorities in my life as I have adopted two children.

   It was sometimes true that the reason for nonattendance was not necessarily because the victim was unwilling but rather because of poor practice. For instance, Maxwell and Morris' (1993) study found that in the early phase of RJ implementation in New Zealand, the low attendance rate was actually related to the fact that the victims were not invited or not adequately noticed or that the time arranged was not suitable for them; in this sample, only 6% of the victims expressed that they did not wish to meet the offender.

3. Satisfaction and Perception of Fairness

   A measure of satisfaction has often been included in evaluation studies. Not surprisingly, high levels of satisfaction with the process and outcomes among victims and offenders have frequently been reported (Maxwell and Morris 1993;

Morris and Maxwell 2000; Umbreit et al. 1994, 2001; Strang 2002; Miers et al. 2001). In particular, the victims' satisfaction has been examined in order to determine the benefits that restorative justice programs may offer them.

The participants' own aims and expectations may influence their satisfaction with RJ schemes (Shapland 2003). Therefore, it might be advisable to determine the needs of these participants beforehand and then to evaluate the extent to which these needs were met in the following restorative justice process. Strang and her colleagues (1999, 2002), using a quasi-experimental design in the Reintegrative Shaming Experiment (RISE) in Canberra, found that conferences satisfy victims' needs far better than the courtroom. Umbreit et al. (1994) evaluated the victim-offender mediation process across four programs in North America. The analysis of the data retrieved through interviews, court record reviews, and observations suggested that the victims (and offenders) were reported to have very high levels of satisfaction and perceptions of fairness with the mediation process. In reviewing 27 VOM victim impact studies covering programs across the USA, Canada, England, and Scotland, Umbreit et al. (2001) concluded that, on the whole, or with very few exceptions, victims who chose to participate in VOM were satisfied with the process and the results of their encounter with the criminal justice system.

Another study examined satisfaction with relation to the participants' experiences and attitudes about mediation. Three aspects are associated with satisfaction: the process, the mediators, and the outcome (Iivari 2010). A study on mediation in Finland based on interviews, observations, and survey methods consistently found that a large majority of victims were satisfied with the mediation process, the mediators, and the compensation for their damages (Iivari 2010). Research in Real Justice conferences in the Netherlands found that most participants (including offenders) were satisfied with the experience and the average marks given to the conference and the coordinators were very high, at 7.8 and 8 out of 10, respectively (Lauwaert and Blad 2010).

A meta-analysis of victims' satisfaction studies by Latimer et al. (2005) showed that victims who participated in restorative processes were significantly more satisfied than those who participated in the traditional justice system. However, they also pointed out that further studies should focus on whether the victims still feel they have experienced some closure and healing at a longer period (6 months or a year) after the restorative process. What is noteworthy in their study is the issue of participation bias – those who agreed to participate in restorative processes had already shown their acceptance of these processes.

The research results on the perception of fairness are rather limited. Research by McCold and Wachtel (2002) demonstrated that offenders' sense of fairness in both conferencing and victim-offender mediation is higher than in the non-restorative justice system. Strang (2002) found that participation in conferences resulted in a high perception of procedural justice among the participants. De Mesmaecker's (2011) study found that no uniform answer can be provided to the question of whether participation in mediation positively or negatively affects perceptions of the criminal justice system.

4. Other Psychological Outcomes
Some researchers have specifically focused on the emotional restoration of the victims who participated in conferences. As Strang (2002) found, participating victims had reduced fear of being revictimized by the same offender; their feelings of fear, anger, and anxiety were reduced; they reported feelings of dignity, self-respect, and self-confidence; they felt they had received an apology from the offender; meanwhile, and most striking, the feelings of vengefulness and unresolved anger were much lower than for those who went to court. Although these positive impacts were reported in the majority of cases, the negative responses, which were found only in a minority of cases, could usually be attributed to poor practice. Overall, the victims' experiences in RJ programs were positive and supportive of their healing. However, these positive outcomes should not overshadow the negative impact these programs can have on victims (Vanfraechem and Bolivar 2015).
Although the above studies achieved methodological soundness and promising outcomes, they do not explain why victims' experiences and opinions have become so vital in assessing the success of an RJ program. They also failed to demonstrate which characteristics or features within the RJ programs satisfied the victims. Furthermore, which of the victims' needs have been met? If satisfying the victims has become the sole objective, why is RJ not incorporated into the whole package of victim support or victim services, rather than being branded separately?

2.2.2 The Offender

As a matter of fact, the most controversial issue in assessing RJ's impact on offenders has been whether reoffending rates, or recidivism, should be given weight. Because they are aware of the "what works" question, RJ advocates have been rather reluctant to make reducing reoffending their program target. Instead, they have suggested that the failure to reduce recidivism should not be used to criticize RJ programs. Yet to prove that a restorative justice process works at least as well or better than a conventional criminal justice process in countering reoffending, numerous research projects have been undertaken to examine the recidivism claim.

Early research very seldom found statistically significant decreases in recidivism (Kurki 2003). Davis, Tichane, and Grayson (1980, as cited in Kurki 2003), in their evaluation of the Brooklyn Dispute Resolution Center, found no difference between the mediation and the court group during a 4-month follow-up period using random sampling. Another research study by Umbreit et al. (1994) also did not reveal significant differences in reoffending between the mediation and the control group (18% vs. 27%) within 1 year. Research at a later period by Nugent and Paddock (1995, 1996, cited in Kurki 2003) and Wiinamaki (1997, cited in Kurki 2003) found reductions in recidivism within a 1-year follow-up period. L.W. Sherman et al. (2000) reported that across the four types of offenses and offenders in RISE (drunk drivers of all ages, violent offenders up to age 29, juvenile property offenders, and juvenile property offenders having organizational victims), only the group of violent offenders were found to have a significant reduction in the average rate of offending in the post-referral period, while the other groups reported no significant court-conference differences.

Shapland et al. (2008) evaluated three schemes in England (CONNECT, JRC, and REMEDI) for adult offenders, some of whom were convicted of very serious offenses. They not only looked at whether the offenders had been reconvicted but also at the differences with relation to the frequency of convictions, the seriousness of convictions, and the cost of offending over a 2-year period. Their research found that offenders who participated in restorative justice (comparing group) committed statistically fewer offenses than the court group (control group), although the overall result for the likelihood of reconviction was not statistically significant. There were variations across the three groups in terms of the cost of convictions and the likelihood and the severity of reconvictions. In terms of "what works for whom," their study provided no evidence that restorative justice works better or worse for any particular demographic group, although the study found a significant relationship between several measures of reoffending and the offenders' views about the conference. In other words, the conference experience itself and the communication with the victim had affected the likelihood of the offenders' reconviction.

Research by Morris and Maxwell (1997) and Maxwell and Morris (1999) also indicated that certain aspects of the conferencing process may reduce the probability of reconviction. The influencing factors were offenders who had apologized, who had participated in conferences that were also attended by the victims, and who felt that they had made amends to their victim. Maxwell and Morris' (2001) research, although based on a relatively small sample of offenders 6 years after their conferences in 1990/1991, found that conferences could contribute toward decreasing the chance of reoffending. The factors related to the conferences were the following: the young people felt they had not been made to feel like bad people; they felt involved in the conference decision-making; they agreed with the conference outcome and completed the tasks to which they had agreed; they felt remorseful for what they had done; they met the victim and apologized to him/her; and they felt they had repaired the damage they had caused. Maxwell and Morris' (2002) study on two other community panel schemes (Project Turnaround and Te Whanau Awhina) also found that restorative processes and practices can have a positive impact on reducing reoffending.

Hayes and Daly (2003), in evaluating South Australian Juvenile Justice (SAJJ), aimed to explain the variability in reoffending based on the variability in the conference process instead of comparing the different effects of court or conference on reoffending. "Restorativeness" was measured by observing how young people behaved during the conference, and procedural justice was measured by observing how the conference was managed. Concurring with Maxwell and Morris' (2001) research in New Zealand, SAJJ also found that conference-specific factors, particularly the offender's remorse and involvement in decision-making, were indicative of reduced reoffending. However, Maxwell and Morris' (2001) study did not supply evidence that identified the elements of the process that induced remorse or that stressed the importance of expressed disapproval in generating remorse. Also, given the small number of interviews, a link between the expression of disapproval and the reported feelings of shame, and reoffending and reintegration, could not be made.

Two additional studies by Latimer et al. (2001, 2005) and Bonta et al. (2006) used meta-analysis to examine the effectiveness of RJ practices in reducing recidivism. Latimer et al. (2005) conducted a meta-analysis of 35 individual restorative justice programs, which showed that restorative justice programs yielded reductions in recidivism, and when compared to the control groups, their results were significantly more successful during the follow-up periods.

Bonta et al. (2006) research covered a broader range of programs, such as court-imposed restitution and community service, as well as newer interventions. Thirty-nine studies met the criteria for inclusion in the review. According to their meta-analysis, on the whole, the effects of RJ interventions on reducing recidivism are relatively small but significant, while court-ordered RJ programs have no impact on recidivism. Moreover, RJ interventions seem to be more effective with low-risk offenders but may be ineffective for high-risk offenders.

Iivari's (2010) research on mediation in Finland reported that face-to-face mediation showed the offenders the consequences of their actions in concrete terms and increased their willingness to provide reparations. According to this study, most of the offenders stated that mediation had discouraged or at least postponed their commission of new offenses.

The relatively new program designed for serious sexual offenders called COSA (Circles of Support and Accountability), which originated in Canada, was established to help released sexual offenders to be better reintegrated into the community and to empower local communities to take responsibility for ensuring that known sex offenders are held accountable (Wilson 2014). In the UK, the model has largely relied on volunteers who have experienced child sexual abuse themselves to create a "community of care" for these offenders. It has been reported that these pilot projects have achieved approximately 90% compliance among registered sex offenders.

The research on recidivism has been extensive, but evidence suggesting that the restorative justice process leads to less reoffending still lacks a strong ground. Returning to theory, especially the reintegrative shaming theory, we are empirically unsure of how the restorative justice process helps the offender to desist from further offending. In particular, in the field, it remains unclear whether the process itself induces the offenders' remorse and sense of shame and whether and how a "reintegration" ceremony, if any, works to prevent further deviance. All of these questions deserve a qualitative examination, as there have been no structured observations on the essential elements of restorative justice. Kurki (2003, p. 297) provided a list of the elements that await further exploration: genuine remorse, apology, consensus, expression of feelings, better understanding of each other, and the like. Walgrave's (2011) suggestion that the questions of "how it works" and "why it works" deserve much more research also rings true.

2.2.3 The Community

It might be unfortunate for RJ that there have rarely been any evaluation studies on how and to what extent communities have benefited from RJ programs. The floating nature of the community may be a reason for this. For instance, the "community" may refer to the support persons on the offender's or the victim's side or to representatives from the local community that have been impacted by the crime. In addition, there seems to be no instrument available to measure the healing of the community. A more serious problem, however, may lie in the participation of the community itself in Western societies, e.g., the difficulties in locating and inviting persons from the community. The role of community representatives in RJ programs has not yet been empirically tested.

2.3 A Process Approach to Restoration

The overwhelming interest in RJ programs demonstrates a strong tendency to restrict restorative justice to a process and efforts to evaluate the satisfaction of participants, and the reduction of recidivism have been unevenly distributed. The restorative justice dialogue itself remains largely unknown in empirical terms with a few exceptions, i.e., Rossner (2011) and Rossner et al. (2013).

The studies, more or less, deal with many aspects of restoration in terms of Braithwaite's republican understanding: "restoring property loss, restoring injury, restoring a sense of security, restoring dignity, restoring a sense of empowerment, restoring deliberative democracy, restoring harmony based on a feeling that justice has been done, and restoring social support" (Braithwaite 2002, p. 12). However, it would be both naïve and unrealistic to expect that a restorative encounter alone could have all these "restoring" effects. Even when restoration is claimed to have been achieved, it remains unknown whether it results from the process itself or from other reasons.

The research has been obsessed with the effects of RJ processes, while the impact of RJ programs in terms of how the outcome of a restorative encounter is related to the decisions has not drawn any attention. Because the restorative justice movement arose as an alternative option for dealing with crime and harmful behaviors, these studies could produce the perception that the criminal justice system is unnecessary and unimportant, despite the fact that the bifurcation between the criminal justice system and restorative justice has been criticized (Daly 2001, 2013).

There is no doubt that a RJ process in the criminal justice context is conceived as consensual, as an option, whereby the affected parties can find a solution on their own, facilitated by an impartial and independent third person. Restoring means giving parties the space to participate in the process and to reach an agreement, through communication, about how to resolve the issue. Thus, the "zero-sum" game or harm infliction situation in the conventional justice system can be reversed to a "win-win" or a harm reparation situation. Through a restorative encounter, the offender gains an understanding of the harm that he/she has caused and the victim maximally retains his/her right to reparations. Moreover, the face-to-face (or indirect) dialogue with the victim also helps the offender recognize his mistakes and hence take responsibility.

3 Restoration Model

Not surprisingly, it is believed that restoration can only be achieved by respecting and enforcing a set of values and principles or adhering to a standard set of practices. The degree of restorativeness, proposed and depicted by McCold and Wachtel's (2002) restorative practices typology, depends on the degree to which the stakeholders (the victims, the offenders, their communities of care) are involved in meaningful emotional exchange and decision-making. The more they are involved, the more restorative the approach becomes. Therefore, a restoration model can be constructed that acts as a forum where the participants can exchange feelings, opinions, and ideas. Sustained by values such as respect, inclusion, and healing, which we addressed in the previous chapter, restoration also must be built upon voluntariness, neutrality, empowerment, and storytelling.

3.1 Voluntariness: What Is Required of Victims and Offenders

The UN Basic Principles on the Use of Restorative Justice Programmes in Criminal Matters (United Nations 2002, II. No.6) specify that "Restorative justice should be used only where there is sufficient evidence to charge the offender and with the free and voluntary consent of the victim and the offender. The victim and the offender should be able to withdraw such consent at any time during the process. Agreements should be arrived at voluntarily and should contain only reasonable and proportionate obligations."

The victim cannot be forced to attend in any case. To address the low attendance rate on the side of the victim, some scholars have suggested various ways of increasing the visibility of RJ in the wider society, including its accessibility to the victim. The idea of using coercion has generally been abandoned, because restoration arises solely from the voluntary nature of the program.

The voluntariness of the offender is built upon his/her admission of the criminal facts and on agreeing to make direct reparations to the victim. Some issues have been raised: To what degree is an offender "coerced" to attend under the threat of a possible criminal sanction? While admitting that offenders may be pressured because the offer comes from a criminal justice agency, some have argued that it is the offender himself (including his lawyer) who decides whether to contact the mediation organization or whether he can be contacted by the mediator by consenting to leave his contact details (Laxminarayan 2014).

Both the victim and the offender can decide to withdraw, and all the decisions arising out of the process ensue from their own deliberations and negotiations. A commonly held opinion is that forcing people to attend (or to participate indirectly) will not lead to a genuine communication process and is unlikely to achieve the goal of restoration (Vanfraechem 2007). On this account, the micro-context of the deliberation process between different stakeholders echoes Habermas's deliberative democracy, although there have been few studies of the degree to which participants appreciate being able to have an influence on the procedures of mediation (De Mesmaecker 2013).

3.2 Neutrality: The Role of the Facilitator/Mediator

Neutrality is a requirement imposed on the facilitator/mediator involved in the restorative process. The UN Principles define the facilitator as "a person whose role is to facilitate, in a fair and impartial manner, the participation of the parties in a restorative process." In the European context, in general, mediators are trained, neutral, and impartial third parties. For example, Recommendation N° R (99)19 on mediation in penal matters of the Council of Europe requires that "mediation should be performed in an impartial manner, based on the facts of the case and on the needs and wishes of the parties" (Article 26). In the Macmillan English Dictionary, "neutrality" has two semantic meanings: the state of not supporting either side in a war, disagreement, etc. and behavior that does not show strong feelings or opinions. Both seem relevant to an understanding of neutrality in a legal process. The facilitator/mediator should not favor one side in deciding on the agreement and should remain equal and upright. However, it is true that no third party is neutral in every sense of the word, because all third parties have their own sets of values. Yet the third party can still be neutral regarding the outcome and the behaviors of the parties within a given range of acceptability (Tidwell 2001).

Here, questions arise with regard to the role of the police in restorative encounters. In both the Wagga Wagga model and the Thames Valley cautioning model, the police led the conferencing as the facilitators. There is no lack of public support for the strong policing character of these encounters, as many people believe that offending should be responded to in an authoritative way. However, RJ scholars oppose it, fearing that police authoritarianism may intrude on the restorative process in nonverbal ways (Young 2001).

3.3 Empowerment: Promise to Victims

Zehr (2002) wrote that "restorative justice is more focused on needs: the victims, the need of communities, the needs of offenders" (p. 18). Victims' needs are of the highest order and have a central place in RJ approaches to crime. It has been suggested that "one aspect of trauma of crime is that the offence and the offender take away power over one's emotional life" (Sawin and Zehr 2007, p. 45); for restoration to take place, the victims "need a sense of control or involvement in the resolution of their own cases" (Zehr 1990, p. 28), which comprises "control over their properties, their bodies, their emotions, their dreams" (Zehr 2002, p. 17).

The empowerment of victims in RJ denounces the forms of secondary victimization to which victims are subject when they attend court procedures. One of its disadvantages for the victim is the role passive engagement plays in conventional criminal procedure. Consequently, the victim's sense of control is further damaged.

Bush and Folger (1994, p. 2) noted that "in simplest terms, empowerment means the restoration to individuals of a sense of their own value and strength and their own capacity to handle life's problems." Empowerment can only be achieved through voluntary and positive participation in the restorative process, in which the victim is given the opportunity for his voice to be heard. The victim cannot be interrupted when speaking, and he feels that his opinion has been taken into account in deciding the outcome of the restorative encounter. In cases involving an indirect meeting, his message should be conveyed to the offender. Aertsen et al. (2011) argued, however, that empowerment implies not merely being able to express feelings but also to be able to "act upon one's environment." Accordingly, Sawin and Zehr (2007) suggested that empowerment is "not only the power to participate but also the ability to draw upon needed resources to make a decision and to follow through on that decision" (p. 48).

3.4 *Storytelling: What Is Supposed to Happen*

Pranis (1998, as cited in Sawin and Zehr 2007, p. 57) reflected on the relationship between storytelling and empowerment: "Listening to someone's story is a way of empowering them, of validating their intrinsic worth as a human being." From the early Mennonite practices to the current mediation in the European context, storytelling is about allowing people to talk about their experiences. Encouraging victims to explain the impact the offense has had on them has been found to have a healing effect. Unlike the victim impact statements used in the American and Dutch legal systems, the storytelling in RJ encounters is "dual directional" in that the victims, in addition to supplying an account of the crime impact, can pose questions to the offenders face-to-face. Arguably, it is not simply their "stories" but also the way that their "stories" are told that enables the process to be restorative for them. Equally, the offender and his supporters (notably his family) should have the space to respond to the victims' questions and to have their own concerns and feelings addressed as well. The advantage of storytelling is that it not only has a function of inclusiveness but also has the potential to transform the relationships between the participants (Parkinson and Roche 2004).

3.5 An Intermediate Reflection

The restoration model found in restorative justice stands out as a way of "doing justice" in today's Western societies, although it claims to have roots in the processes for resolving conflicts in both premodern times and present day indigenous non-Western societies. The communication process, which embraces approaches categorized as restorative, is not value-free. Tidwell (2001, p. 149) argued that "most processes of conflict resolution grow from and support the ideals of democratic liberalism." As he suggested, it is the philosophical foundations and consensus of values that contribute to success in resolving conflicts. Walgrave (2008, p. 99) advanced the notion that "social life ethics," on the basis of respect, solidarity, and responsibility, "[deal with] how citizens participate decisively in the way society and community are governed through social, economic, welfare and cultural policies, and about how they are committed and interact in daily life." The RJ processes we have presented so far in this and the preceding chapter have been fundamentally shaped by the broad context of democratic liberal societies. This context also makes the promotion of RJ possible as a way to deal with intercultural conflict in a Europe characterized by multiculturalism and diversity.

The stepping stone for democratic liberalism is that individual rights and freedoms are respected. Doing justice in a restorative way requires each individual's free consent to be sought and secured. Not only is equal participation necessary, but also no one can exercise dominant power in the deliberation process leading to the decision-making. This approach inevitably echoes the broader political and social context in democratic societies (Parkinson and Roche 2004).

However, the weaknesses in this restoration model are worthy of attention. First, in this concept, society appears to be absent, or in other words, the voice of the society is ignored in this restoration model. As a community-based approach, the community (or the society) should be equally if not more important than the other parties. However, in the predominant RJ processes and models, the restoration of the community is so abstract that it seems to indicate that "if both sides are restored, so is the community." If this is true, then what is needed is probably not RJ but victim support or offender assistance programs.

Second, in this restoration model, the victims' needs and satisfaction are given a paramount place. Zehr, who is considered a zealous spiritual leader in the RJ movement, strongly called for victims' needs to be met (Zehr 2002). Admittedly, today, it is almost impossible to dissociate the emergence of RJ from the victim movement. Yet it is argued here that a harm-focused approach does not necessarily indicate a "victim orientation." Indeed, showing solidarity with others' sufferings is salient in an individual right-based society. However, both victimology and the RJ field may need to reflect on the labeling process of the victim and maintain distance from the stereotypical notions of victims (Van Dijk 2009). Luckily, there is a concurrent reflection about whether the translation of victims' interests into rights can best address victims' experiences and expectations, as victims' advocates may believe (Pemberton and Vanfraechem 2015). It is possible that a different society may have a different notion of victims and victimization; hence, one needs to bear in mind other approaches to restoring victims. For example, Riger (1993) argued that underlying the concept of empowerment is individualism, where individual interests lie above those of the group. Thus, in another society, in which individuals' conformity to the group or the community is greatly valued, the idea of individual empowerment may lose its applicability.

The above analysis brings us to a fundamental question: To what extent is this restoration model suitable for other societies that do not concur with liberal traditions? The question regarding RJ's cultural variability was examined by Hamlin and Hokamura (2014) in terms of implementing an RJ model in Japan. Cultural difference is an important issue for RJ: If it has roots in non-Western societies, then how can it reenter these societies, or is this return not really necessary? In the next chapter, we will examine whether this model is feasible in today's Chinese society. Before doing so, we need to examine two diverging conceptions of RJ: the maximalist and the minimalist understandings.

4 A Maximalist or Minimalist Understanding of Restoration

In a nutshell, the core concepts of restoration have remained difficult and complicated. There are at least two dimensions of restoration that play an active role as depicted in the RJ story. First is the "satisfaction" of the clients. Restorative justice programs, such as mediation, are conceived as a service offered to clients – the general public in the society and the consumers of the conventional criminal justice system. Just as criminal agencies "are being conjoined to care about lay people using their 'services'" (Jefferson and Shapland 1990, p. 12, as cited in Mawby and Walklate 1994), restorative justice also sells its restorative ideas and practices and uses the clients' satisfaction as a measure of its intended outcome. In so doing, it exposes itself to the suspicion that satisfaction is used to compare it with the "services" provided by the conventional criminal justice system, rather than as a real indication of restoration. Among these clients, the most numerous have been the victims and offenders but primarily the victims. According to Zehr (2002), the needs of the victims must be addressed first. Contrary to the needs of victims propagated by law-and-order politicians and campaigners, RJ focuses on the concrete needs of individual victims and the elements that are the most important for them. In doing this, RJ stands as a humanistic approach that takes victims into account and initiates the road to recovery for them.

The second dimension of restoration, which is usually neglected, but obvious in mediation within the criminal context, is probably related to the social order itself. As suggested by the very few in-depth studies, the need for a quick response (despite the need for much more time) to less serious crimes or even felonies explains why judicial authorities try to use alternative measures. Nevertheless, the benefits of RJ for the state, for instance, in countering the problem of overcrowded prisons, seem to have been diluted in the wake of the sweeping literature that has focused on individual victims and offenders.

This divide in the concept of restoration – the focus on victims as consumers or the focus on societal interests – can be seen as a reflection of contrasting concerns about whether coercive sanctions can be accepted in a restorative frame. McCold (2000) rejected the possible inclusion of coercive sanctions because it would shift restorative justice back toward punitiveness, while Daly (2000) and Duff (2003) integrated the restorative models into a punishment philosophy. Walgrave (2003) agreed with using coerced restorative sanctions but disagreed with Duff in that he believed punishment is not necessary to achieve restoration.

The contrasting views on restorative justice are later described as "purist" (or minimalist) and "maximalist." The former attaches significance to the encounter between the perpetrator, the offended, and other stakeholders. Advocates of the purist approach argue that the parties to a crime should be offered an opportunity to meet and decide about what is the most satisfactory response to that crime. The reasons why the proponents of restorative justice argue in favor of encounters vary, but the most convincing may be that "such processes are useful for achieving a whole range of beneficial outcomes" (Johnstone and Van Ness 2007, p. 10). In other words, what restoration means in a specific context is determined by the deliberations of the stakeholders (Dignan 2003).

The maximalist, outcome-oriented adherents of RJ attach importance to repairing the harm from the crime as much as possible. The way of responding to the crime should be oriented toward healing and empowering, because victimization results in a series of impacts on the victims' lives and well-being. Crime also disturbs the offender and the community as such. Traditional criminal justice systems, which impose pain on the offenders, are neither necessary nor sufficient (Johnstone and Van Ness 2007). RJ advocates may also adhere to the transformative value of the resolution of the crime. They believe that the ultimate goal of this restorative process is to transform the relationship one has with others and with society at large. In this respect, the interests of society should be served as well. Without doubt, the negative incident of crime is conceived as providing a great opportunity.

The different conceptions of RJ mentioned above do not contrast with each other fundamentally; rather, they only vary in emphasis. Both embrace encounter, repair, and transformation (Johnstone and Van Ness 2007). All would agree that communication processes, dialogue, and deliberation are essential to restorative justice. As a maximalist, Walgrave (2003) believed that face-to-face, informal, and voluntary meetings provide the best prospects for restoration.

This unsettled issue regarding the minimalist and maximalist views was revisited in a recent overview study of RJ and mediation in 36 European countries. While adopting the maximalist vision of restorative justice, which may include imposed reparation orders, community service orders, or legal provisions allowing prosecutorial or court diversion on the grounds that amends have been made, Dünkel et al. (2015) also acknowledged that these initiatives "have to be performed voluntarily, implemented in a manner that is neither stigmatizing nor repressive, and should not to be classified as forms of punishment, but rather as interventions that serve to foster offender responsibility and reintegration through the experience of making amends" (p. 8).

References

Aertsen, I., Bolivar, D., De Mesmaecker, V., & Lauwers, N. (2011). Restorative justice and the active victim: Exploring the concept of empowerment. *Temida Journal on Victimisation, Human Rights and Gender, 14*(1), 5–19.

Bonta, J., Jesseman, R., Rugge, T., & Cormier, R. (2006). Restorative justice and recidivism: Promises made, promises kept. In D. Sullivan & L. Tifft (Eds.), *Handbook of restorative justice: A global perspective* (Vol. 108–120). London/New York: Routledge.

Braithwaite, J. (2002). *Restorative justice and responsive regulation*. Oxford: Oxford University Press.

Bush, R. A. B., & Folger, J. P. (1994). *The promise of mediation: Responding to conflict through empowerment and recognition*. San Francisco, CA: Jossey-Bass.

Campbell, C., Devlin, R., O'Mahony, D., Doak, J., Jackson, J., Corrigan, T., et al. (2005). *Evaluation of the northern Ireland youth conference service*. NIO research and Statistical Series: Report No. 12. Belfast: Statistics and Research Branch of the Northern Ireland Office.

Coates, R. B., & Gehm, J. (1989). Victim meets offender: An empirical assessment. In M. Wright & B. Galaway (Eds.), *Mediation and criminal justice*. London: Sage.

Crawford, A., & Newburn, T. (2003). *Youth offending and restorative justice: Implementing reform in youth justice*. Cullompton: Willan Publishing.

Crawford, A., & Newburn, T. (2013). *Youth offending and restorative justice*. Cullompton: Willan Publishing.

Crosland, P., & Liebmann, M. (2003). *40 cases: Restorative justice and victim-offender mediation*. Bristol: Mediation UK.

Daly, K. (2000). Revisiting the relationship between retributive and restorative justice. In H. Strang & J. Braithwaite (Eds.), *Restorative justice: From philosophy to practice* (pp. 33–54). Dartmouth: Ashgate.

Daly, K. (2001). Conferencing in Australia and New Zealand: Variations, research findings and prospects. In A. Morris & G. Maxwell (Eds.), *Restorative justice for juveniles: Conferencing, mediation & circles* (pp. 59–83). Oxford/Portland, OR: Hart Publishing.

Daly, K. (2013). The punishment debate in restorative justice. In *The Sage handbook of punishment and society* (pp. 356–375). London: Sage Publications.

De Mesmaecker, V. (2011). *Perceptions of justice and fairness in criminal proceedings and restorative encounters: Extending theories of procedural justice*. Leuven: KU Leuven.

De Mesmaecker, V. (2013). Victim-offender mediation participants' opinions on the restorative justice values of confidentiality, impartiality and voluntariness. *Restorative Justice: An International Journal, 1*(3), 334–361. doi:10.5235/20504721.1.3.334.

Dignan, J. (2003). Towards a systemic model of restorative justice: Reflections on the concept, its context and the need for clear constraints. In A. v. Hirsch, J. Roberts, A. E. Bottoms, K. Roach, & M. Schiff (Eds.), *Restorative justice & criminal justice: Competing or reconcilable paradigms?* (pp. 135–156). Oxford/Portland, OR: Hart Publishing.

Doak, J., & O'Mahony, D. (2006). The vengeful victim? Assessing the attitudes of victims participating in restorative youth conferencing. *International Review of Victimology, 13*(2), 157–177.

Duff, A. (2003). Restoration and retribution. In A. v. Hirsch, J. V. Roberts, & A. Bottoms (Eds.), *Restorative justice and criminal justice: Competing or reconcilable paradigms?* (Vol. 43–59). Oxford/Portland, OR: Hart Publishing.

Dünkel, F., Grzywa-Holten, J., & Horsfield, P. (Eds.). (2015). *Restorative Justice and Mediation in Penal Matters in Europe: A stock-taking of legal issues, implementation strategies and outcomes in 36 European countries*. Mönchengladbach: Forum Verlag Godesberg GmbH.

Fellegi, B., & Szegö, D. (2013). *Handbook for facilitating peacemaking circles*. Budapest: PT Mũhely.

Hamlin, J. B., & Hokamura, A. (2014). The cultural context of restorative justice: Journeys through our cultural forests to a well-spring of healing. *International Journal for Semiot Law, 2014*(27), 291–310.

Hayes, H., & Daly, K. (2003). Youth justice conferencing and reoffending. *Justice Quarterly, 20*(4), 725–764. doi:10.1080/07418820300095681.

Iivari, J. (2010). Providing mediation as a nation-wide service: Empirical research on restorative justice in Finland. In I. Vanfraechem, I. Aertsen, & J. Willemsens (Eds.), *Restorative justice realities: Empirical research in a European context* (pp. 95–120). The Hague: Eleven International Publishing.

Johnstone, G., & Van Ness, D. (Eds.). (2007). *Handbook of restorative justice*. Cullompton: Willan Publishing.

Kurki, L. (2003). Evaluating restorative justice practices. In A. Von Hirsch, J. Roberts, A. E. Bottoms, K. Roach, & M. Schiff (Eds.), *Restorative justice and criminal justice: Competing or reconcilable paradigms* (pp. 293–314). Oxford: Hart Publishing.

Latimer, J., Dowden, C., & Muise, D. (2001). *The effectiveness of restorative justice practices: A meta-analysis*. Ottawa: Canadian Department of Justice.

Latimer, J., Dowden, C., & Muise, D. (2005). The effectiveness of restorative justice practices: A meta-analysis. *The Prison Journal, 85*(2), 127–144. doi:10.1177/0032885505276969.

Lauwaert, K., & Blad, J. (2010). Evidence based policies? In I. Vanfraechem, I. Aertsen, & J. Willemsens (Eds.), *Restorative justice realities. Empirical research in a European context* (pp. 185–216). The Hague: Eleven International Publishing.

Laxminarayan, M. (2014). *Accessibility and initiation of restorative justice*. Leuven: European Forum for Restorative Justice.

Liebmann, M. (2007). *Restorative justice: How it works*. London: Jessica Kingsley Publishers.

Mawby, R. I., & Walklate, S. (1994). *Critical victimology: International perspectives*. London: Sage Publications.

Maxwell, G., & Morris, A. (2001). Family group conferences and reoffending. In A. Morris & G. Maxwell (Eds.), *Restorative justice for juveniles: Conferencing, mediation and circles* (pp. 243–263). Oxford: Hart Publishing.

Maxwell, G., & Morris, A. (2002). Restorative justice and reconviction. *Contemporary Justice Review, 5*(2), 133–146. doi:10.1080/10282580212702.

Maxwell, G. M., & Morris, A. (1993). *Families, victims and culture: Youth justice in New Zealand*. Wellington: Social Policy Agency and Institute of Criminology, Victoria University of Wellington.

Maxwell, G. M., & Morris, A. (1999). *Understanding Reoffending*. Wellington: Institute of Criminology.

McCold, P. (2000). Toward a holistic vision of restorative juvenile justice: A reply to the maximalist model. *Contemporary Justice Review, 3*(4), 357–414.

McCold, P., & Wachtel, T. (2002). Restorative justice theory validation. In E. Weitekamp & H.-J. Kerner (Eds.), *Restorative justice: Theoretical foundations* (pp. 110–142). Cullompton: Willan Publishing.

Miers, D. R., Maguire, M., Goldie, S., Sharpe, K., Hale, C., Netten, A., et al. (2001). *An exploratory evaluation of restorative justice schemes* (Vol. 9). London: Home Office.

Morris, A., & Maxwell, G. (2000). The practice of family group conferences in New Zealand: Assessing the place, potential and pitfalls of restorative justice. In A. Crawford & J. Goodey (Eds.), *Integrating a victim perspective within criminal justice: International debates* (pp. 207–226). Aldershot: Ashgate Publishing.

Morris, A., & Maxwell, G. M. (1997). *Family group conferences and convictions*. Occasional Papers in Criminology New Series: No. 5. Wellington: Institute of Criminology.

Newburn, T., & Britain, G. (2002). *The introduction of referral orders into the youth justice system: Final report*. London: Home Office Research, Development and Statistics Directorate.

Parkinson, J., & Roche, D. (2004). Restorative justice: Deliberative democracy in action? *Australian Journal of Political Science, 39*(3), 505–518. doi:10.1080/1036114042000295101.

Pemberton, A., & Vanfraechem, I. (2015). Victims' victimization experiences and their need for justice. In I. Vanfraechem, D. Bolivar, & I. Aertsen (Eds.), *Victims and restorative justice* (pp. 15–47). London/New York: Routledge.

Riger, S. (1993). What's wrong with empowerment. *American Journal of Community Psychology, 21*(3), 279–292.

Rossner, M. (2011). Emotions and interaction ritual: A micro analysis of restorative justice. *British Journal of Criminology, 51*(1), 95–119. doi:10.1093/bjc/azq075.

Rossner, M., Bruce, J., & Meher, M. M. (2013). *The process and dynamics of restorative justice: Research on forum sentencing*. Sydney: University of Western Sydney.

Sawin, J. L., & Zehr, H. (2007). The ideas of engagement and empowerment. In G. Johnstone & D. W. V. Ness (Eds.), *Handbook of restorative justice* (pp. 41–58). London/New York: Routledge.

Shapland, J. (2003). Restorative justice and criminal justice: Just responses to crime? In J. V. R. Andrew von Hirsch & A. Bottoms (Eds.), *Restorative justice and criminal justice: Competing or reconcilable paradigms?* (pp. 195–217). Oxford: Hart Publishing.

Shapland, J., Atkinson, A., Atkinson, H., Dignan, J., Edwards, L., Hibbert, J., et al. (2008). *Does restorative justice affect reconviction. The fourth report from the evaluation of three schemes*. London: Ministry of Justice.

Sherman, L. W., & Strang, H. (2007). *Restorative justice: The evidence*. London: Smith Institute.

Sherman, L. W., Strang, H., & Woods, D. J. (2000). *Recidivism patterns in the Canberra reintegrative shaming experiments (RISE)*. Canberra: Centre for Restorative Justice, Australian National University.

Strang, H. (2002). *Repair or revenge: Victims and restorative justice*. Oxford: Clarendon Press.

Strang, H., Barnes, G., Braithwaite, J., & Sherman, L. (1999). *Experiments in restorative policing: A progress report on the Canberra reintegrative shaming experiments (RISE)*. Canberra: Australian National University.

Tidwell, A. (2001). *Conflict resolved?: A critical assessment of conflict resolution*. London: Bloomsbury Publishing.

Umbreit, M. S., Coates, R. B., & Kalanj, B. (1994). *Victim meets offender: The impact of restorative justice and mediation*. Monsey, NY: Criminal Justice Press.

Umbreit, M. S., Coates, R. B., & Vos, B. (2001). Victim impact of meeting with young offenders: Two decades of victim offender mediation practice and research. In A. Morris & G. Maxwell (Eds.), *Restorative justice for juveniles: Conferencing, mediation and circles* (pp. 121–143). Oxford: Hart Publishing.

Umbreit, M. S., Coates, R. B., & Vos, B. (2006). Victim offender mediation: An evolving evidence-based practice. In D. Sullivan & L. Tifft (Eds.), *Handbook of restorative justice: A global perspective* (pp. 52–62). London/New York: Routledge.

Umbreit, M. S., Coates, R. B., & Vos, B. (2007). Restorative justice dialogue: A multi-dimensional, evidence-based practice theory. *Contemporary Justice Review, 10*(1), 23–41. doi:10.1080/10282580601157521.

Umbreit, M. S., Vos, B., Coates, R. B., & Lightfoot, E. (2005). Restorative justice in the twenty-first century: A social movement full of opportunities and pitfalls. *Marquette Law Review, 89*, 251.

United Nations (2002). *Basic Principles on the Use of Restorative Justice Programmes in Criminal Matters*. New York.

Van Dijk, J. (2009). Free the victim: A critique of the western conception of victimhood. *International Review of Victimology, 16*(1), 1–33.

Vanfraechem, I. (2007). Community, society and state in restorative justice: An exploration. In R. Mackay, M. Bosnjak, J. Deklerck, C. Pelikan, B. v. Stokkom, & M. Wright (Eds.), *Images of restorative justice theory* (pp. 73–91). Frankfurt am Main: Verlag fur Polizeiwissenschaft.

Vanfraechem, I., & Bolivar, D. (2015). Restorative justice and victims of crime. In I. Vanfraechem, D. Bolivar, & I. Aertsen (Eds.), *Victims and restorative justice* (pp. 48–75). London/New York: Routledge.

Walgrave, L. (2003). Imposing restoration instead of inflicting pain: Reflections on the judicial reaction to crime. In A. v. Hirsch, J. v. Roberts, A. Bttoms, K. Roach, & M. Schiff (Eds.), *Restorative justice and criminal justice: Competing or reconcilable paradigms?* (pp. 61–78). Oxford: Hart Publishing.

Walgrave, L. (2008). *Restorative justice, self-interest and responsible citizenship*. Cullompton: Willan Publishing.
Walgrave, L. (2011). Investigating the potentials of restorative justice practice. *Journal of Law & Policy, 36*(9), 91–139.
Wilson, C. (2014). *The restorative nature of circles of support and accountability.* Paper presented at the Exploring the potential of restorative justice for sexual violence, Leuven, Belgium, November 12–14, 2014.
Young, R. (2001). Just cops doing "shameful" Business?: Police-led restorative justice and the lessons of research. In A. Morris & G. Maxwell (Eds.), *Restorative justice for juveniles: Conferencing, mediation & circles* (pp. 195–225). Oxford/Portland, OR: Hart Publishing.
Zehr, H. (1990). *Changing lenses: A new focus for crime and justice*. Scottdale, PA: Herald Press.
Zehr, H. (2002). *The little book of restorative justice*. Intercourse, PA: Good Books.

Chapter 10
A Dialogue Between China and the West on Doing Restorative Justice

1 Introduction

This chapter is dedicated to making the dialogue between China and the West on doing justice in a restorative way more constructive and fruitful. In highlighting and bringing together the previous chapters, we will start with the following questions: In what ways do China's mediation practices diverge and converge vis-à-vis the assumptions and concepts of RJ in the West? Does China need the Western RJ model? If the answer is yes, how likely is it that restorative justice processes will be implemented in China?

2 Does China Need the Restoration Model?

This study starts with the domestic scholar's question of whether to adopt "restorative justice or not." From a Western perspective, the Chinese harmony approach to conflict and the dependence on the authority over individual choice seem contrary to the application of the Western model of RJ. It is indeed pointed out by Chinese scholars that a neutral communication process between the victim and the offender is lacking. Nevertheless, if we recognize that RJ has only been under development for a few decades in the West, it might be too early to exclude the practices in Chinese society from the RJ camp. Yet measuring another society's local practices and programs against a Western-centered conception is fundamentally flawed and leads to suspicions of colonialism. If we respect the domestic practice of any society and allow diversity, then there is not much concern about not conforming to the standard, as evidenced in the first chapter. It is not naïve to construct two, three, or even more sets of definitions of RJ. It is important not to impose the concept on any people who do not share the same ideology.

There is no intention here to replicate the efforts made by RJ advocates to trace its roots to any premodern Western society or non-Western indigenous societies, although

X. Yuan, *Restorative Justice in China*, Springer Series on Asian Criminology and Criminal Justice Research, DOI 10.1007/978-3-319-63922-2_10

Chinese history, which is characterized by the tension between Confucian benevolence and legalist punishment, paints a picture of RJ for humankind (Braithwaite 1999). Chinese legal history and culture have sustained community-based mediation up to the present. China's culturally embedded practices do not differ much from the definition of RJ as a community-based response to harm. The former emphasizes the engagement of all sides in resolving the problem to restore harmony for the sake of society. However, this is largely absent in the current restoration model in the West. Given the criticism of the lack of liberal rights raised by liberal scholars in China and abroad, this study stands as a conservative counterattack, calling for serious attention to be given to the preservation of the virtues of justice seeking.

Nevertheless, this study is not in favor of any "Orientalism" (Said 1978) that romanticizes the Chinese culture and approach and rejects any exchange. Westernization probably is not perceived to be as horrible a plague as it would have been 40 years ago, given the fact that the Chinese government is making great strides toward bringing its domestic legal system in line with Western models. It may be interesting for readers to know that, during our 5-month stay in the field, we occasionally heard and witnessed several related anecdotes: Some places were experimenting with the jury system, and during a lecture, several scholars called for the establishment of special courts for traffic disputes in China, inspired by the justice courts (治安法庭) in some states in America. There was an intern at court with a research topic on shared guardianship in divorce cases – another Western-inspired practice. While "looking to the West" is admirable, this study suggests that "looking to the East" is equally important.

Indeed, both the Western restoration model and Chinese mediation practices value harm restoration, although the latter attaches more importance to restoring harmony to the collective than to repairing the relationship between the victim, the offender, and the community. At this point, this study argues that if a harmonious society is to be built in contemporary China, the restoration model should be implemented.

In China, rising societal discord in the form of mass events (群体性事件) or group conflicts has entered domestic discussions and debates, despite heavy state control over the media. It is not that these different voices and opinions have disturbed social harmony; rather, the repression of these voices has stirred public dissatisfaction. The Chinese society of today is not the one of 40 years ago, in which totalitarianism prevailed, and it is not even like the one of 20 years ago, when Qiuju had to travel day and night to the city in order to seek justice. A more civilized and transparent Chinese criminal justice system is on the horizon. For example, the reeducation through labor (劳动教养), which had been in existence for half a century, was finally abolished at the end of 2013. The number of crimes that are subject to the death penalty in the criminal code has been reduced in recent years with every amendment (Hoyle and Miao 2014; Hood and Hoyle 2014).

On the other hand, it remains undisputed that the societal transformation China is currently experiencing is unprecedented. The result has been a gap between the rich and the poor, diversifying demands for interests and rights, and a rising awareness of individual freedom and autonomy. Indeed, there has been evidence indicating that China is departing from its communitarian roots to a more individualistic society (Anderson and Gil 1998; Rojek 2001; Lu and Miethe 2003). This is evident in the 2012 revision of the Law on Protection of the Rights and Interests of the Elderly, which made visits to elderly parents a legal obligation and was a sign that it needed reinforcement. What is evident in the current empirical study is that citizens have the need to express their opinions and feelings, to communicate and to be heard. Thus, the Western restoration model, as a participatory civic forum, has great potential for harmonizing interpersonal relationships and contributing to a healthy and harmonious society.

3 Implementing the Restoration Model in China

This study concurs with Hamlin and Hokamura (2014) conclusion that cultural considerations must be taken into account if RJ is to work in an Eastern culture. Nuances are likely if there is an attempt to implement the restoration model in China. Below, an analysis of the implementation of this model is offered. First, it takes the political, societal, and cultural conditions in China as a given fact. The idea is not to give them an overhaul but to bring them under the spotlight.

Chinese society is essentially communitarian, notwithstanding the gradual trend of disintegration spurred by economic development and modernization, and people recognize each other through various strands of relationships behind the "face." The "in group" or the "out group" differentiates the closeness in any social relationship. Group cohesion is prioritized over individual needs. Thus, the restoration model is primarily directed by what community harmony requires, rather than by individual desires.

This argument seems to preclude the government officials, in the vernacular, *gong jia ren* (公家人), who wield state power from being involved in the restorative process. However, given the fact that the restoration model is situated within the criminal justice system, contact with the "system" – the government officials – seems inevitable. In this context, it is likely that the presence of the state authority in the restorative process will result in additional humiliation. Although statute and policy limit their discretion, it is still advisable to situate the process as a diversion measure entrusted to a trained third party. The outcome reached through the process is then sent back to the justice system, and its supervision ensures that public interests are not violated. It requires, however, the mediator/facilitator at the community level to work independently of the justice system.

In the implementation of the restoration model, some of its typical features need to be adapted to Chinese societal and cultural conditions.

3.1 Impartiality

We start from the concept of impartiality. In democratic societies, the mediator/facilitator is often secured by NGOs or local services that are independent of the central state authority, with the aim of providing full participation and engagement of citizens or communities. The citizens are left with the decision-making capability. By contrast, as raised by many Western RJ scholars, the involvement of a police officer or other state authority may influence the impartiality of a mediator/facilitator, because they can make decisions, take sides, or use coercion.

Impartiality rests on the assumption that the victim and the offender have an equal footing. However, the criminal justice context determines that the offender is in a weaker position: An agreement successfully reached during the process will influence the final judicial decision regarding him. The labeling effect of the criminal justice system is quite stigmatizing. On the other hand, the cultural underpinnings seem to suggest that the victim's side has the moral upper hand, because he was wronged by another's behavior; however, the victim is supposed to pardon when the perpetrator has offered an apology and reparations. Hence, it is possible that the victim will appear assertive and have a strong opinion. While the benefit of the restorative process is that the victims have an opportunity to talk about their experiences, it is also important to avoid further harm to the offender. Thus, in principle, the mediator cannot take sides; but in reality, if attention is otherwise given to attaching blame to the offender's wrongful behavior, this may create a perception of being partial to the victim. In other words, the mediator/facilitator needs to be careful to consider the status of the relationship between the victim's side and the offender. Traditionally, in Chinese society, the mediator appears assertive and directive (Wang et al. 2007); hence, an adaptation can be made to place more trust in the citizens, enabling them to deal with the matter and make decisions on their own.

3.2 *Voluntariness*

The closer the conflict is to the end of the criminal justice spectrum, the lesser the degree of voluntariness the participants may have. Chinese practices have shown that when conflicts have remained in the mediation room, people have had more freedom to fail and have gone on to seek justice from the court. Certainly, pressure is felt by both sides at the police stage when the official sanction is pending. For instance, one threat by the police has been "if he does not accept mediation, we will lock him up."

Within the ongoing process, until the conflict moves into the courtroom, people have had less freedom because of the pressure they have felt: for the victim, either adopting the normal procedure or accepting the agreement with the offender, and for the offender, choosing between a prison sentence or a non-prison sentence.

Pressure was felt throughout the criminal justice settings. Although voluntariness in making reparations to the victims is used to assess the performance of the offender, the latter cannot be expected to enjoy the resulting pain. Economic compensation by the offender is meant to be a punishment; because it is pain that is imposed on him, how pleasant is it likely to be?

Thus, informed by practice, discussions on "voluntariness" as opposed to "coercion" should bear the criminal justice context in mind. Not all RJ scholars have rejected "coercion" as a proper institutional tool when a voluntary encounter has failed. Braithwaite's (2002) "should be on the broad base; on the narrower top, deterrence and incapacitation should be utilized only when the restorative attempts have failed. Indeed, the voluntariness in RJ programs comes in degrees, depending on the stage at which the restorative encounter is situated. Offenders may be less voluntary during the diversion or the presentence stages than at the post-sentencing stage.

3.3 Storytelling

Although individuals have an obligation to contribute to collective harmony, the process needs to begin with allowing the participants to ask questions and tell stories. A similar dialogue can be found in Chinese mediation practices; often, the mediation starts with "what has happened? What are both sides' arguments? And what are their ideas?" Yet in our field observation, the mediators were reluctant to allow both sides to argue about what happened, because this makes the final conclusion of the disputes more difficult. An authoritarian style also renders personal accounts of an individual's opinions and arguments less important. This study suggests that a more participatory forum should be available for citizens to express their opinions and feelings. Victims need to be acknowledged for their losses, both material and emotional.

Nevertheless, it is possible that a boundary should exist to circumscribe the ambit of storytelling; as we are reminded by L. W. Pye (1996), the Chinese act based on standards rather than feelings. Emotions constitute an important part of human feelings (人情), but the latter do not rest upon the former. It is essentially the "face" and human feelings that coordinate one's behavior and regulate the interaction. Thus, a victim is supposed to allow his perpetrator not to lose face if the latter is to be expected to behave in a better way (Hu 1944). The victim may explain his experiences but should avoid directly criticizing the offender for the sake of the latter's and his families' face.

Open communication, as an exchange of ideas and opinions – when it happened – was applauded and valued by the participants. The current study suggests that the primary concern for victims was that the offenders had truly realized the wrongfulness of their behavior and had learned a lesson. Whether this concern is addressed determines whether the victims can reach an agreement with the other side.

3.4 Empowerment or Power Balance

The idea of empowering victims through storytelling may not necessarily gain the same support in China, due to the cultural differences, i.e., an emphasis on mastery and control and an orientation toward interdependence and connectedness. In some RJ programs, the overemphasis on the victims' well-being in a restoration model has been criticized (Daems 2010). The assumption of the universality of the victims' trauma tends to ignore the coping strategies present in other cultures. The Chinese conception of "a mature man" is that he does not show emotion in front of those with whom he is unfamiliar, because doing so would publicly expose weakness in his character. Being judged as immature is something about which he would be teased and should feel ashamed (Lin 1936). This might not be easily apprehensible to a Westerner. To illustrate, an elder who is fond of ice cream and eats it in public would probably not be judged at all in the West, but a Chinese elder who still enjoys ice cream would not only lower his status by doing so but would also likely be the subject of laughter. Similarly, a person will express his true feelings within his family rather than openly share them with a stranger. This explains why therapeutic storytelling to empower victims may not be applicable in China.

Instead of empowering the individual, the family's opinions and needs must be taken into account. In the relationship that has been broken as a result of the event, there can be no winners, as both sides have suffered losses from the damaged harmony. To empower the victims, one should first ask who the victims are (Van Dijk 2009), though the answer is not very clear-cut in a damaged relationship and the boundaries between offenders and victims are sometimes blurred (Dignan 2005). To the extent that the crime affects the families of both sides, rebuilding the relationships concerns two families rather than two persons.

Rather than the empowerment of victims, the power balance is perhaps more urgent and predominant in Chinese practices in the current social context (Wu 2014). As a result of modernization and economic development, Chinese society is undergoing a transition from an "acquaintance society" to a "stranger society." The result is a low level of trust among citizens and a gap between the rich and the poor, which makes dialogue more difficult. This situation is exacerbated by the rising awareness of rights and the assertion of individual interests. The traditional value of *qing li* (feelings and reasonableness) and *rang bu.* (compromise) must yield to the modern discussion of money and interests. In RJ programs, victims can directly ask for reparations from the offenders, and the offenders can propose arguments concerning whether their requests are reasonable or not. However, they may fail to address the issue of the social inequalities that may be present in the restorative process.

3.4.1 Making a Decision or Dependence on the Authority

In Chinese history, the mediator was usually a person who had high moral standards and was well respected in the community. Not long ago, this moral authority was destroyed in the period of Communist China and was lost in the harsh campaigns launched against Confucianism, the climax being the Great Proletarian Cultural Revolution. Deference to moral authority was replaced by allegiance to the Communist Party (Rojek 1989, 2001). The mediators who used to sit on local mediation committees were replaced by party cadres, politically correct and eager to resolve matters for the masses. In spite of rejecting Confucianism, Mao was a genius in borrowing from the traditional social organizations in Confucianism and in creating a "mass line," in which power flowed from the bottom-up rather than the top-down (Rojek 2001). Following the "mass line," every social organization controlled by the party was required to be active in identifying disputes and extinguishing them. The institutionalization of the people's mediation committees during the early years of the socialist state tightened the control over Chinese society.

Although the satisfaction of both sides is highly important in RJ in the Western world, our study shows that this cannot be said in the case of China. To illustrate, in the mediation room, we witnessed that the victims' complaints and voices were often repressed in order to achieve a final agreement. We also observed that the perpetrators were asked, or more accurately, ordered by the police to go to the mediation room in order for their "problem" to be resolved. In spite of their dissatisfaction, the disputants had to accept the agreement. My requests to interview these disputants were refused by the mediator because "there is always one side (at least) who is not satisfied with it." He disclosed that he was afraid that the interview might stir up their emotions, leading to one or both sides to resurrect the dispute.

The mediators who mediated the conflicts in the context presented in our study did not represent themselves but, instead, the state authority. The police office was only a few meters away, and police officers interfered tremendously in both the process and outcomes of the mediation. Likewise, when political authorities such as state judges and prosecutors take over the mediation between the offender and the victim, absolute deference is required from the disputants. There was hardly any mutual exchange between the disputants when a political authority was present. This could especially be a disadvantage for the offenders, because they could only defer and could not express any dissenting opinions.

Nevertheless, obedience to authority is culturally more predetermined in China than in the West. Overall, the concept of paternalism in Asia does not have the stigma it has in the West (Pye and Pye 1985). In the latter, individuals are skeptical about state power and embrace freedom in self-decision-making, but in the former, making decisions means taking risks, and there is security in having no choices to make (Pye and Pye 1985). The Chinese largely rely on the authorities to maintain their well-being and order, as well as to make decisions on behalf of the collectivity.

4 Going Beyond the Restoration Model

So far, we have discussed that in an attempt to implement a Western restoration model, some cultural considerations must be taken into account, such as the importance of the family, the need for a balance of power instead of empowerment, harmony-driven manners of communication, the importance of "face," and the inevitable dominance of the political authority. These may suggest that a pure restoration model cannot be realized in contemporary China. In sum, the pure restoration model diverges from the Chinese context, not least because the traditional conceptions and the current rapid social transformation are entangled. Certainly, for China, the implication of the restoration model would be to increase respect for the participants, that is, to allow them to be heard and informed and their opinions to be considered.

This idea is not new. If we return to a consideration of the reconciliation center, it can be said that a participatory restorative process was laid down as its guideline for implementation. The fundamental obstacle, perhaps, lies in the lack of awareness of and forums for civic participation at the societal level. Who will act as a facilitator/mediator to engage all sides? Who can be a bridge between the state authority and the individual citizen? How, again, can one ensure that such a restorative process will be free from political interference and individual abuse? In contemporary China, the restoration of relationships requires balance in the roles of the victim, the offender, the community, and the government.

The Western RJ experience appears to suggest that the community is similar to civil society (Van Ness 2002) and comprises community volunteers from NGOs such as the victims' service or the offender support groups, as opposed to departments under a branch of the government. This is not currently the case in China. Due to the monopoly power exercised by the party, the trend toward community participation remains marginal (Plummer and Taylor 2004; Taylor 2004). However, the lack of such a sphere has not prevented the Chinese people from forming group recognition. Essentially, the Chinese people are group oriented in that the people view themselves as belonging to a group rather than as autonomous individuals. The group is so diverse and fluid that it can be a locality, an entity, an occupation, or even someone who is commonly known. Within the group, mutual obligation is reinforced, and group harmony is maintained. The community, in this sense, is closer to society and is permeated with all kinds of social relationships, which differs from the understanding of civil society in Western RJ (Metzger 1998; Heberer 2012; Yu and Guo 2012; Strang and Braithwaite 2001).

When implementing the restoration model, the most significant practical issue is probably the relationship between the community and the government. The status quo of community correction (社区矫正) in China (Zhou 2005; Zhang 2009) suggests that although it began only after the 2003 Notice Concerning the Work of Implementing Community Correction (关于开展社区矫正试点工作的通知), due to a lack of involvement by societal organizations, it is likely that community correction has been reduced to the continuation of prison sentences. There has been a dearth of concrete measures aimed at helping offenders to reintegrate into society. The community organizations in China, the street offices (街道办事处), and the residence committees (居民委员会) lack autonomy in self-governance. Thus, the nature of the administration (行政化) of community correction has been transformed into managing instead of correcting prisoners (Ruan 2011).

Given all the foregoing considerations, any expectation that there could be a relatively mature social group (社会团体) to organize and facilitate the restorative process in China is far from the reality. In light of the fact that the meaning of community remains ambiguous in Western RJ programs (Crawford and Clear 2001) and controversy exists around community involvement (Fonseca Rosenblatt 2015), is a "community"-based RJ process necessary? I agree with Van Ness (2002) that the role of the government needs to be reexamined. A justice system can still work in a restorative way even if a community-based communicative restorative process is not available.

5 A "Restorative" Justice System

Perhaps no one can evaluate exactly how "restorative" a system can be. This calls attention to the unsettled struggle between process and outcome. That is, the outcome can be beneficial and restorative for all sides, giving the interests of each side consideration, rather than merely satisfying the punitive nature of the system. One can also accept that state officials can initiate the procedure to produce a restorative outcome on the basis of the voluntariness of each side.

As analyzed in Chap. 6, reconciliation between the victim and the offender does not always produce a transformation in their interpersonal relationship. After all, an individualized effort to work with both sides to address their personal feelings and needs is lacking. Nevertheless, confrontation is minimized, and harmony through compromise is valued. The state officials operate as the third person to engage both sides in resolving the conflict. The aim is to reduce the harm by making reparations to the victim and saving the offender from punitive sanctions. Perhaps the Chinese practices do not differ significantly from the definition of RJ "as a response to crime oriented by reducing the harm." The harm includes both the broken relationships in particular and, more generally, the loss and damage to others. If the aim is to repair the individual relationships between the victim, the offender, and the community, then the restorative model is needed. If the aim is to reintegrate rather than punish the offender, to restore the victim rather than leave his losses unaddressed, and to restore social harmony, then state-centered justice can be as restorative as expected.

References

Anderson, A. F., & Gil, V. E. (1998). China's modernization and the decline of communitarianism the control of sex crimes and implications for the fate of informal social control. *Journal of Contemporary Criminal Justice, 14*(3), 248–261.

Braithwaite, J. (1999). Restorative justice: Assessing optimistic and pessimistic accounts. *Crime and Justice, 25*, 1–127. doi:10.2307/1147608.

Braithwaite, J. (2002). In search of restorative jurisprudence. In L. Walgrave (Ed.), *Restorative justice and the law* (pp. 150–167). Cullompton: Willan Publishing.

Crawford, A., & Clear, T. (2001). Community justice: Transforming communities through restorative justice. In G. Bazemore & M. Schiff (Eds.), *Restorative community justice. Repairing harm and transforming communities* (pp. 127–149). Cincinnati, OH: Anderson Publishing.

Daems, T. (2010). Death of a metaphor? Healing victims and restorative justice. In S. G. Shoham, P. Knepper, & M. Kett (Eds.), *International handbook of victimology*. Boca Raton, FL: CRC Press/Taylor & Francis Group.

Dignan, J. (2005). *Understanding victims and restorative justice*. Maidenhead: Open University Press.

Fonseca Rosenblatt, F. (2015). *The role of community in restorative justice*. London/New York: Routledge.

Hamlin, J. B., & Hokamura, A. (2014). The cultural context of restorative justice: Journeys through our cultural forests to a well-spring of healing. *International Journal for Semiot Law, 2014*(27), 291–310.

Heberer, T. (2012). Creating civil-society structures top-down? In J. Yu & S. Guo (Eds.), *Civil society and governance in China* (pp. 63–84). New York: Palgrave Macmillan.

Hood, R., & Hoyle, C. (2014). *The death penalty: A worldwide perspective*. Oxford: Oxford University Press.
Hoyle, C., & Miao, M. (2014). Thinking beyond death penalty abolitionist reform: Lessons from abroad and the options for China. *China Legal Science, 2*, 121.
Hu, H. C. (1944). The Chinese concepts of "face". *American Anthropologist, 46*(1), 45–64.
Lin, Y. (1936). *My country and my people*. New York: The John Day Company.
Lu, H., & Miethe, T. D. (2003). Confessions and criminal case disposition in China. *Law & Society Review, 37*(3), 549–578. doi:10.1111/1540-5893.3703003.
Metzger, T. A. (1998). *The western concept of a civil society in the context of Chinese history*. Stanford, CA: Stanford University Press.
Plummer, J., & Taylor, J. G. (2004). The characteristics of community participation in China. In J. Plummer & J. G. Taylor (Eds.), *Community participation in China: Issues and processes for capacity building* (pp. 36–54). London: Earthscan.
Pye, L. W. (1996). The state and the individual: An overview interpretation. In B. Hook (Ed.), *The individual and the state in China* (pp. 16–42). Oxford: Clarendon Press.
Pye, M. W., & Pye, L. W. (1985). *Asian power and politics: The cultural dimensions of authority*. Cambridge, MA: Harvard University Press.
Rojek, D. G. (1989). Confucianism, maoism, and the coming of delinquency to China. In R. J. Troyer, J. P. Clark, & D. G. Rojek (Eds.), *Social control in the People's Republic of China* (pp. 84–96). New York: Praeger.
Rojek, D. G. (2001). Chinese social control: From shaming and reintegration to 'getting rich is glorious'. In J. Liu, L. Zhang, & S. F. Messner (Eds.), *Crime and social control in a changing China* (pp. 89–103). Westport, CT/London: Greenwood Press.
Ruan, C. (2011). Community correction in China: causes, problems and improvement [*woguo shequ jiaozheng zhidu: yuanqi, wenti yu wanshan*]. *Journal of Peking Administration College, 2011*(1), 98–102.
Said, E. (1978). *Orientalism*. New York: Random House.
Strang, H., & Braithwaite, J. (2001). *Restorative justice and civil society*. Cambridge: Cambridge University Press.
Taylor, J. G. (2004). The context for community participation in China. In J. Plummer & J. G. Taylor (Eds.), *Community participation in China: Issues and processes for capacity building* (pp. 23–35). London: Earthscan.
Van Dijk, J. (2009). Free the victim: A critique of the western conception of victimhood. *International Review of Victimology, 16*(1), 1–33.
Van Ness, D. W. (2002). Creating restorative system. In L. Walgrave (Ed.), *Restorative justice and the law* (pp. 130–149). Cullompton: Willan Publishing.
Wang, P., Di, X., & Wan, K. H. (2007). Regional reviews (section b Asia). In G. Johnstone & D. W. V. Ness (Eds.), *Handbook of restorative justice* (pp. 477–488). London/New York: Routledge.
Wu, Y. (2014). People's mediation in China. In L. Cao, I. Y. Sun, & B. Hebenton (Eds.), *The handbook of Chinese criminology* (pp. 116–129). New York: Routledge.
Yu, J., & Guo, S. (2012). *Civil society and governance in China*. New York: Palgrave Macmillan.
Zhang, C. (2009). Comparative analysis and choice of the formation of community correction between Beijing and Shanghai [*woguo shequ jiaozheng jinghu moshi de bijiao fenxi yu xuanze*]. *Peking Social Sciences, 2009*(1), 55–61.
Zhou, X. (2005). The policy of community correction of released prisoners from the empowerment perspective [*shehui gongzuo chongquan shijiao xia de shifan shequ jiaozheng zhengce fenxi*]. *Journal of University of Science and Technology Beijing (Social Sciences Edition), 21*(4), 45–52.

Chapter 11
Conclusion

1 Introduction

In this final chapter, I will start by summarizing the answers to the research questions raised in the first chapter – how are the restoration of harm and interpersonal relationships embodied in the current criminal mediation as a means of conflict resolution in China; in what ways do Chinese mediation practices converge with and diverge from RJ in the West; to what extent can the restoration model in the West be replicated in China; and what adaptations should be made? At the same time, this concluding chapter tries to highlight the implications of the Chinese way of implementing restorative justice for its Western counterparts and to offer some possible solutions to improve Chinese mediation practices. It will also reflect upon the methodology for the sake of future study. Finally, this chapter will advance the analysis of how to enrich the current understanding of RJ through the case study of China.

2 A Brief Response to the Research Questions

It may be a worthwhile endeavor to stress the points flowing from the previous chapters. A simple repetition of each chapter's conclusion would be redundant; rather, I will synthesize them and argue that the answers to the three questions should be treated integrally, as reflected in the following sections.

Chinese mediation practices are oriented toward resolving conflict by engaging all sides. Instead of placing individual needs at the center, the practices are directed toward achieving harmony in social relationships. In this process, the state exerts a predominant role, demanding absolute deference from the disputants and rendering the individuals' real needs less important than the needs of socicty. This approach finds its roots in the Chinese legal tradition, in which the primary consideration is given to the collectivity – the communal interests shared by groups or communities.

X. Yuan, *Restorative Justice in China*, Springer Series on Asian Criminology and Criminal Justice Research, DOI 10.1007/978-3-319-63922-2_11

In contemporary China, it appears that the collectivity is reinforced, driven by a political will aimed at maintaining the stability of the social order. As a consequence, individual autonomy is further weakened, which becomes even more clear in a context in which there is a rising demand for the protection of personal interests and rights.

Both the literature review and the empirical study suggest that in China, the resolution of conflicts through the engagement of all sides does not reflect the restoration model of the West, which is built upon voluntariness, impartiality, empowerment, and storytelling. As argued above, the restoration model of the West has been deeply shaped by its societal context. If its restoration model is to be replicated in China, there definitely will be some hurdles. Therefore, an adaptation is needed that takes Chinese cultural, political, and societal conditions into account.

Next, we will move to the implications that the "lived" experiences in China might have for its Western counterparts and how Chinese practices have enriched or challenged the understanding of restorative justice in theory and in practice at the international level.

3 The Implications of the "Lived" Experiences for Western Counterparts

The Chinese experiences captured in this study may appear both communitarian and authoritarian. A liberal scholar is likely to see such situations as problematic and as violations of personal freedom. Scholars tend to trace restorative justice back to premodern times, upholding reparative history as the predecessor to modern restorative justice practices (Weitekamp 2000; Braithwaite 2002). Thus, why would the restorative justice camp reject an approach which derives from a society's own traditions and cultural values? Here, some of the characteristics of current Chinese mediation practices are outlined with the hope that there might be some useful implications.

3.1 Social Harmony Comes First

Chinese practice seems to be driven by a "society" mindset rather than an "individual" mindset. People are embedded in all sorts of social relationships, and it is best not to fight; even when a conflict is inevitable, it is best to resolve it rather than to persist in the dispute. Making peace concerns the stability of society and harmony over the long term. There is also pressure on the disputants from their families, relatives, and other social networks to resolve the matter and move on. It seems that the starting point is not individual autonomy but how the "community of care" responds and reacts to the affair. The success rates of mediation are high; "failure" occurs only when the victims believe their perpetrators have failed to take (sufficient) responsibility. Respect does not necessarily mean advocating for one's autonomy and free will; respect also means believing in the goodness of human nature and guiding and educating a delinquent toward good behavior after he has made a mistake. The pressure to resolve the matter and bring peace to everyone involved is understandable.

3.2 Shame and Reintegration

This study does not join the debate about the exact role of shame in restorative justice, but it is still worthwhile to refer to the shaming and reintegration practices observed in this study. Shaming the offender is not exclusive to Chinese society and its justice apparatuses, although admittedly, in both the public trial and sentencing assemblies (公审公判大会) in the early years (roughly 1949–1978) and the strike hard campaigns (严打斗争) in recent years (1978–present), brutal scenes of the condemnation of offenders have never been out of sight. Shaming by the state apparatuses can easily result in stigmatization rather than reintegration. In contrast to the punitive public opinions active on online outlets, the relatively lenient opinions voiced by the victims in this study may suggest a different picture, although they must be considered with caution.

In a society categorized by interdependence and mutual obligation, the shame culture encourages a wrongdoer to repent. As voiced by those who have been directly harmed, seeing the wrongdoer renew himself through an apology and reparations is important. Direct censure from the victims was rarely seen; even the mediator avoided directly criticizing the wrongdoer. Instead, persuasion and mild education were the strategies that were often used. Arguably, this reflects the idea of separating the self from the act in order to preserve the self-esteem of the wrongdoer.

The cultural expectation of repentance from the offender may explain the weight given to the offender's remorsefulness, which in most cases, is shown by his reparative efforts toward the victim. Although the assessment is produced by the community correction section of the local justice bureau that is assisting the justice agency, the criminal justice staff sometimes may feel obligated to verify the trustworthiness of the assessment report, given the possible lack of expertise of the start-up community correction service.

To the extent that patriarchy persists, the family as an institution plays a key role in taking responsibility for their delinquent members. There is no controversy about whether the crime impacts the offender's family members; in fact, the crime harms the offender's relationship with his family, and, thus, the bond of mutual obligation requires them all to assume the responsibility for making reparation to the victims. In this study, shaming did come from the young offenders' families; the young offenders also feel ashamed because of the reactions of their parents, teachers, and friends. To the extent that society excludes the offenders, e.g., by expelling them from school or work, reintegration should be seen as providing them the option of staying out of prison, although under the supervision of their family.

The victim's acceptance makes the reintegration of the offender possible after a crime has happened. It should be noted that victims may not always have positive opinions of their perpetrators for various reasons, including gossip. For example, they may have heard something bad about the perpetrator from someone else and thus have a negative opinion of him. Nevertheless, the victims choose to settle the dispute in a peaceful way and let the matter go. It follows that the political context of building a "harmonious society" reinforces the group orientation of each person with respect to the responsibilities and commitments to the larger social collective (Delury 2008).

The implications of Chinese mediation practices for the West do not lie in democratic processes but in the fact that space is given for informal controls to occur that emphasize the role of the community, the family, and the culture in disciplining the offender and reshaping his behavior.

4 Enriching the Understanding of RJ

If we agree with Cain (2000) that "the deep presumption of western theories may be harmful for non-western consumers of them" (p. 239), any form of Occidentalism that denies the differences should also be rejected. Equally, as mentioned before, this study has no intention of returning to romanticism in order to advocate the beauty of Chinese practices. Our thinking is aimed toward understanding how Chinese experience can further expand the understanding of RJ or raise some challenges to it.

We wonder first if we can reject the mindset of either "victim" or "offender"; that is, harm may first affect the victim as an individual but can also affect the offender to an equal extent. Moreover, it is not only individuals that are impacted by the harm but also the networks around the family. Therefore, more reflection on how the "victim" is socially constructed (Van Dijk 2009) in the West, both in victimological research and restorative justice, is probably needed. On the other hand, due to the Chinese legal tradition, which places a premium on social order and collective harmony (Ren 1997), concern about the harm to the community may be placed above that to the individual.

Secondly, human sentiment (*qing*) and reasonableness (*li*) remain vigorous forces that challenge the law promoted by the state within the Chinese criminal justice system, as manifested in the mediation practices. "Essentially, what is equal may not be justice. In a sense, justice is a relative rather than an absolute concept. After all, each society not only prefers one principle over another but also culturally defines what is fair, just and equal" (Ren 1997, p. 63). How Chinese society's own traditions interact with the formal justice system will perhaps shape the form that justice reform in China should adopt. While this issue might be pressing in contemporary China, it certainly carries the pursuit of harmony and justice into the future. Thus, restorative justice research will likely gain much by being patient and providing sufficient support to the examination of how a society under transformation, which is struggling with its formal justice system, can successfully provide justice to all.

It is probably best to view restorative justice as a compass, rather than as a panacea (Walgrave 2014). Essentially, it is a set of ideas that challenge the established criminal justice system (Johnstone 2004). This study opposes the perception of restorative justice as a magical way to achieve apology, forgiveness, healing, etc. This perception may have some appeal to some victims or offenders, but it risks characterizing the problem-solving itself as an elixir. The virtue of forgiveness may be shared across some cultures and religious doctrines, but advocating restorative justice as a place where it can be found is not a mistake.

There is no "right" way to do restorative justice (Morris 2002), and each nation may decide how to implement it in its own way (Braithwaite 2000). In a communitarian society, harmony and compromise, deriving from the traditional culture, are reproduced by the socialist state. All the social relationships bring people together to resolve the conflict in order to achieve harmony. Thus, if we try to devise a definition of RJ deriving from the mediation practices in this study, it could simply be the following: "RJ is a process to restore harm in society in an inclusive way." This consists of two elements: first, harm at the societal level has priority over harm to individuals and, second, inclusion should be maximized to reach the various stakeholders, among which the state is a prominent player.

5 Some Challenges

The critical issues surrounding Chinese practices can return the discussion to the field of restorative justice. First, who should the mediator be? Volunteer mediators who have no sanctioning power are active in Western RJ programs, while the police-led family group conferences have been criticized on the basis that there is likely to be excessive coercion and shaming (Young 2001). This study provides a different perspective about the role of the state in restorative justice practices or, to be more accurate, the role of the state as the mediator. An ambivalent attitude is captured: Although there is a general dependence on paternalistic authority in Chinese society, acceptance of authoritarian rule does not always occur smoothly. Nevertheless, interestingly, studies comparing the level of trust in legal authorities between mainland China and Taiwan have found that Chinese respondents who live in an authoritarian regime report higher levels of trust in the police, the court, and the criminal justice system as a whole, compared to their Taiwanese counterparts, who live in a democratic regime (Hsieh and Boateng 2015; Lai et al. 2010). This is not intended as a comment about which one is preferable but simply to draw attention to the complexity of the discussion on the role of the state in RJ.

A second challenge relates to the inclusion of the offender in a society that labels, denounces, and stigmatizes him. It might be fair to point out that the aim of inclusion in many RJ programs is met with the harsh reality that societal conditions categorized by discrimination and rejection have not been sufficiently addressed. Indeed, it is unrealistic to expect that a restorative process can fundamentally change the penal ethos. In the case of China, Braithwaite (1999) believed that Chinese practices involve excessive stigmatization, which led him to eliminate the section on China in the book *Crime, Shame and Reintegration*. It is likely that fostering a restorative culture within a society not only necessitates social support for RJ practices but also the resolve by policy-makers not to demonize the offender in various ways as is often negatively portrayed in state-controlled media.

A third challenge is raised regarding the evaluation studies on the effects of RJ. Despite the abundant literature, there are unfortunately many issues that remain unresolved. A key theme is how we should circumscribe the process. First, it tends to neglect the pre-encounter situations in which shaming has probably already taken place. The existing international literature seems to focus largely on the offender-victim encounter and how both sides have experienced it. But where then does the process start? Secondly, although individual harm has been given substantial attention in the evaluative studies, it remains unclear how the public interest and harm can be restored and assessed.

Nevertheless, in the conclusion of this study, we seek to offer some possible solutions aimed at improving Chinese mediation practices. As China is in transition, the needs and demands of its citizens deserve serious attention.

6 The Way Out for Chinese Practices: Possible Solutions

Restorative justice in the West stands as a symbol of a movement "from state to citizen" (Green 2014), suggesting that the responsibility for crime control has shifted away from the state and toward the community. In China, the increasing conflict produced by the societal transition has strained the justice system. As it is not independent from the justice system, the reconciliation of the victim and the offender risks being taken over to serve an instrumental rationale for the state (Bonafé-Schmitt 2013). It is necessary to prevent the "irrationality of rationality" (Trevaskes 2009), which would turn reconciliation into a formality, thus losing its original meaning.

The current study suggests that in contemporary China, informal controls, on the basis of tradition and culture, still underlie the criminal justice system, which negotiates the relationships between the victim, the offender, and the society. Although this study suggests that a purely Western restoration model will not necessarily fit within Chinese realities, are there any useful implications for Chinese practices?

6.1 Toward Better Communication

We do not consider the Western restoration model to be the best one or one that will work for all. Drawing on the field study, however, we indeed found that people have the need to communicate with their victims or perpetrators about the crime event, the impact, consequences, etc. Nevertheless, their communication is being obstructed or not facilitated. Among others, some of the reasons for this are the following: the authoritarian style that inhibits the narratives, the limited time and busy schedules of the state authorities, and pressure from the environment. This does not suggest that the Western expressive healing style of the restoration model will work perfectly in China. What matters the most is whether the offenders have an apologetic attitude and whether they have learned a lesson following their criminal behavior. This is what must be communicated. Moreover, not all victims prefer to meet the offenders: Direct confrontation is sometimes an obstacle to reconciliation.

In the Western restoration model, communication, in most cases, is facilitated by a third person – professionally trained mediators/facilitators or volunteers working in local communities. Such an organization, which is independent of the state, might not be realistic for China. However, the state-controlled mediation committees exist extensively in workplaces, residences, neighborhoods, etc. An effective channel that bridges these community organizations and the criminal justice apparatuses might facilitate conflict resolution. Nevertheless, this issue merits extensive study in the future. Although there has been a critique of the phenomenon of "justice by geography" (Ashworth 2002), the networks into which Chinese people are woven may favor geographical proximity and familiarity in the resolution of conflicts.

To maximize the possibility of communication, two judicial measures are considered supplementary and therefore have not yet been promoted. First, diversion measures can be used more frequently, in tandem with community work or other correction measures. In other words, giving offenders a grace period to fulfill the obligations imposed on them toward the victim and the community can help guide them toward earning leniency through diverse reparative measures. Given the irreversible labeling effect of criminal convictions, the study asserts that diversion measures should be used more often prior to court.

Second, the state is not devoid of responsibility for supporting victims who have been severely impacted by crime. In victim-offender reconciliation, an overly high burden is placed on the offender and, consequently, his entire family. Tension is unavoidable when too heavy of a financial burden is placed on the offender's side. Needy victims may be more hopeful of obtaining compensation than seeing their offenders punished.

6.2 *Satisfaction of Participants*

The citizens' satisfaction tests the nerve of the state authority, and it is not easily achieved. How can busy justice organs truly satisfy the needs of the citizens? There are almost no citizen organizations working with them to relieve the burden, e.g., by taking on the mediation work. Satisfaction does not necessarily lie in the full expression of emotions but in whether the citizens receive respectful treatment and an acceptable final outcome. Unlike the restoration model in the West, where the citizens make the decision themselves through deliberation and negotiations, in China, the decision-making lies in the authority, who takes the outcome of the mediation agreement into account. We did find that some victims were happy when they were contacted and their opinions were consulted, but still, they were not properly informed about the final decision on their offenders.

Achieving satisfaction is probably built upon the respect for procedural rights: to be heard, to be informed, and to be ensured that the participants' opinions are being taken into consideration. In China, there has been a rising awareness of personal freedom and rights; this is reflected in the case study, where the participants expected to be treated with more respect and more recognition of their status. We hence argue that it is necessary to strive for the rights of both offenders and victims, not to check the state's power but to earn more respect for the citizens when they are dealing directly with the state authority. In particular, the law should be oriented toward more effectively promoting the victims' rights and interests; in this way, the top-down legislation has the potential and receives the legitimacy for practical implementation. It is true that citizens want to have a voice so that their opinions can be heard during the conflict resolution process. Facilitating this does not threaten the authority but reinforces the citizens' recognition of the authority.

6.3 Judicial Reform in China

All this might suggest the need for judicial reform in China, where there is an increasing domestic demand for the better delivery of justice. In learning from Western justice systems, the Chinese justice system has primarily shifted toward becoming offender focused, thus divorcing itself from its long tradition (Fan 2011) and departing from the conception of justice harbored by ordinary citizens. Victim-offender reconciliation does return the conflict to the disputants, but the authoritarian state has strongly embedded its ideology and will. The outcome may not be equally perceived as beneficial by the citizens but as primarily for the sake of the system, through which the state achieves its political goals.

China is not short of legislation and reform initiatives; however, learning how to implement the reforms does not come from books but from action. The endeavors to more effectively resolve conflicts should be more attentive to the real needs of the participants. Chinese citizens are not opposed to authority, but in respecting authority, they also want their autonomy to be respected. In the interactions between the individuals and the state, more time and energy should be given to the citizens. This will require the depoliticalization and the de-administration of the justice system; that is, the state authorities should not be required to attend all sorts of political education or ideological assemblies or be used as tools to serve governmental goals. They should be responsible only for the cases they are currently handling. The party structure, such as the prosecution committees or adjudication committees, should not be a stumbling block to any non-prosecution decision or judicial discretion. Social harmony, as the political goal to be achieved by the state apparatuses, cannot be used as an excuse to impinge on the citizens' autonomy and rights.

A formalized justice system is a precondition for safeguarding individual rights. This implies that both the state actors and the citizens have formed a conviction that the law is fair and equal to everyone, rather than manipulated by one side. Such a consensus, however, is currently lacking, in spite of the various legislation and regulations in place. This has led to the impression that mediation may have become a hotbed for judicial corruption and penal trade. Improving the justice system, therefore, requires a more transparent forum and wider participation by the citizens in supervising the process and the outcomes. Civic participation, rather than one dominant voice, has the potential to make the system more restorative and potent.

7 Methodology Revisited

7.1 A Chinese and a Non-Chinese Perspective

What is truth? It is usually believed that truth can only be discovered if a scientific methodology is followed. I am not taking issue with this view, but I would rather take a bit of time to reflect upon the methodology at this point and how it has impacted the "truth" or the story told in this study.

It has been three decades since Clifford Geertz first published the book *Local Knowledge* and two decades since the story of *Qiuju* became a symbol of contrast between a localized view of justice and the government-initiated law program. This study hardly falls under the scholarly tradition of interpretive anthropology, although it tries to interpret the practice from the perspective of the local people. Fundamentally, this study tries to understand the "local" practice in its own context. A naturalistic qualitative study was thus employed, which is not devoid of shortcomings.

7.2 "Twist" of the Methodology

Serving the aim of our field investigation, a naturalistic inquiry allowed flexibility and adaptability, contingent on the access and the resources available. Interaction between the researcher, the participants, and the researched institutions is important. However, the scope of sight is likely to be narrowed to what the researcher is allowed to see. Nevertheless, while the contingency of access may have been a constraint in this study, the study may contribute to the knowledge of how to get "inside" and conduct criminology fieldwork in China.

This study concedes that deriving from its own social science traditions, the empirical studies on RJ practices in the West have been, comparatively speaking, well designed and conducted. There was, by contrast, no ready-made instrument that could be directly applied to an examination of Chinese mediation practices. Deeply influenced by Western studies, I adopted the same ideology at the outset, which was to examine the victims' and offenders' experiences before and after the mediation. This approach was essentially found to be completely unrealistic due to the constraints that existed in practice. Consequently, I had to abandon that methodology and base the interviews on general questions (the themes to be investigated were presented in the data collection chapter). These questions still gave a great deal of attention to people's experiences. In critical retrospect, however, this approach may not be a good starting point for examining criminal mediation in China. Why? First, mediation was largely annexed to the formal judicial procedure across its different stages; hence, the experience with mediation cannot be easily distinguished from the ongoing normal procedure. Secondly, related to the first issue, people had a tendency to voice their opinions about the final disposition rather than the process. Certainly, we were not aware of these issues until we spoke with our respondents about their experiences. Thus, the shortcomings with this approach may, in the meantime, be treated as an added benefit for future study. At the risk of being too simplistic, the current study suggests some research topics for further examination, such as the extent to which Chinese judicial actors embrace and define restoration and punishment, respectively, how the image of the victim is constructed within the criminal justice system, etc. We speculate that the first question is well suited to a quantitative research design and the second favors both the descriptive and explorative approaches.

7.3 A Little Confession

As a Chinese person, I have ever fallen into the trap of Western RJ ideology. Yes, liberalism and individualism are like magnets that easily transform a person. I felt ashamed that I had ever judged the Chinese experience from a Western perspective, considering it coercive and unbearably authoritarian. My bias remained with me until almost the last moment, until the last day, when I wrote in my field diary: "Today, I understand why Confucius is considered the greatest thinker of restorative justice (citing Braithwaite 1999)." This feeling only arose in that moment. When I was back in Leuven, I lost that "wisdom" once again, because I needed to think along the lines of my Western training, which considers "how to undertake analysis," "how to report findings," etc. I am not saying that Western methodology is bad, but as a learner, Mencius (372 BC–289 BC) always said: "[I] t would be better to be without the Book of History than to give entire credit to it."[1] I think I may have to stop here; I will not stop reading, but for this moment, I want to stop thinking. If RJ has ever been guided by any ideology, then I must conclude that every advocate should stop "hijacking" it, because it might only cater to individual appetites. Stop.

[1] Translated by James Legge, retrieved from http://ctext.org, on February 10, 2016. The original in Chinese: 孟子曰:"尽信《书》,则不如无《书》."

References

Ashworth, A. (2002). Responsibilities, rights and restorative justice. *British Journal of Criminology, 42*(3), 578–595. doi:10.1093/bjc/42.3.578.

Bonafé-Schmitt, J.-P. (2013). Restorative justice and penal mediation: The French exception. In D. Cornwell, J. Blad, & M. Wright (Eds.), *Civilising criminal justice: An international restorative agenda for penal reform*. Hampshire: Waterside Press.

Braithwaite, J. (1999). Restorative justice: Assessing optimistic and pessimistic accounts. *Crime and Justice, 25*, 1–127. doi:10.2307/1147608.

Braithwaite, J. (2000). Repentance rituals and restorative justice. *Journal of Political Philosophy, 8*(1), 115–131.

Braithwaite, J. (2002). *Restorative justice and responsive regulation*. Oxford: Oxford University Press.

Cain, M. (2000). Orientalism, occidentalism and the sociology of crime. *British Journal of Criminology, 40*(2), 239–260. doi:10.1093/bjc/40.2.239.

Delury, J. (2008). "Harmonious" in China. *Policy Review*, (148), 35–44.

Fan, Z. (2011). *Law of feelings and the Chinese [Qingli fa he zhongguo ren]*. Beijing: Peking University Press.

Green, S. (2014). *Crime, community and morality*. New York: Routledge.

Hsieh, M. L., & Boateng, F. D. (2015). Perceptions of democracy and trust in the criminal justice system: A comparison between Mainland China and Taiwan. *International Criminal Justice Review, 25*(2), 153–173. doi:10.1177/1057567715570050.

Johnstone, G. (2004). How, and in what terms, should restorative justice be conceived? In H. Zehr & B. Toews (Eds.), *Critical issues in restorative justice* (pp. 5–15). Cullompton: Willan Publishing.

Lai, Y. L., Cao, L., & Zhao, J. S. (2010). The impact of political entity on confidence in legal authorities: A comparison between China and Taiwan. *Journal of Criminal Justice, 38*(5), 934–941.

Morris, A. (2002). Critiquing the critics. A brief response to critics of restorative justice. *British Journal of Criminology, 42*(3), 596–615.

Ren, X. (1997). *Tradition of the law and law of the tradition: Law, state and social control in China*. Westport, CT: Greenwood Press.

Trevaskes, S. (2009). Restorative justice or mcjustice with Chinese characteristics? In M. Farquhar (Ed.), *21st century China: Views from Australia* (pp. 77–96). Newcastle upon Tyne: Cambridge Scholars Publishing.

Van Dijk, J. (2009). Free the victim: A critique of the western conception of victimhood. *International Review of Victimology, 16*(1), 1–33.

Walgrave, L. (2014). *Restorative justice is not a panacea against all social evils*. Paper presented at the ESF exploratory workshop on critical justice, Leuven, October 15–17, 2014.

Weitekamp, E. G. M. (2000). Research on victim-offender mediation. Findings and needs for the future. In T. E. F. f. V.-O. Mediation (Ed.), *Victim-offender mediation in Europe* (pp. 99–121). Leuven: Leuven University Press.

Young, R. (2001). Just cops doing "shameful" business?: Police-led restorative justice and the lessons of research. In A. Morris & G. Maxwell (Eds.), *Restorative justice for juveniles: Conferencing, mediation & circles* (pp. 195–225). Oxford/Portland, OR: Hart Publishing.

Appendix: Guideline for Reconciliation Center for Juvenile and Young Adult Crimes (Excerpts, Translated by Xiaoyu Yuan)

Article 3

This guideline shall be applicable to crimes committed by juveniles and young adults (aged between 14 and 25) when the following requirements are met:

1. Illegal or criminal facts are clear and undisputed.
2. Both sides are clear about the legal stipulations and possible outcomes and are willing to reconcile.
3. The acts violate the administrative laws or are misdemeanors, and the perpetrator is remorseful.

Article 7

The reconciliation center shall, based on the distribution and the amount of events, select the mediator from the university/college, the street office, the justice bureau, etc.

The mediator should meet the following requirements: (1) has the qualification of a mediator, psychiatrist, or school teacher, (2) has at least 2 years' experience in mediation or has work experience dealing with students' affairs, and (3) has passed the training for being a mediator.

As for the mediators that have been selected, the reconciliation center should make a list for the convenience of the disputing parties when they choose their mediators. The list should specify the mediators' names, occupations, specialties, etc.

Article 8

For the applicable cases, after fulfilling the obligation of informing both parties of the reconciliation option and the disputing parties realize that there is the possibility of reconciliation but they are still unsure, the police and the judicial staff can entrust

X. Yuan, *Restorative Justice in China*, Springer Series on Asian Criminology and Criminal Justice Research, DOI 10.1007/978-3-319-63922-2 the case to the reconciliation center. The latter can negotiate between the disputing sides to enhance their willingness to reconcile.

When the mediator negotiates between the two parties, he can do so by getting in touch with each party respectively and facilitating a back-to-back communication in order to provide additional information necessary for both sides to decide whether or not they will opt for mediation. The mediator cannot impose pressure on either side in any form, nor can he/she require or hint that both sides should reconcile in the name of the police or the judicial staff.

Article 13

The participants of the reconciliation conferences include those who are obligated to attend and those who are not.

Those who are obligated to attend include: (1) the victim or his representative, (2) the perpetrator or his representative, (3) the police officer who is in charge of referring the case for prosecution or the prosecutor who is in charge of the case, (4) the mediator, and (5) the minute-taker.

The following people can be invited to be present when necessary: (1) the families, relatives, or teachers of both sides, (2) representatives from the school or community where the event occurred, and (3) others who have been impacted by the event.

When inviting both sides' supporters to the conferences, the convenor should inform them of the requirements beforehand, as well as ask for the opinions of both parties. The number of participants should remain balanced for both sides.

Article 15

The reconciliation center is equipped with a special conference room, where an oval or rectangle table large enough for 10–16 persons is placed. The staff from the police or the judiciary should sit across from the mediator and the minute-taker, and the disputing parties should sit, respectively, on the left and right hand of the mediator and the minute-taker. The seats of the perpetrator and the victim should remain the form of a right angle, and they should sit between their supporters.

The "flow chart for criminal reconciliation," "principles of criminal reconciliation," and "responsibilities of the mediator" should be put up on the wall of the conference room. At the outset, leaflets, such as the brochure of criminal reconciliation, should be provided for the convenience of all the participants.

Article 16

The mediator shall respect the following principles when organizing and presiding over the conference.

1. Respect. Arrive at the conference ahead of time and receive all the participants warmly; be kind and gentle, and have no discrimination against any side.
2. Impartiality. Treat each side equally and make sure all sides have opportunities to fully express their opinions; intervene and facilitate the agreement to be reached, make sure that both sides communicate with each other on a voluntary basis, and refrain from any interference.
3. Confidentiality. The mediator must not disclose to others any information about the cases or the disputing parties. The mediator must not provide any information that is unfavorable to reconciliation, nor should he vent his anger in front of the disputing parties.

Article 17

All the participants shall abide by the following principles:

1. Equal communication. All the participants are equal, and no side may discriminate against the other or humiliate the other. All the participants may speak up in a specified sequence, and no one may interrupt the others. A participant should raise his hand when he wants to speak.
2. Be rational and gentle. Listen to the guidance from the mediator. No one may attack the other side verbally or nonverbally.
3. Be honest and act in good faith. Openly express one's opinion, and fulfill one's promises with good faith.

Article 19

The conference should proceed in the following sequence:

1. The mediator initiates the conference and introduces the police or judicial staff, the victim, the perpetrator, and other participants; the mediator should repeat the rules that all the participants should respect; all the participants should promise that they will respect the rules.
2. The discussion of the first round is in the following order: the police or judicial staff, the victim, the perpetrator, the supporters of the victim, the supporters of the perpetrator, and the community representatives:

   The police or judicial staff briefly introduces the crime event.

   The victim describes his experience and the losses and harm suffered because of the crime, expresses his willingness, and, if he wants, asks the perpetrator questions.

   The perpetrator explains his motives or purposes, the reasons for his crime, states how he has reflected on his behavior, and responds to the victim's questions.

The supporters of each side, the community representatives, and others can express their opinions about the crime and the harm and can ask questions of the perpetrator.

The perpetrator can make his statement again and respond to the questions raised by each participant.

3. The mediator summarizes the first-round discussion and invites further discussion on diverging ideas, especially concerning the perpetrator's responsibility. The order of the second-round discussion is the same as above.

   When necessary, the mediator can guide participants who hold different opinions into further elucidating their ideas. Under unusual circumstances, the mediator can have a recess for back-to-back negotiations before resuming face-to-face communication.
4. On the basis of full communication, all the participants can draft an agreement if all have agreed on the apology, restitution, community service, etc.
5. The minute-taker is responsible for noting down the whole process. All the participants place their signatures on it after they have approved the content.

Index

X. Yuan, *Restorative Justice in China*, Springer Series on Asian Criminology and Criminal Justice Research, DOI 10.1007/978-3-319-63922-2

Printed by Printforce, the Netherlands